FOUR PLAYS FROM NORTH AFRICA

Fatima Gaillare, *House of Women,* U.S. premiere
University of Massachusetts Curtain Theatre, 2002

Tayeb Saddiki, *The Folies Berberes,* world premiere
Institut du Monde Arab, Paris, 1993

FOUR PLAYS FROM NORTH AFRICA

Edited with an Introduction
by
Marvin Carlson

Martin E. Segal Theatre Center Publications
New York

Library of Congress Cataloging-in-Publication Data

Four plays from North Africa / edited with an introduction by Marvin Carlson.
   p. cm.
  ISBN 978-0-9790570-2-1
  1. North African drama (French)--Translations into English. I. Carlson, Marvin A., 1935-

PQ3988.5.N62F68 2008
842'.91408961--dc22

2007048928

Translations by Marvin Carlson (The Veil and The Folies Berbers, David Looseley (Araberlin), Carolyn and Tom Shread (House of Wives),

Copy-editing by Margaret Araneo

TABLE OF CONTENTS

For Abdelkader Alloula

Editor's Introduction
Four Plays from North Africa

Theatre from the Arab World, almost unknown to English-language scholars and readers two decades ago, is gradually coming to be recognized as an important part of the world dramatic heritage. The *Routledge World Encyclopedia of Contemporary Theatre* devotes an invaluable full volume to the Arab World,[1] and three English-language anthologies provide a modest but important sampling of the rich theatrical fare available in this hitherto neglected part of the world of drama. The first of these, the truly pioneering collection, *Arabic Writing Today: The Drama*, was published as early as 1977 by the American Research Center in Cairo. It performed a most praiseworthy service in making such work available for the first time to English readers, but given the potential field, its range of selections was extremely narrow. Eight of the nine plays it contained were from Egypt, and the other from Syria.

There is no disputing the dominance of Egypt in the history of the modern Arab theatre, but given the geographical and cultural range of that theatre, this volume gives an extremely narrow picture of its subject. Two more recent collections present a much more extended and thus more accurate representation of the modern Arabic drama. The first, *Modern Arabic Drama*, appeared in 1995 as part of the Indiana University series in Arab and Islamic Studies.[2] Again, Egypt held a deserved first place, contributing four out of the twelve plays in this collection, but the rest presented a commendable geographic sampling, with three works from Syria, and one each from Iraq, Tunisia, Lebanon, Palestine, and Kuwait. A second volume, *Short Arabic Plays*, published in 2003[3] by Interlink Books, expanded the geographical range still further, with five plays each from Egypt and Syria, two from Lebanon, and one each from Iraq, Palestine, Libya, and the United Arab Emirates.

Although naturally these collections represent only a very small

---

1. Volume 4, ed. Don Rubin (London: Routledge, 1999).
2. Ed. Salma Khadra Jayyusi and Roger Allen.
3. Ed. Salma Khadra Jayyusi.

part of the dramatic material available from the Arab world, one very important part of that world remains seriously under-represented in English translation, and that is the substantial theatre tradition of Western North Africa, the region known to Arabs as the Maghreb. In Arabic, *Maghreb* means "place where the sun sets" and is opposed to the much less commonly encountered term *Mashriq*, the "place where the sun rises." The Mashriq refers to what Westerners call the Middle East and sometimes the Orient as well, while the Maghreb, according to the narrowest definition, includes the three Northwest African countries bordered by the Atlas Mountains: Morocco, Algeria, and Tunisia. A broader definition would include also the two bordering countries with significant indigenous Berber populations and cultures: Mauritania and Libya.

Although all three of the core Maghreb nations have a significant modern drama tradition, their virtual exclusion from the existing anthologies is doubtless due in part to geography and in part to language. Geographically, they are, at least in the Arabic-speaking world, the countries most remote from Egypt and Syria, the centers of the modern Arabic theatre. Linguistically their dramatic tradition shares the tensions of theatrical expression throughout the Arab world, but in a form that adds to their marginalization in international scholarly study of the drama. In all three countries, Arabic is the official language and is spoken by the vast majority of the population, with various Berber languages taking a distinct second place. French is a distant third, but it remains in all three countries basic to much economic, political, and cultural activities.

From the beginning of the modern era, Maghreb dramatists, like those elsewhere in the Arab world, have wrestled with the linguistic tension within Arabic itself. Traditional Arabic poetic expression remained close to the classical Arabic of the Koran, but this generally seemed stilted and artificial in the theatre, and today most Arabic dramatists, including those in Tunisia, Algeria, and Morocco, write in a style fairly close to the Arabic spoken in their own communities, even when this means that their plays may be very difficult for Arabic speakers in other countries to understand. Playwrights from the Berber populations have another, more serious problem. Although there is a small, and growing, amount of Berber drama, and words or passages in various Berber languages often find their way into basically Arabic plays, a dramatist whose native language is a Berber one can only hope to gain a reputation by writing in one of two foreign languages, Arabic or French. Usually, like Algeria's Kateb Yacine, they select French.

French is, however, also the language often selected by Arabic speaking dramatists in these countries, and many of the best-known dramatists of the Maghreb, including the four represented in this volume, have created their dramatic works, wholly or in part, in that language. Although most of the leading dramatists of Egypt, for example, have some fluency in English, and the leading Egyptian dramatist of the late twentieth century, Alfred Farag, in fact lived in London, an Egyptian dramatist would scarcely think of writing a play in English, while French is the preferred language for many leading dramatists in Morocco, Algeria, and Tunisia. Given the troubled colonial history of this region, and especially of Algeria, this choice might seem surprising, but there are a number of reasons for this, even for dramatists who, unlike those of a Berber background, could as easily write in Arabic as French.

This phenomenon has been addressed by a number of Maghreb authors, and one of the most comprehensive analyses of their choice of French has been provided by the Tunisian poet Tahar Bekri in an essay entitled "Ecrire en Français au Maghreb" (Writing in French in the Maghreb). He begins by noting that the colonial tradition remains a powerful one, especially in Algeria, where from 1830 to 1962 only French was taught in the schools and for more than a century the literary tradition was entirely a French one. This domination was far less in Tunisia and Morocco. They were only French protectorates, for shorter periods of time (Tunisia 1881 to 1956 and Morocco 1912 to 1956), and both French and Arabic were taught in the schools. Still this gave most students a bilingual background, reinforced in some cases by households where one parent was from the Maghreb and the other French.

Bekri notes a number of other reasons for a special interest in French in the Maghreb, however. First, unlike Francophone or mixed-language writers in, for example, Belgium or Quebec, the Maghreb author using French is not resisting a dominant language but utilizing the "language of the Other" to achieve certain cultural or literary effects. The range of linguistic expression offered by choosing or mixing local Arabic, literary Arabic, Berber, and French gives the Maghreb writer a challenging palette of linguistic possibilities. The different if complementary literary traditions also allow such dramatists to decide if they wish to present a love story, for example, in the very different terms of French or Arabic literature. On a less positive note, the possibility of political, or more recently religious, censorship has sometimes encouraged Maghreb dramatists to publish possibly troubling works in French and indeed in France. Finally, and I suggest most importantly in the case of theatre, writing in French offers to the Maghreb author the possibility of an international reputation that would not be possible for work written in the local tongue. Nor is this only a matter of one's international reputation. There is enough post-colonial residue even in the United States that many young American dramatists or experimental companies have not attracted serious critical attention until they have been presented in Europe, and especially in London, and the relationship of the Maghreb theatre to Paris is even more powerful. Bekri concludes: "It is no exaggeration to say that Paris has become, whether one wished this or not, the necessary way to get oneself read and to make contacts among those from the Maghreb."[4]   Although each country has produced a good deal of drama in Arabic, as well as some in the various Berber languages, many of the best-known dramatists of the Mahgreb, especially those in Algeria and Morocco, are most widely known for their work in French.

Thus, both geography and linguistics have worked to marginalize Maghreb theatre for those relatively few scholars who have opened the modern study of Arabic drama. This marginalization is clearly reflected in the three current anthologies of Arabic drama in English, although their presentation has usually neither admitted nor explained this tradition's lack of representation. The introduction to the most recent collection, *Short Arabic Plays*, for example, begins: "Interlink is here presenting a collection of twenty short plays, nineteen in English translation and one in original English, written by sixteen Arab playwrights . . . from various Arab states." While this is true, it does not acknowledge that only Arabic language plays (except for the one English example) have been included. The reader is thus given no warning

---

4. In *De la literature tunisienne et maghrébine* (Paris: L'Harmattan, 1999), 5–13.

that there are a substantial number of other "Arab playwrights" in other "Arab states," who are not represented because their work is not actually written in Arabic, or because their Arabic is apparently too remote, linguistically or geographically. This is all the more surprising since one English-language play is included, undermining the presumed even if unstated dedication to only Arabic language drama.

This ignorance of or indifference to the drama of the Maghreb is unfortunately commonly found not only in standard anthologies but even in standard histories and reference works. A striking example is the section on "Arabic Drama Since the Thirties" in the *Modern Arabic Literature* volume of the *Cambridge History of Arabic Literature*. This essay is written by M. M. Badawi, also editor of this volume and unquestionably the leading modern authority on Arabic theatre writing in English. Badawi's forty-five-page essay devotes only two pages to Tunisian theatre, one paragraph to Algeria, and two short paragraphs to Morocco. The treatment of Algeria, with its substantial dramatic repertoire in both French and Arabic, is particularly uninformed. From the beginning, Badawi asserts, "Algerian intellectuals were too much taken up with French culture" to give Arabic drama any encouragement, while the general public "did not much like literary drama," preferring the "Algerian national dramatic entertainment, which was a mixture of song, laughter, and improvised scenes." He cites two dramatists as in his opinion the only Algerian "men of the theatre," Kateb Yacine and Kaki Wil Abd al-Rahman, both of whom had to "bow to popular demand" and give up writing "well-constructed plays." The "younger generation," of unnamed dramatists, have given up playwriting, according to Badawi, in favor of collective authorship and improvisation.   In fact, Kaki's experiments with traditional forms were of enormous importance and influenced a whole generation of Maghreb playwrights, while Yacine, like Abdelkar Alloulah, whom Badawi does not even mention, has an international reputation as one of the leading dramatists from the Arab world in the late twentieth century.

This marginalization of a significant part of Arabic drama even

---

5. (Cambridge: Cambridge University Press, 2006), 402.

by Arabic scholars is all the more unfortunate because the Francophone theatre of the Maghreb is similarly marginalized by English-language scholars interested in French-language theatre. Only in very recent years has the study of Francophone literature, French literature produced outside of France, become an important part of French studies in England and America, and although French-language plays from Canada, the Caribbean, and sub-Saharan Africa have been translated into English and some at least are becoming increasingly well known, the dramatic work of the Maghreb still remains almost unknown in English translation. This is the case even though the leading dramatists of this region are in many cases known and produced in France itself. So far, the study of Francophone theatre in Africa has been devoted almost exclusively to sub-Saharan Africa, once again ignoring or marginalizing the major cultural world of the Maghreb, which does fit the easy totalizing Western idea of "African theatre." Thus, John Conteh-Morgan's 1994 *Theatre and Drama in Francophone Africa*,[6] at this point the basic English text on this subject, is quite devoid of any mention of the rich Francophone theatre of the Maghreb. French scholarship is no better. M. Fiangon Rogo Koffi's even more recent (2002) *Le Théâtre Africain Francophone*[7] is not much better on this score. It discusses the work of more than one hundred Francophone dramatists in Africa, only five of which come from the Maghreb (three from Algeria and two from Morocco). There are more dramatists discussed from Madagascar than from the entire Maghreb. The only significant study of the theatre of this region readily available is Laura Chakravarty Box's excellent and ground-breaking 2005 *Strategies of Resistance in the Dramatic Texts of North African Women*.[8]

The present volume is planned to help alleviate this neglect and to introduce the important theatrical culture of the Maghreb to English-language readers. It includes translations from four of the best-known and most-honored dramatists of this region, two from Algeria and one each from Morocco and Tunisia. Before speaking briefly of their specific careers, a quick overview of the modern

---

6. (Cambridge: Cambridge University Press, 1994).
7. (Paris: L'Harmattan, 2002).
8. (London and Paris: Routledge, 2005),

dramatic tradition of the Maghreb may be useful.

Although both a live performance tradition and a thriving shadow-puppet theatre can be traced back for many centuries in many parts of the Arabic world, Arabic theatre in the European style was, not surprisingly, a product of the colonial period. For many years, the modern Arabic theatre was said to have begun with the production in 1847 of Marun Al-Naqqash's *al-Bakhil* (The Miser) in Beirut. Despite the title, the work was not, as has sometimes been claimed, an adaptation of Molière's play, but a staging of several popular stories in a European dramatic style. Recently, Shmuel Moreh and Philip Sadgrove have discovered an equally early Algerian play that combines elements of traditional Arabic live performance with European practice, Abraham Daninos's *Nazahat al-Mishtaq wa-Ghussat al-Ushshaq fi Madinat Tiryaq fi'l-Iraq* (The Pleasure Trip of the Enamoured and the Agony of Lovers in the City of Tiryaq in Iraq). This was the first play in Arabic to be published (in Algiers in 1847) anywhere in the Arab world, the next not appearing until some twenty-six years later, in 1863 in Beirut.[9]

Despite this early start, European-style theatre in the Arabic language did not develop in the late nineteenth century in the Maghreb as it did in Egypt and Syria. Instead, such theatre was confined to productions in French or Spanish, presented by amateur actors from the foreign-language communities for soldiers and the early European settlers in these countries. A large theatre was built in Algiers as early as 1853 by the French government and a Spanish theatre in Tetouan in Morocco about ten years later, but their public was essentially, if not entirely, a European one. The Chicago World's Fair of 1893 featured an "Algerian and Tunisian village," the only specific buildings of which mentioned in the Fair's official guidebook were a "truly Oriental . . . Algerian theatre, seating six hundred persons" and a Tunisian, holding three hundred.[10] The theatrical fare of these theatres, however, was primarily belly dancers, one of the biggest attractions of the Fair.

---

9. Shmuel Moreh and Philip Sadgrove, *Jewish Contributions to Nineteenth-Century Arabic Theatre* (Oxford: Oxford University Press, 1996), 45.
10. Julian Ralph, *Chicago and the World's Fair* (New York: Harper, 1893), 208.

The next phase of theatrical activity in this region came early in the twentieth century, as a part of the cultural renaissance called *al-Nahda* (Awakening) centered in Egypt. Colonial theatre for the colonials continued, at such sites as the Spanish Theatre Cervantes, built in Tangier in 1913, the French Masrah al-Balady (Public Theatre) built in Casablanca in 1922, the Rossini Theatre (1903), and Municipal Theatre (1909) in Tunis. At the same time, however, the Maghreb was visited by touring theatrical companies from Egypt, which provided examples of an Arabic-language theatre that could participate in the general cultural awakening taking place at this time. From around 1910 onward, first Tunisia, then Algeria, welcomed a series of such companies, which in turn inspired local theatrical companies to form, especially around the universities. In Tunisia, ach-Chahama (Gallantry) was formed by Tunisian and Egyptian amateurs as early as 1910, and Algiers saw the founding of the first and most important such group, the Society of Muslim Students, in 1919. Professional Arabic-language touring companies first appeared in Morocco in 1923, from both Tunisia and Egypt. Members of one of these companies remained in Marrakesh and established a company there in 1924.

During the 1920s and 1930s, largely under the influence of the touring Egyptian companies, small companies were formed and a number of plays, some in classical Arabic and others in the local dialect, were formed in the Maghreb. Tunisia was particularly active, with a dozen or so ongoing companies operating in Tunis. Female directors, headed by Wassila Sabri, began to appear in the late 1920s as part of a growing interest in Tunisia in female equality. By the 1940s, a number of specifically women's companies had been organized, with all roles played by women. Although a wide variety of dramas, comedies, and musicals were produced by these companies, Mahmoud Messadi's *al-Sudd* (The Barrier, 1940) has been called the first truly Tunisian play, an ambitious attempt to combine Muslim with contemporary existentialist thought and a visionary hero who has been compared with Ibsen's *Brand*. Tunisian playwrighting developed rapidly during the next decade, much of it either historical plays dealing with Tunisia, the Maghreb, or Andalusia, or plays of social criticism in the Tunisian dialect. Both types of drama encouraged nationalist sentiments and contributed significantly to the stuggle against French colonialism of the early

1950s, culminating in violent resistance beginning in 1954 and independence in 1956. During these turbulent years, in 1953, Tunis founded the first municipally funded professional company in the country.

The first significant Algerian man of the theatre was Salaali Ali, a director and actor, whose popular play *Juha* (1926) launched a wave of political dramas contributing to the struggle for independence. Significantly, it appeared the same year as the founding of the first Algerian political party dedicated to that cause, the Najm Shmall Afriqiya (Star of North Africa). That year also saw the return to Algeria from schooling in France of Rasheed Qasanteeni, the author of more than thirty popular plays, who has been called the "Father of the Algerian Theatre." The following year another major pioneer, the actor-singer Maheddine Bachetarzi, produced his first of many plays. During the 1930s, Algiers became a significant theatre center, with well-established local companies and traveling troupes form Egypt, Tunisia, and Morocco. In 1935, the Star of North Africa party sent a troupe to France to perform for immigrant communities, but it ran into trouble with French authorities, who feared it was enouraging Algerian nationalism.

The 1940s and 1950s saw a growing consolidation of theatre throughout the Maghreb, despite the violent upheavals in Algeria, in which theatre artists were often deeply involved. After deadly clashes with freedom-seeking demonstrators in 1945, the French occupation of Algeria became more repressive, although the colonial authorities sought some conciliation by establishing the Algerian Theatre Company at the Algiers Municipal Opera House in 1947, with Maheddine Bachetarzi as its director. Not surprisingly, however, funding was cut off within a year, out of concern for the political content of much of the work offered. Plays of social commentary were very popular, as were historical dramas such as Ahmed Tufeeq al-Madani's 1948 *Hannibal*, since these allowed political commentary under the guise of historical distance. Revolutionary sentiments were more and more openly expressed in the theatre until the actual outbreak of the revolution in 1956.

Two years later, as the revolution continued, Mutafa Kaatib, who had served as deputy to Bachetarzi in the Algerian Theatre Company, established in recently independent Tunisia an Algerian company in exile called the National Liberation Front Arts

Company. Prior to this time they had been based for three years in Paris. This company became the theatrical voice of Algerian independence, encouraging revolutionary plays with which it toured to such sympathetic countries as China, Russia, Libya, Morocco, and Iraq. Its most dedicated revolutionary dramatist was Abd ul-Haleem, but surely the best-known dramatist encouraged by this company was Katib Yacine.

Although the NLF performed in either classical Arabic or the Algerian dialect, many of the plays they presented were originally written in French and translated. Yacine is a central example of this. Yacine's native language is the Berber Tamazight, a language that would not allow either publication nor dissemination of his work. Thus, like his fellow Tamazight playwright Mouloud Mammeri, he has chosen French as his language of literary creation. Both authors have subsequently been translated in colloquial Arabic for production by the NLF and others.

The long Algerian War of Independence finally concluded in March of 1962. The following January, a decree from the new Algerian government established an Algerian National Theatre and organized theatrical activities throughout the country. The NLF theatre returned from exile to become this National Theatre. Its productions and the many festivals it organized dominated theatrical culture in Algeria for the next decade and a half, although in the late 1970s, the government strongly encouraged theatrical decentralization, giving strong support to the regional theatres in Oran, Anna, Constantine, and Sidi-bel-Abbas.

The figure most associated with this movement is one of the leading dramatists of modern Algeria, Abdelkader Alloula, whose play *The Veil* appears in this volume. Alloula, born in 1929 in a small village near Oran, studied theatre with Jean Vilar in Paris from 1960 to 1962, but returned to Algeria when independence was declared and joined the newly formed National Theatre there, first as an actor, then as a director, and eventually, as an adaptor and playwright. When attention shifted to regional theatre, he became director of the Regional Theatre of Oran, where he gained his first major success directing his own play *El Khozea* (Bread).

After three years as director in Oran, Alloula was invited to direct the National Theatre in Tunis, but he had disagreements with the ministerial authorities there and returned to Oran, where he remained as director until his assassination by a religious fundamentalist in March of 1994. It was during this second administration in Oran that he created his best-known work, a trilogy of socially engaged dramas that are collectively known as The Generous Trilogy, from the title of the middle play, *Les Généreux* (*Al-Ajwad*, 1984) meaning "The Good People" or "The Generous Ones." The series began in 1980 with *Les Dires* (*Al-Agwal*, The Sayings) and concluded with the play translated for this volume, *Le Voile* (*Al-Lithem*, The Veil). Although a few names recur in the plays, they present quite separate stories, all concerned with the tribulations of "the good people" in a corrupt and repressive society. The use of songs, narrative, and episodic structure will doubtlessly suggest Brecht to a Western reader, and the German dramatist was certainly among Alloula's models, but equally important was the storytelling tradition and conventions of his native country.

Since his death, Alloula's reputation has steadily grown both in Algeria and France, and one of the major events of "Djazair 2003," a year-long celebration of Algerian culture in France, was a national tour of a company of young actors from Oran performing Alloula's *The Veil*. The following year, the tenth anniversary of his assassination, his plays and career were celebrated throughout Algeria and France.

The other Algerian dramatist represented in this volume, Fatima Gallaire, has a much different background, though like Alloula, she was born in 1944 in a small village, near the city of Constantine. She grew up in Algeria, but in 1967, frustrated by the misogynist attitudes that she had found first in her home community and then as a student at the University of Algiers, she departed for France, where, except for a few years in the early 1970s, she has lived since, marrying a Frenchman in 1980. She first created for the cinema, but turned to theatre in 1985 with a powerful first play about a fatal tension between traditional culture and modernism among Algerian women, *Ah, vous êtes venus là où il y a quelques tombes* (Ah, You Have Come to Where There Are Tombs). *Co-épouses* (Co-Spouses), which appears in this volume, was her second play, published in 1992. Although much lighter in tone, it deals with an equally serious social question, the tensions within a polygamous household.

Despite Gallaire's exile, her plays all deal in some way with her homeland, and many are set there. She has always been centrally interested in women's issues, and the continuing oppression of women in Algeria has provided inspiration for much of her work. Traditional Algerian culture had been strongly repressed during the years of French rule, and was not surprisingly strongly reasserted after independence. Unfortunately, for Algerian women, this often meant a strong emphasis upon highly conservative Islamic social and religious beliefs. In 1984, a Family Code was passed, forbidding marriage between a Muslim woman and a non-Muslim man and allowing polygamy, both of which have inspired plays by Gallaire. The new constitution of 1988 dropped all references to the rights of women. In the early 1990s, the fundamentalist Islamic Salvation Front made major electoral gains, threatening a further erosion in the situation of women. A military takeover and guerilla warfare marked the next decade, and stability was still not totally restored at the beginning of the new century. During this turbulent period, Gallaire was denied permission to return to her homeland, although she did set up a fruitful collaboration with academic and cultural colleagues in Morocco and made several trips there. Finally, in 1999, she was granted a visa to visit her family and home.

The author to date of more than thirty plays, more than twenty novels, a number of films, poems and other writings, and the recipient of a number of major French literary awards, among them the Arletty Prize in 1990 and the AMIC Prize from the French Academy in 1994, Gallaire is today one of the best-known writers from the Maghreb.

In Tunisia, as in Algeria, independence was followed at first by strong governmental support of the arts. Under the ministerial leadership of Chedly Klibi, the arts in general and theatre in particular were encouraged by funding, construction of new facilities, and establishment of major festivals, most of which continue today. This "golden age" of modern Tunisian theatre lasted until the late 1970s, when decreased funding and increased censorship began to make theatrical production more difficult. The year 1982 saw a number of major developments, the establishment of the Tunisian National Theatre Company; the founding of the country's first serious theatre journal, *Fadha'aat Masrahiyya* (Theatrical Areas); and the creation of the Carthage Theatre Days Festival, which has become a major international event.

Even so, censorship has remained a serious problem for Tunisian theatres, and its pressures are felt in different ways in what a recent study has described as the three major types of theatre in Tunisia today.[11]   First are the official state-supported theatres, such as the TNT, that emphasize art and craft and avoid controversial material. Second are the groups such as the Gafsa Theatre Company (founded 1973) or the Théâtre Maghreb Arabe (founded 1974), that frequently challenge governmental positions and as a result either perform outside Tunisia or risk censorship or even imprisonment. A third group is the private theatres, more like experimental companies in Europe, but that generally avoid politically sensitive matters. Jalila Baccar, represented in this volume, has been a pioneer and leading figure in both the oppositional and private theatres.

Born in Tunis in 1952, she attended the university there and was one of the founders of the Gafsa Theatre Company.   She worked with a number of other groups before founding with her continuing partner, Fadhel Jaibi, the first private professional theatre in Tunisia, the Nouveau Théâtre, in 1976. Here she served as both leading actress and dramatist. Again with Jaibi, she established in 1994 her current group, Familia, which has gained a major international reputation, traveling first to Cairo, Beirut, and Damascus, then through much of Europe and as far as Argentina, Japan, and South Korea. They appeared at the Avignon Festival in 2002 and at the Berlin Festival in September of that same year, where three of their previous productions and three of their films were shown at various theatres and where Baccar and her company created *Araberlin*, the play included in this volume. Its theme is the difficulty of Arab immigrants living in a city like Berlin amid contemporary fears of Arab terrorism.   In 2003 *Araberlin* won the annual award for outstanding Francophone drama given by the French Société des Auteurs et Compositeurs Dramatiques.

Although Baccar, like almost all Tunisian dramatists, has had to negotiate often with governmental censorship, only her most recent drama, *Corps-otages*, has been actually banned for production at

11. Badra B'Chir, "Evolution des formes de créativité et dynamique sociale: l'apport de la comédienne tunisienne au théâtre en Tunsie. In *Théâtre et changements sociaux*. Procedings of the Quatrième Congrès International de Sociologie du Théâtre, Institut Supérieur d'Art Dramatique, 7–12 (Tunis: Editions Sahar, 1995), 82–91.

home, although it enjoyed a very successful performance at the Odéon in Paris, where it was the first Arabic play ever presented in that major theatre. Created in conjunction with the fiftieth anniversary of Tunisian independence, it looked back over that period and the many specific references to political figures and key events proved unacceptable to the Tunisian authorities. In an interview in the on-line Tunisian journal *Kalima* in October of 2006 Baccar urged the censor to relent, since her play was written "for Tunisians and should be seen by Tunisians." The website itself however, remains blocked in Tunisia.

Although Morocco has had a less substantial modern theatrical tradition than Algeria or Tunisia, and its dramatists have, like those in other parts of the Maghreb, had a somewhat uneasy relationship with state censors, on the whole dramatic expression has been rather less troubled there. The French protectorate established censorship in 1934, but as time passed, it became more tolerant of the developing Moroccan theatre, and in 1950 even provided a French theatre expert, André Voisin, to study and enourage theatre in that country. He remained for six years, traveling throughout Morocco, studying local performance traditions, and establishing workshops for theatre study. Many of the leading Moroccan theatre artists of the next generation were his students, among them Tayeb al-Saddiki, born in 1938, the best-known contemporary Moroccan dramatist, one of whose works appears in this collection.

The first professional theatre in Morocco, al-Ma'moura, the National Theatre, was founded just before independence in 1954 and was Morocco's leading encourager of young actors and dramatists until it lost the support of the Ministry of Cultural Affairs and was forced to close in 1974. A core of its actors then founded the Troupe du Théâtre National, which took up residence at the Théâtre Mohamed V in Rabat, where it performs today. Saddiki, who had founded a successful alternative troupe, the People's Theatre, in 1961, was invited to serve as artistic director, but, always an independent spirit, he found this position too restrictive and left to form his own theatre in Casablanca, where he is still located.

Saddiki, although he studied theatre with Jean Vilar in France,

---

12. Interview with Sihem Bensedrine, *Kalima*, October 18, 2006.

began his career as a designer and architect. He is well known as both a painter and a calligrapher, an actor and director, and a designer of scenery for theatre and cinema. He is best known throughout the Arab world, however, as a playwright, the author of some fifty original works and adaptations in both Arabic and French. Among the European authors he has translated into Arabic are Molière, Aristophanes, Goldoni, Ben Johnson, Marivaux, Gogol, Ionesco, and Beckett. His interest in Moroccan traditional performance is equally strong, however, and he has been a pioneer in developing interest in early performance texts and traditions.

From the beginning of his career, Saddiki has had a special affection for and sympathy with Molière, who, he has remarked, is a Mediterranean author and thus much closer to the Moroccan spirit than a dramatist like Shakespeare, for example. Saddiki's first adaptations were of the Molière farces *Le Medecine Volant* and *Ja Jalousie du Barbouille*, in 1955, and he continued to translate the French playwright and to present his works in the Mogador Theatre in Casablanca, where he was artistic director. In the mid-1990s, he wrote two original plays which featured Molière as a character, one simply named *Molière*, in 1992, and another with the more complicated title, *Nous Sommes Faits pour Nous Entendre* (We were Created to Understand Each Other), the following year. The first deals directly with Molière's illness and death, focusing upon his struggles with his social and religious enemies whom Saddiki specifically likens to Arab fundamentalists who oppose the theatre in his own time. The second, which is included in this collection, deals with the visit of the first Moroccan ambassador to the court of Louis XIV and focuses less on intolerance and censorship and more on cultural conflict. As translator, I have taken the liberty of changing the title to the more lively *The Folies Berbers*, a pun from the play itself.

Here then is offered a wide-ranging selection of dramas by some of the leading dramatists from this section of the world. It is a small sampling of the riches available, but it may, we hope, encourage those interested in the theatre to look further into the fascinating experiments and achievements of the Maghreb dramatic tradition.

Marvin Carlson

Abdelkader Alloula

THE VEIL

by Abdelkader Alloula

Translated by Marvin Carlson

THE VEIL

by Abdelkader Alloula
1987

CHARACTERS

THE NARRATOR

BERHOUM THE TIMID

CHERIFA, his wife

SI-KHELIFA, their neighbor

AN ORDERLY at the hospital

LAAREDJ, FILALI, BEKKOUCHE, neighbors

LIVE-AS-SHE-PLEASES

LOOK-FOR-THE-GOOD

SEEK-THE-PEACE

DOCTOR

POLICEMEN

INSPECTOR

VISITOR

FEMALE VISITOR

PRISONER

THE NARRATOR:
Djelloul, the worker, my brother, has a downcast heart,
His strength is exhausted, his desires thwarted,
His clear rights trampled upon, his opinions silenced.
Djelloul, the worker, my brother, his spirit is chained.

He walks, bent and staggering, bearing the weight of his suffering;
Over his head, like hawks, dark visions circle.
His foundations shake, a volcano erupts within him.
His distracted thought is plunged in a sea of speculation.
His feet drag, always hampered by his trials;
He advances weighted down by his life, his misfortunes.
Spring warbles around him, but he burns with anger.
Suffering has marked his features, has left furrows in them.
Worries lie behind and before him, a weight lies on his shoulders;
He bids farewell to a problem at the factory door
And finds it awaiting him at the door of his home.
When things clear up so that his stomach settles for a moment,
Disorders push into his flat, proliferating.
When he rolls up his sleeves to confront the problem of
        unemployment,
His children abuse him, demanding clothing.
When he has victoriously seized control of production,
The grocer appears with his bill in his hand.

Djelloul, the worker, my brother, has a downcast heart,
His strength is exhausted, his desires thwarted,
His clear rights trampled upon, his opinions silenced.
Djelloul, the worker, my brother, his spirit is chained.

He meets with those like him, the workers: that is his fate.
He rolls up his sleeves and plunges into action,
Drawn to the horizon, dazzled by the taking of positions.
He realizes his strength, takes fire, thrusts out his chest,
Openly embraces his comrades and cries: "I am yours!
Illumine my path, explain to me my task!"
They have walked through the history of humanity,
They have revealed the past and its hidden stages
And have recounted the journey since its beginning.

The explanations of the workers enlarge his spirit and vision
And, in the cradle of their movement he finds confidence.
He views society with a fresh eye and sees how it is organized:

One class in frustration and pain, selling its strength,
And another, living at its expense, in ease and comfort.
He understands the wrath of his peers and grasps the dimensions
        of their commitment.
Their struggles make sense and the obstacles appear clearly.
He raises his head, he comes to support his comrades,
Full of their power, subjugated to the movement.

Othmane, the worker, my brother, has a downcast heart,
His strength is exhausted, his desires thwarted,
His clear rights trampled upon, his opinions silenced.
Kaddour, the worker, my brother, his spirit is chained.

He enters the movement to become totally devoted to it.
He commits his knowledge and discrimination to its service.
He is impatient, as if wanting to remove a debt.
When he has some business in mind,
He sometimes forgets his hearth
And, if necessary, gives up lunch and dinner.
Sometimes he exhausts his own funds for the good of the movement.
He has sounded the depths of his militancy and is delighted with
        its secrets;
He immersed himself in it, its ambiance pleased him, solidarity
        conquered him.
As soon as he buried a problem, some transaction appeared to him.
He learned lessons of nobility from the workers;
He appreciated the value of courage in militancy;
He tested his knowledge and evaluated his experience.
Each step that he took increased his will.
When he is hard-pressed or when circumstances become difficult,
He turns to his friends to discuss and consult with them:
He knows they are with him in good and bad times.

Berhoum the Timid, son of Ayoub the Dry, was born about forty-
two years ago. His mother, El-Farzia, brought him into the world at

the dawn of a spring day in a thick forest. When the child saw the day, he was welcomed neither by *youyous* nor by dances of celebration.

He was wrapped in his father's turban and placed beneath a pine tree amid asparagus plants, poppies, and wild artichokes. At this time Ayoub the Dry, the father of Berhoum the Timid, was a farmworker for the colonials, but he was also a flamboyant and prestigious union director: he was known to every farmworker and every sharecropper from Sidi-bel-Abbes to Sidi-Boumediene.

One week before the birth of Berhoum the Timid, a general strike was organized in this region.   Matters then became complicated and took a turn for the worse.   The workers rose, and,after having set fire to the barns and haystacks of the colonials, they laid siege to the police headquarters with cries of "Allah is great," and armed with pitchforks, they broke in the gate of the prison and set free the prisoners. Then the mounted guard arrived in reinforcement and at full gallop from the city, armed to the teeth, and spread out over the region like a swarm of locusts.

Ayoub the Dry tied up his *gandoura* and threw it over his right shoulder, hid his face with the tail of his turban, and fled into the forest, desperate.

El-Farzia ran along the tracks of her husband, carrying her children, a bag of hard wheat under her arm, a leather bottle of water on her back, and in her womb, silent, Berhoum. Thus the whole family of Ayoub found itself in flight, hiding among the trees and bushes, wandering in the forest.

After two nights spent under the stars, Ayoub the Dry, the *paterfamilias*, decided to call a halt and ordered the youngest of his children to return to the village. He said to them: "Remain with me only El-Farzia and El-Ghalia, your older sister who will help her mother. As for you, young ones, it is enough! Return to your family: two of your go to the home of your paternal uncle, the other two to the home of your maternal aunt."

Ayoub the Dry, El-Ghalia, and El-Farzia could not close their eyes at night because of the jackels that circled them and never ceased howling. They could not rest by day because of the police and their tracking dogs on their trail. And yet in spite of all this, Berhoum the Timid did not flinch or twist about in the belly of El-

Farzia, his mother.

During one of these execrable nights, while stretched out on the earth, they considered their suffering by dim starlight. Ayoub placed a trembling hand on the belly of his pregnant wife and said to her: "This one is not like the others! He is angry! He is sulking! The world as it is will not satisfy him! To judge by his discretion, he is preparing to resist; he is armed! He will set up an ambush for the police!" El-Farzia answered: "If he is a boy, we will called him Bessam . . . " "No! No!" Ayoub interrupted. "We will give him a ringing name, a virile, generous name . . . We will call him Deham!"

Berhoum, timid, poked out his nose just after the breaking of dawn, in total silence. His mother gritted her teeth and tears rolled down her cheeks. After assisting her mother, El-Ghalia ran to announce the news to her father. Ayoub the Dry arrived running, happy, and firmly repeating: "Deham! . . . Deham! . . . Deham!" The mountains returned the echo. He found Berhoum, his tiny arms folded over his eyes, hiding his face as if he feared to receive blows. Ayoub took his son tenderly in his arms and drew him against his chest; and as he sought to embrace him, at the moment Ayoub lowered his head, the police seized him by the neck.

Berhoum the Timid, who was first named Deham, did not remember his father. He was deprived of him by the men of violence who carried him off bareheaded, who apprehended him just as he was going to embrace his son for the first time.

Ayoub the Dry was tried a week after his arrest by armed judges. He was condemned to deportation and banished, in chains, to Cayenne. Two years after, sad tidings came to the village. It was reported to Ghalem, his brother, that Ayoub had escaped from prison and perished at sea; the fish had eaten him. It was said that he had been devoured by a shark . . .

Berhoum the Timid was brought up by his uncle Ghalem, but the unfortunate uncle, oppressed by the burden of the family and his problems, was no longer in full possession of his senses. He forgot to enroll his nephew in the French civil list. It must be noted, however, that since he was very small, indeed from his infancy, Berhoum the Timid was always retiring, forgotten; it was rare that anyone paid him any attention or was concerned with him. Berhoum never raised his voice, never wept with strength, even when his cousins pinched his back, resolutely trampled on him, or softly pinched him.   When he was suffering, Berhoum wept internally, his face undistorted and without a trace of tears. Timid, shy Berhoum.   Only rarely did he join in to the games of the children his own age. He sat apart and observed from afar, a spectator. He loved to watch things from afar, as a spectator, but an informed spectator.   He analyzed the play shrewdly.   He knew who was exercising force, who was bluffing, but he never pointed anyone out or involved himself in the game.

It was quite by chance that Ghalem recalled that his nephew was not registered at his home. He remembered this the day when he summoned him to be circumcised. He then struck his forehead, having planted the knife in the trunk of a tree, and said to the orphan: "Do not soil your gandoura and wait here, near the olive tree. I am going to register you before they notice and condemn me to pay a fine. When I return, I will circumcise you." Ghalem departed running and swearing to himself. When he entered the town hall he was seized with panic to the point of forgetting the forename of the son of his departed brother, and his distraction increased when the foreigner began to interrogate him about "Ayoub the Felon," and inquired about the name of the midwife . . .

Ghalem began to mouth words at random and to stammer. Luck was with him however. The infidel was a bit tipsy. But Ghalem stumbled over his nephew's name. He had completely forgotten it! He remained for a long moment, his head in his hands. He knew that his brother had chosen for his son a galvanizing name, a symbol of audacity and offense, a resounding name . . . Ghalem sought repeatedly in his memory but could not recall that dear name.   Fear paralyzed his thought and the functionary was pressuring him!   Then, to remain faithful to the desire of the deceased, he blurted out: "Berhoum!" like the blast of a cannon, which made the foreigner wince! Before the name was out of his mouth, many others raced through his head: "Baroudi! Haddam! Derdak! Boucif! Antar!" The important thing was that he register his nephew and leave unscathed from the town hall, but it was a close shave! And thus, Deham the Timid became Berhoum; he grew up amid general indifference.   He attended the Koran School, but without a slate and seated behind the last row in the entry porch. He went twice a night across the courtyard of the communal school with his cousins to urinate in the stalls of the foreigners.

Berhoum the Timid, son of Ayoub the Dry, worked the land and tended the goats. And when the land no longer offered work, he went to the village to try to earn some money. There he met "The Alsatian," the carpenter, who hired him for a while and called him "Varum!" He also met "Grenadin," the baker, who employed him from time to time and called him "Baron!" Sometimes also he worked for the miller, but the latter communicated with him only by gestures.

Berhoum applied himself industriously to his work; while engaged, he was attentive, precise and spoke to no one. His only weakness? Once a day, for a minute or two, he became distracted, lost in his thoughts. He spoke to himself in order to set free the words that had accumulated within him.

BERHOUM: I would do . . . I would do . . . I would do some small deed in my life. Open your ranks so that I too can for once at least do something in my life!

—You can do nothing, fool! Your fate is in the hands of others! What can you hope to do, when you yourself are made by others. Made, unmade, and remade.
—Let me become a lubricator and clean the machines in the shop.
—Forbidden!
—After working hours!
—Impossible!
—For nothing! Free of charge!
—Why? Do you fancy yourself at home here?
—Let me teach the young the trade and the love of work. The factory could be shown off, piece by piece, shown again, cleaned, tidied up until it shined. It would be like the masters: "Hold on here, you! You, there! You, stand in front! You, there, under the machine! Go, slide in carefully! You, stand facing me and lift with me . . . You, turn the other way! . . . Go, kids, flood the factory! You, come here! You, come here! . . ."
—Fantasies! All these are fantasies, oh, son of Dry!
—I want to do! But how to go about it! Ah, sir! When I want to do something I feel a pressure growing and growing within me. But as soon as I seek to do it, the pressure immediately disappears, and I

draw back! It is as if there were another person within me! Go
away! Leave me in peace!
—You have no strength, Berhoum! You have no confidence in
yourself! Do your small bit and disappear! Ask God's mercy!
—If I could do something, I would want to do nothing more, I would
do nothing more . . .

THE NARRATOR: Berhoum the Timid, son of Ayoub the Dry, was
strongly beset by misfortunes, but he clung to life. As he clung to
the windows of the communal school, through which he could
snatch a few words of French. He knew how to be attentive and to
listen to people with interest. He loved to take pleasure in the
sweetness of words. When his uncle Ghalem lectured the members
of the family on freedom, saying to them: "In the society of the
future, you will all be free men . . . And this unhappy people,
muzzled in front and with a gun in their back, will all the same
liberate themselves and work miracles!" These words of his uncle
inspired Berhoum and ran through him like a breath of life, like a
zephyr that brought peace to the soul. When Berhoum heard his
uncle hold forth on the society of the future, on the liberty of thought
and of expression, he would hiccup with pleasure and lean against
the wall . . . He felt a tingling in his feet and felt himself soaring
through the house, between the matting and the ceiling.
    Berhoum the Timid, son of Ayoub the Dry, was married by
his family with Cherifa, his cousin, the daughter of his uncle
Ghalem. His family said: "She is enterprising and of age and he is
timid, an orphan, and a laborer; they will understand each other at
once." When they were children, Cherifa loved and defended him.
Thus, their relatives married them. A week after the proclamation
of independance, they said: "This is the propitious moment; the
occasion of victory is a good omen! Let them consummate their
union while the nation is jubilant.
    Berhoum and Cherifa understood and loved each other. They
knew how to support each other. He, head lowered, said his prayers
and stopped his ears when she raised her voice to speak rapidly and
angrily about their social situation. She jumping about and
swooning when he haltingly informed her that he had just received
his license to work.
    In brief, Cherifa and the son of Ayoub lived in this way,

mutually supporting each other, crossing difficult passages, but always giving thanks to the Almighty, while the years passed,

The Almighty blessed them with three daughters: Daouia, Halima, and El-Aounia, and two sons, Larbi and Tayeb, who were all born in rapid succession.

Berhoum and Cherifa left the countryside, misery pushing them from one side and the village calling them from the other. Economic improvement exerted its attraction. Cherifa said: "It bewitched and drew us like a lover." They looked around the village for a long time before being able to settle at its edge. They lived behind the cemetery, then below the town dump, then near the swamps, in caves and in slums. Then the Almighty gave them his blessing and they ended by finding two rooms and a kitchen in a building on the point of collapse with a staircase composed of shaky or missing steps, and a single toilet on the landing of the third floor.

Berhoum the Timid, the husband of Cherifa, daughter of Ghalem, was as a qualified laborer in the paper mill. He had now been there ten years. The factory had recently opened and its European machines were still excellent. He worked there for a long time before finding his niche and obtaining his qualifications.

But before finding this work in a public enterprise, the unhappy Berhoum had stumbled, and more than once. At first he was a slaughterer, then a half-price officer. Sometimes he worked for the glory of God, sometimes he was paid with entrails. He hawked fish and Barbary figs in the streets. He was a house painter, a mattress worker. He worked for masters in the private sector and drank his bitter cup to the dregs. He was a mason, building with blue stone and marble while living in danger of caveins. He was a plumber, ironworker, mechanic . . . machinery suited him perfectly, sending all day under a motor, occupied with pieces of metal, without anyone coming to bother him . . .

Berhoum the Timid was much appreciated in the pubic sector for his dedication to his work. He was assigned to the area where the paste was being washed. Despite all the calamities that befell him there, he never cheated on his hours, was never behind on his tasks and was never absent.

BERHOUM: Cherifa! Oh, Cherifa! Quick! Quick! Save me!

CHERIFA: What is it, Berhoum? You are hiccuping and white as a sheet.

BERHOUM: Ah! Cherifa! A catastrophe! Ah! Cherifa! A catastrophe!

CHERIFA: By the Prophet! Speak! What is it, son of Dry?

BERHOUM: Alas! How can I speak? Panic! It is panic, be quick!

CHERIFA: But what do you want me to do? Why must I be quick, you wretch?

BERHOUM: Sprinkle me! Pour water on me, Cherifa! Quickly!

CHERIFA: All right . . .All right . . . Courage! Here's some cool water In God's name . . . In God's name . . .Dear God, Berhoum . . . .

BERHOUM: Dear God! Dear God! The catastrophe that I am trying to escape, Cherifa!

CHERIFA: Just speak! Speak! I am terrified!

BERHOUM: The hiccups! Cherifa, the hiccups! Quick! Quick!

CHERIFA: What do you want me to do? Do you want a little more water? I'm trembling all over!

BERHOUM: I must hide! Disappear! Quick, wife! Hurry up! Quick!

CHERIFA: Disappear? Have you done something?

BERHOUM: Where can I hide? Oh, Cherifa, help me!

CHERIFA: But what's going on? Berhoum, you frighten me! What have you done? Speak! I am your wife and your cousin! Tell me!

BERHOUM: What can I tell you,, wife! Help me! Hide me! Make me disappear! Spirit me away! Bestir yourself and save me!

CHERIFA: It looks to me now as if you have assassinated someone and you are in flight!

BERHOUM: Me, an assassin? Me, an assassin? Don't you know me? Me, a quarter of a man? Me, oh Cherfia, who when I hear a mosquito buzzing around me expose my cheek so as not to trouble him. Me, kill someone? Look at my knees and you will understand. See how they tremble. Am I a man capable of killing? Hurry up, Cherifa, hurry up!

CHERIFA: You are going to tell me right now what is going on, or I will set up a howling that will freeze the spines of the whole neighborhood!

BERHOUM: No! Where? A little more water! Quick, quick . . . just see what a state I'm in! Half of me is stretched out on the ground and the other is standing, but trembling.

CHERIFA: It's the police, isn't it? The police are at your heels; that is why you are fleeing and seeking to hide!

BERHOUM: Wrap me in a blanket, or better, stuff me in a sack and close it up. Hide me, daughter of Ghalem, hide me! Hurry! The hiccups . . .

CHERIFA: Here, drink! Now! You've succeeded in making me tremble all over.

BERHOUM: Bolt the door, put out the light, and smother your breath! Don't open to anyone. I'm going to hide in the wardrobe.

CHERIFA: I've never seen you in such a state! You must have committed some terrible act to be so eager to hide! Have you killed or wounded somebody?

BERHOUM: Calm down, wife! Help me! Help me open this wardrobe and stop hiccuping! Me, kill or wound somebody? The Timid get into a fight? Me, who whenever I happen to catch sight of myself in a mirror become ashamed and hang my head! When someone happens to step on my toes, it is me who asks pardon and who lowers my head! The window, Cherifa, close it too and draw the curtains. But do it quickly, quickly!

CHERIFA: In the name of the God's Messenger, Berhoum, tell me what's going on!

BERHOUM: I have nothing to tell you, wife! Catastrophe! What can I do? How could I expect this situation? By what trick can I escape the trap? They are out to get me! If they don't catch me at home, they will corner me at the factory. No one can do anything against their way of scheming and plotting. Help me, God, help me!

CHERIFA: Berhoum, son of Dry, either you tell me what has happened to you or I am going to take a hatchet and stand guard at the door . . .

BERHOUM: Calm down, wife! Try to help your husband . . . See how I tremble! You would think I had caught cold. How can I get away? What can I do to escape them? Ah! I will slide between the matting and the mattress and you put pillows and sheep skins over it.

CHERIFA: Who are these people you are so afraid of? Speak! Just speak! Do you want to drive me crazy?

BERHOUM: Have pity on me, wife! The hiccups! They will choke me!

CHERIFA: Who is out to get you? Speak or I will freeze the neighbors will fear!

BERHOUM: They are . . . Ah, Cherifa, My lips tremble and no longer obey me . . . no longer obey . . .

CHERIFA: Calm down! You want a little more water! Breathe slowly!

BERHOUM: My shoes are firmly on my feet?

CHERIFA: Yes, you want to escape, is that it?

BERHOUM: No! My shirt and pants look alright?

CHERIFA: Certainly! Have you broken out or what?

BERHOUM: No! I am terrified and I have the feeling that my body and feet are naked! Timidity and fear have taken possession of me.

CHERIFA: Don't be afraid! I am here! I have only to scream and the whole neighborhood will be here! Just tell me who are these old folk who are harrassing you.

BERHOUM: Not old folk! Some are my own age, others even younger than I am! They are called the "con . . . gregation," or perhaps the "congruences?" or perhaps the "conspicuous." Oh, these hiccups, Cherifa! The "conspirators."

CHERIFA: You must arm yourself, son of Dry! The situation is serious, it seems! Here, take a bottle. I will take the hatchet!

BERHOUM: My ears! My ears, Cherifa, how do they look?

CHERIFA: These "complications," or these "constipations," do they know where you live?

BERHOUM: They know where I live, the day of my birth, and the contents of my belly. Nothing escapes them, these "complicators!" My knees, Cherifa! Am I standing on one leg or on two?

CHERIFA: Berhoum, certainly this is a serious matter! To battle, Berhoum, to battle! Today we no longer reckon the number of the fallen! Rare are those who remain standing! Today the room will be bathed in blood! You watch the window and I will stay by the door. Cheer up, son of Ghalem. The blood that has not flowed in your house during the last three sheepless festivals can be redeemed today, son of a hero! How? Do you dare to conspire against my husband while I am here? If one of you dares to show me the end of his nose, I will kill him! These "concertinos." That's all we needed, concertina players! And these people with concertinas, is this some new movement? It's the first I've heard of it! Every year there is some new fashion that catches us by surprise! By the head of El-Farzia, my uncle's wife, I swear that they won't touch a hair of your head. Their concertinas will fall in a row at my feet . . .You, just watch out the window. I will take care of their reception and their departure . . . Whoever steps through the door will see his family weeping for him!

BERHOUM: Be calm, wife! Your blood is boiling! You will be the end of me! That bottle you've armed me with, if I ever throw it, I will fly off along with it! My body is melted . . . extinguished . . . absent! I no longer have any feeling! Look at me; I seem to be inhabiting another body! Look at the bottle! See how it moves about on its own! I no longer know if it is I who is holding it or if it is the bottle that holds me by the hand and makes me dance . . . Be calm, cousin! These conspirators, they are laborers who work with me in the business and who live in our neighborhood; they could be thought of as neighbors. Put up the hatchet and take the bottle from my hand; I will tell you everything just as it happened. Now, the hiccups are clearing up . . .

CHERIFA: Quick, tell me, before they arrive and overwhelm us!

BERHOUM: Put away the weapons, wife, and lower your voice; these people are not coming to fight with me. I am the one who is fleeing them, even though they like me well enough. They have nothing against me and have no intention at all of harming me. It is me who is afraid of them! I am afraid that they will attach me to themselves, to their movement!

CHERIFA: You need to reject the concertina and take up some other instrument. Then they will leave you in peace.

BERHOUM: It's not a question of concertinas, Cherifa! Calm down and put away the hatchet.

CHERIFA: There, it's done. Now, explain yourself!

BERHOUM: Quiet! They're coming up the stairs!

CHERIFA: No. It's our neighbor who is bringing up water. He always stumbles between the first and second floor, poor fellow. Go on, explain!

BERHOUM: Come closer so that I can speak softly; no one must hear. And when they knock at the door, stop breathing and hold me close in your arms! Open to no one, you understand, even if the children want to come in . . . Come closer . . . Closer . . . and as you as you hear a knocking, hold me close . . .

CHERIFA: Berhoum! So, it's love that stimulates you, not fear! You are excited!

BERHOUM: Everything is mixed up in me, Cherifa!

CHERIFA: There, here is my knee; rest your elbow on it and tell me.

BERHOUM: The national manufactury of cellulose where we work was set up by foreigners. It began operations in 1972 and has suffered from problems ever since. Until now, in particular, it has never reached the production level for which it was planned and built. The water is inadequate and comes from the river. In winter, at the slightest rise in water level, we have to stop work. In the summer, during the periods of great heat and dryness, we have to stop production again. The factory is built next to the sea, and yet it is always lacking, always thirsty! The pulp from which we make paper comes to us in too small quantities; they say that no one can be found any longer to gather the pulp. Electricity is also lacking. There is never enough. Twice a year we are surprised by discharges of high tension! . . . Then there is the excavation at the doors of the factory, at the entrance and exit. Six directors have followed each other in heading the enterprise. As for the administrative personnel, they have no concern other than to advance their own interest and to mock the others. Others seek only the interests of the private sector and work underhandly to weaken the state sector. Some work for the general good, but with fear in their belly. The workers in the factory are as if under a state of siege: fear — terror even —

possesses them and there is no solution in sight.   Whoever is unfortunate enough to raise his head receives a broadside of bullets. Among them there are those who stand up to pray for rain; others who ask the Lord's pardon before blaspheming; others who enter into a sort of trance when they hear the word "productivity"; others also who say "Workers! Let us organize! We can . . . " but who, even before completing their phrase, cover their mouths; others who say that we must plan prayers on the beach, since that would be closer; others who say "Ach! The authorities are coming!" and "We are like chess pieces, manipulated by the imperialists for their own amusement."   Some have requested increased salaries to compensate, they say, for their humiliation!   Others say that it is torture, that it is the end of the world and that we are dying away, and there are those who say "Take care of the paper, we are importing it from abroad! . . .

CHERIFA: Quiet! I hear footsteps!

BERHOUM: It's them! It's them, Cherifa! Come close again!

CHERIFA: No, it's the sound of boots . . . It's our neighbor from above. And these "committers" that you are running away from. Who are they?

BERHOUM: There are three of them: Filali, Laaredj, and Bekkouche. They are accused of being agitators, while in fact, they are men of integrity who would give their lives for their country and who want only the good and happiness for the workers. They are devils of men! They have marvelous understanding! No one can resist them! Their goal? That the factory be forced to increase its productivity or if not, that it be closed.

CHERIFA: Are these workers or bosses?

BERHOUM: You've put your finger on the sore point! That's the way they talk. They can't say two words without repeating "The workers must manage their own factory!" They are devils, I tell you, Cherifa! And they keep up with everything that happens in the organization!

CHERIFA: Do you think they are capable of directing the factory?

BERHOUM: They are devils, I tell you. They know the whole factory, from its foundations up to its management!

CHERIFA: Are they members of the trustees?

BERHOUM: They have a foot among the trustees, but elsewhere also.

CHERIFA: And what interests them in you? Why are they looking for you?

BERHOUM: The big boiler, the one that washes and grinds up the pulp is not working. They want me to fix it. They have circulated their propaganda saying that Berhoum, son of Ayoub the Dry, is an ace mechanic, and they say he is the only one able to repair it . . .

CHERIFA: Hurrah for my husband Berhoum, the Ace Mechanic!

BERHOUM: Wife! Wife! You have lost your mind! Be quiet! You will get me spotted! Be quiet! I tell you . . .

CHERIFA: I am going to put the water on the fire to make them some tea!

BERHOUM: Oh, daughter of Ghalem, listen to me! This is a risky business. Lower your voice and listen to me. I am going to explain.

CHERIFA: You see this hatchet? If you don't open the door to them and receive them as you ought to, this night I will chop you into pieces! This night I will make you perform on the concertina! They are coming to ask for you help for the good of all and you run off, terrified! The mighty oak has produced only an acorn!
BERHOUM: In the name of all you hold dear, just listen to me for a minute!

CHERIFA: Speak quickly, then!

BERHOUM: This boiler, it is forbidden to go near it and its mechanism is complicated. Much of the factory is stopped because of it. The administrators have warned the workers that whoever touches the boiler must be licensed. They say that they are going to call in a specialist technician from abroad to repair it. And our friends, for whom you want to make tea, want to repair this boiler secretly at night!

CHERIFA: Go buy them some rolls before they arrive! Quick, get up!

BERHOUM: Wife, where do you think I can find rolls at this hour? Why do you think I told you all this?

CHERIFA: As soon as they arrive, show them in and I will run out and buy some little pastries from the baker.

BERHOUM: My hiccups, Cherifa!

CHERIFA: They will pass! As soon as they knock at the door, they will pass . . . But you, who told you they were looking for you to repair the boiler?

BERHOUM: Messaoud, the night watchman at the factory. They all worked on him and have enrolled him in their movement. He is in the organization! They are devils, Cherifa! Devils! And this Messaoud, now he speaks like them of social justice and workers' rights! . . . He told me "This is our factory! We own it! We are going to show them that we are capable of running it and making it work." They are demons! . . . And our neighbor, the one who lives just at the end of the terrace, is their friend! From time to time they visit him to get advice!

CHERIFA: Our neighbor? Which one?

BERHOUM: Ho Chi Minh!

CHERIFA: Si-Khelifa, the Indochinese?

BERHOUM: Right! Daughter of respectable people! They are devils! And you knew nothing about it!

CHERIFA: Ah . . . Ah . . . Ah . . .

BERHOUM: The hiccups have stopped, Cherifa!

CHERIFA: Steps! Listen! It's them! Three of them! Open the door!

BERHOUM: Take the hatchet!

CHERIFA: They avoided the hole as if they knew the stairway perfectly!

BERHOUM: But . . . haven't I told you enough about them?

CHERIFA: Their step is pleasant enough. They are coming up without hurrying . . . I am going to prepare a couscous with butter for them; I have some excellent semolina put aside.

THE NARRATOR: Berhoum the Timid, son of Ayoub the Dry, opened the door, trembling, as soon as he heard a knock . . . He froze when he saw Filali, Laaredj, and Bekkouche standing there, lined up like posts on the doorsill. They said: "Peace be with you!" and he answered: "May God hear you!" swallowing his breath. His blood rushed to his head and his ears began to ring. He wanted to say to them, "I am an inoffensive soul, messieurs. Why do you come to trouble me?" But behind the door, Cherifa pinched him and he said: "Please, messieurs, come in! I am alone with my wife . . . Enter! Welcome! We were expecting you!" Berhoum the Timid showed them in, and after inviting them to sit, he began to go to the kitchen and back, following Cherifa, as if he had lost something. He sat a plate before them, brought them a jug of water, and said to them: "I am going to bring you a jug of milk." He continued coming and going in this way. Cherifa looked at him with wide eyes and said "Just go sit with them men! When the couscous is ready, I will let you know." Filali called to him: "Dear Berhoum! Please, come and sit! Let the milk go! Come, we have things to talk about!"--"My wife is fxsing us a good couscous . . . with sugar . . . honey, you know, is out of range." "You are celebrating some happy event?" said Laaredj. "We heard your wife's cries on the stairway." — "It is just that my wife cries out like that from time to time, training herself so as no to lose her voice." — "And the couscous?" asked Bekkouche. "Why is that? Are you saying that you were expecting us?" — "It is the first time that you have visited us, and moreover you are coming about a serious matter . . . "Berhoum answered. "We are going to break bread together; a little couscous will confirm our good humor and prepare the ground for discussion." They laughed. Filali seized the moment, leaned forward on his bent knee and opened discussions about the large boiler.

The son of Ayoub sat and embraced his legs. He placed his chin on his knees, wrinkled his brow, and pricked up his ears. He devoted himself to the spectacle of these men, drank in their words, and observed the particular vocal strategies of each. He noticed how they leaned upon each other, as if they were born from the same womb. He noted how each thrust out his chin and hardened his expression when he used the word "enemies," how each shrugged his shoulders and made a fist whenever he said "we," how each thrust out his chest and expanded his arms when he spoke of "social justice." Berhoum sat there, hugging his chest and breathing very, very softly, savoring their words and digesting them as if he were in a delicious dream. From time to time, his eyes were misted with tears; his vision clouded and they appeared to him like lions roaring and shaking their manes.

Cherifa, daughter of Ghalem, happy in her kitchen, mixed butter into the couscous. Her hands swimming in the large plate, she was proud of her husband, the son of Ayoub the Bannished. The situation recalled her past and her youth to her; she recalled the countryside at the time of shooting and sacrifices. She was happy and occupied herself skipping back and forth. She quietly brought her children into the kitchen and said to them: "Your father is resolved! He has renounced his timidity and has moved into action! He is going to enter into a mission to benefit the people. I can hardly keep from crying out. If we did not have guests I would make the walls ring!"

Berhoum the Timid, son of Ayoub the Dry, and his comrades studied carefully each stage of their mission. During their discussion they always came back to the boiler. Laaredj nicknamed it "the washerwoman," Bekkouche "the festive pot," and Filai "Miss Steamer." After having eaten and finished their discussion about this operation, they got up and prepared to depart. They made their good-byes to Berhoum; Laaredj shook his hand vigorously and slapped him on the shoulder; Bekkouche kissed him on both cheeks; and Filai pulled out of his shirt some folded documents and gave them to him, saying: "These are the plans for the boiler and the chart of its internal apparatus; we have obtained them from the administration. Study them and be careful; we have got to put them back."

"How can I read them?" Berhoum said. "You are mistaken, my friends! You take me for an engineer? Your brother here present is a simple manual worker!"

"But your experience! What is important to us is your experience! Just cast a glace over these plans, perhaps you will gain something from it," answered Filali.

They went away, leaving behind them the son of Ayoub standing, dazed, the documents in his hands, as if chained. His children and Cherifa surrounded him. He did not look at them, did not speak to them. He remained a long time, standing like a statue, absently, imagining himself facing the disciplinary committee and listening to their voices abusing him: "What possessed you to go along with those agitators? You have stolen official documents from the files of the administration and you were planning to steal the great boiler! Yes, to steal it to sell it to the Japanese for scrap metal! This is sabotage—economic sabotage. You are the leader of this group! That is why you have always been so silent and solitary! But the Almighty has unmasked you, and you have fallen into our hands. We will be finished with you today! And the union, you say? What use is it? It seems to be inoffensive and stupid, while it promotes sabotage! May God curse you, traitor! You Japanese dog, enemy of the people . . . "

Berhoum the Timid, son of Ayoub the Dry, pushed aside his children and ran to the home of Si-Khelifa, "the Indochinese." He pushed upon the door violently, entered, then threw down the crumpled documents to the ground. He stood behind his neighbor, his face blood-red, shaken by hiccups . . .

Si-Khelifa, "Ho Chi Minh," his neighbor, did not flinch, did

not utter a word. His back was turned to the door and he looked out
through the open window toward the distant sea, lost in his
thoughts.   He wore a hat in the form of an upside-down
couscoussier to protect his head. His home, truth to say, was almost
in ruins, and from time to time, a tile fell from the roof. He was
sitting with his legs folded under him, his hands on his knees.
Beside him was a small low table on which was set a glass of tea and
a bit of barley bread. The hiccuping had taken control of Berhoum,
and his words were drowned in the bottom of his throat. The silence
of Ho Chi Minh, sitting there like a curio, added to his impatience
and his fright. He stamped three times on the floor with his heel to
mark his presence and to attract his neighbor's attention.

Si-Khelifa was an old man; he was past sixty and had
experienced strange adventures during his life. From his earliest
years he had tasted beatings and prison, had known hunger and
haevy blows, sickness and wounds; he had suffered martyrdom.
Called up by France during the forties, he had been sent to fight in
Indochina. He deserted the French army and joined the Vietnamese
beside whom he fought against France and then America: sixteen
years of exile and combat. He returned to his dear fatherland after
independence, saying: "Now I am old, and I have seen enough. I
must return home. When my time comes, I can be buried near my
father and my grandparents." In the neighborhood, Si-Khelifa was
loved and respected. He was consulted and visited like a saint.
Some called him "the Sage," others, "Indochina," some named him
"Vietnam," others "Ho Chi Minh." Berhoum stamped his heel on the
ground. Two words escaped from his lips: "Si-Ho!"

BERHOUM: Oh, Si-Ho!

SI-KHELIFA: Stop stamping on the ground with your foot, or the
roof will fall in!

BERHOUM: Oh, Si-Ho, this is dangerous business! These
documents have been stolen from the directors.

SI-KHELIFA: Please have a glass of tea and breathe the sea air.

BERHOUM: I am about to smell the odor of prison. I see the police rollig up their sleeves and hear my children weeping for me.

SI-KHELIFA: To the devil with ill omens! Calm yourself, Si-Berhoum, and lower your voice a bit. The neighbors' children are small and at this hour they should be asleep. Our poor building is so dilapidated that if you sneeze tiles fall from it.

BERHOUM: Your friends . . . they came to my house . . . they put this bomb in my hands and left..in a hurry!

SI-KHELIFA: Would you like me to pour you a bit of tea! It is warm and thick: just at the perfect point to enjoy!

BERHOUM: Oh, Di-Khelifa, I have come to see you so that you can explain, can clarify things for me! My soul is petrified; it has no means to appreciate intoxication or to seek pleasure! These documents have been stolen from the administration!

SI-KHELIFA: How?

BERHOUM: I don't know how they were taken! But it is a serious theft whose author will pay for in the most serious manner, without pity or mercy. Your friends . . . Your friends have left this poisonous thing with me and gone off to sleep in peace! "So that you can study the interior of the boiler," they said . . .

SI-KHELIFA: Their aim is noble and right is on their side.

BERHOUM: . . . The interior of the boiler! Rather say that I should study the best way to get into prison! Perfect! I must think it over and decide if I will go to prison with my chest out or on my side, if I will go there alone or if I will take my comrades with me!

SI-KHELIFA: This task, oh Si-Berhoum, is a noble one. If you are able to undertake it with confidence, calm, and judgement, there will be no prison or punishment . . . Quite the contrary! You will have helped out your business, and at the same time, you will have saved thirty families!

BERHOUM: But, Si-Khelifa, the administration has forbidden us to go near the boiler! Moreover, they have said that they are going to bring in a specialist from Germany to look over the evil thing.

SI-KHELIFA: And the water . . . The problem of water! How are they going to solve that difficulty?

BERHOUM: They say that they are going to take care of it once and for all; they plan to dig wells.

SI-KHELIFA: And the pulp? What are they planning to do to stop the desert sands that are eating it up? And where are they going to get someone to harvest it? Tell me!

BERHOUM: How should I know, I, how to solve the pulp problem?

SI-KHELIFA: Perhaps they plan to recite incantations? To create pulp by magic and sorcery?

BERHOUM: Oh, Si-Ho Chi Minh! What have I to do with . . .

SI-KHELIFA: Your factory is in peril! There will be no specialist for the boiler, nor the means necessary to make the factory run! You would see this clearly if you thought a bit about it! There are men inside and outside the factory who are working against the general good and who put pressure on our business and our future! Among them, there are those who serve the national private sector, others who serve foreign capital, and even some who serve both! Such people are like a serpent in our bosom! If they could, they would sell the factory out from under you! Your factory irritates them and the boiler is only a pretext to license thirty workers. After the boiler, they will make the pulp a pretext to license thirty others. Oh, Si-Berhoum, your bread is now threatened. If you are not licensed with the first group, you will be so with the second. And your pride, oh Si-Berhoum? If you repair the boiler, you will provide proof of your power and effectiveness! If you repair the boiler, you will force these people to retreat, and the pretext that they have put forward to license the works will no longer be worth anything! So, what do you think, Chief?

BERHOUM: Excuse me, I am trying to breathe. I seem to have a noose around my neck! I am stunned. I would like to breathe the sea air a bit; yes, that is true.

SI-KHELIFA: The tea is cold! Do you want me to make you a small glass?

BERHOUM: No, your words have intoxicated me! It is as if I drank two teapots full! While you were speaking, I felt myself in battle, attacking, a machine gun in hand, decimating the enemy.

SI-KHELIFA: It is a battle, truly! And the boiler is one stage in this battle!

BERHOUM: Our friends, the agitators, left me on the river bank and you have immersed me.

SI-KHELIFA: Laaredj, Bekkouche, and Filali love you and have the greatest confidence in you.

BERHOUM: You are all in agreement!

SI-KHELIFA: Explain!

BERHOUM: What I mean is . . . you are all so confident . . . You seem engaged in the matter and you know the factory better than I do, who lives there!

SI-KHELIFA: These documents? What are they for?

BERHOUM: I know very little! Only an engineer can read these plans. I am only a simple manual laborer.

SI-KHELIFA: Look carefully: perhaps you will gain something. The workers are counting on you.

BERHOUM: They would be better off relying on God . . . An operation carried out at night, hidden away, is not an easy thing . . . Let them rely on God! Even in the full light of day I can't pull this off!

SI-KHELIFA: The bottle of gas . . . for soldering . . . That should be under the boiler, wrapped in a sack.

BERHOUM: How can they get a bottle of gas into the factory?

SI-KHELIFA: The administration's employee who got the plans for us and informed us about the project will take care of the bottle. He will get one from the radiators in the offices.

BERHOUM: Ah, my ancestors! And the soldering tubes?

SI-KHELIFA: Bekkouche will bring them. He will wear them around his waist.

BERHOUM: Ah, a good trick! . . . and the copper?

SI-KHELIFA: Filali will put a tube of lead in one of the wheels of his bicycle and will roll up two meters of copper tubing in his turban.

BERHOUM: Prodigious! The clever devils! Who could keep up with them! Those people who plan to empty the factory and sell it for their profit, let them pay out of their own pockets to provide for the factory!

SI-KHELIFA: You will find flashlights near the entrance. The tools will be in an iron chest near the gas bottle. On the rim of the boiler you will find water, honeycakes, and coffee, a gift from the workers.

BERHOUM: If you were only present, oh Ayoub the Dry!

SI-KHELIFA: What? What are you saying?
BERHOUM: You have set up a regular ambush!

SI-KHELIFA: Organization is the secret of success!

BERHOUM: The boiler, how high is it? How many meters did you say?

SI-KHELIFA: Three meters, fifty-six.

BERHOUM: Have you even studied the plans?

SI-KHELIFA: No. We have studied the surroundings of the boiler. The rest is for you! Here, take them.

BERHOUM: There are the entrails . . . Water circulates through these conduits . . . This is the opening for it to escape . . . If I were not afraid of being mistaken I would say that this is the vapor chamber and that the motor . . . And this would be the mechanism for changing gears . . . A ladder! A ladder, uncle Vietnam! You didn't think of that, did you! How am I going to get up there?

SI-KHELIFA: You will make a pyramid. Laaredj and Bekkouche on the bottom, Filali on their shoulders and you on Filali's shoulders. The ladders in the factory are all out of commission; the administration borrows them for personal use!

BERHOUM: Then you didn't find any trick to get a ladder in?

SI-KHELIFA: No, we have much less time than you think. If we had enough time, we could have brought in an entire crane, piece by piece!

BERHOUM: Prodigious!

SI-KHELIFA: You can leave the plans with me if you are afraid or if you want to travel more lightly.

BERHOUM: No. I will take them along to study at home. My children will lend a hand. And besides, I can do myself proud before Cherifa. The smell of the sea at your home, oh Si-Khelifa, tickles the nostrils!

SI-KHELIFA: Be careful not to sneeze! You risk getting a tile on the head!

THE NARRATOR: From this moment on, Berhoum, son of Ayoub

the Dry, began to be treated with an unaccustomed consideration and with great respect by his wife and children. He appeared to his family as a hero of fantasy, planning terrible offensives against the enemy. For three consecutive evenings upon his return from work, he remained shut up in his room, carefully studying the plans of the boiler. His children had to go study their lessons at the homes of neighbors, giving up to him the low table, while Cherifa sat on watch near the door of the room. Whenever her husband sighed or yawned, she asked him if he needed anything. Three consecutive nights were passed by the son of Ayoub the Dry in studying and verifying. From time to time, he spoke to his conscience: "It is a curse that God has laid upon me! If the operation succeeds, I will be licensed; if it fails, I will be licensed . . . These men are devils! These agitators work underground! Like an earthquake!

The fourth evening, that of the operation, Berhoum the Timid, son of Ayoub the Dry, left before evening prayers. Cherifa guided his steps and threw a casserole of water behind him as favorable omens. He entered the factory and proceeded toward his working post, hiccuping, running with sweat, his feet dragging as if he were carrying a boiler on his back, while the workers watched him in admiration. He walked as if rattling chains were already attached to his ankles . . . He approached his working post while the growling of the factory sounded in his ears. As he walked, it seemed to him that he heard Ayoub the Dry calling to him in these words: "This is what men do, my son! Act and defend your dignity and your power will grow!"

Berhoum painfully passed two hours working at his machine, and when the agreed-upon moment arrived, he said to his working companion: "Keep an eye on the machine, please. I am going to go to the toilet, begging your pardon. If I am a bit slow, don't worry. I have an upset stomach."

"It's the water," his companion replied. "The water is poisoned and it is ravaging us! Go empty your boiler, and when you return, it will be my turn."

Berhoum crossed the court, and arriving at the shut-down wing, he slipped unobtrusively into the darkness of the shop and was careful to be seen by no one. There, he said in a weak and disguised voice: "Oh, Si-Mohamed, watcher of the night! Have you no knife to lend us. We need it. Speak!" No one answered him. He took a flashlight and turned it on.   A bat flew above his head, frightening him.   Dropping to one knee, he said: "I swear by God that I will not begin again, oh, my uncle!"   He asked God's pardon, arose, took several steps.   He was in front of the boiler: large, glack, cylindrical, high . . . He directed his light toward it and began to consider it.   White graffiti could be read on its surface: "May a day come without breakdowns and without troubles," and on the other side: "Our dignity lies fallow and our hopes are in the boiler!"   He opened wide his arms, embraced the machine and laying his cheek against it, spoke tenderly to it: "Ah, my dark one!   This night the son of Ayoub has decided!   This night, Berhoum will penetrate your entrails and stimulate you, you who inflame your creatures! Tonight your joints will tremble, Miss Steamer!   Tonight you will bellow or I am not a man!"

The breast of Berhoum the Timid, son of Ayoub the Dry, filled with joy and power when he saw the refreshments spread out as promised on the lip of the machine.   He stepped back three paces from the boiler and, without being aware of it, began to dance, spinning in a lively manner, his arms held out like a hawk, his neck extended, as if he controlled every part of this factory, as if he acquired worth from them.

Laaredj, Filali and Bekkouche arrived running and out of breath; in the twinkling of an eye, they attached ropes, sorted out the tools, and said: "In the Name of the Prophet!"   They helped each other up and formed a human ladder in the form of a pyramid, each bearing the other on his shoulders.   "Ay, Filali, you are crushing my bones!" — "Let go of my leg and hold my belt; you're tickling me!" — "My friends, my knee is giving way!   Your shoulders are rough and your feet smell!"

Rapidly, Berhoum climbed up to the boiler.   He lifted the lid and fumbled about among the hoses.   He seized the tubes and checked the pieces out one by one.   He was not long in finding the source of the breakdown.   From the belly of the boiler he called out: "Easy . . . Easy . . . while the boiler echoed "Easy . . .Easy . . ."   He had found the motor open.   The pieces had been removed that lay long its sides and the electric wires were exposed.   Filali called to him and asked questions.   Berhoum replied "Sabotage!"   The machine echoed "Outrage . . . Outrage . . ."   He repaired the motor and left the machine covered in sweat.   He sat with his legs crossed on the rim and said to his companions: "We've won! This really deserved the honey cakes. Press that green button on the side and we'll try out the beast!"

Filali leaned on the button. The machine started, the motor hummed, water surged into the interior of the vat, and the boiler shook as if there were an earthquake. The men below leaped for joy. Bekkouche shrugged his shoulders and Laaredj broke into dancing. Berhoum, who was sitting on the edge at the top of the boiler, was shaken violently from side to side. He started to slide and found nothing to hang on to. He leapt into darkness and emptiness. He fell badly and broke his leg; the unhappy fellow almost lost consciousness. His companions ran to him, helped him to sit up, and wiped the sweat from his brow. They saw that his leg was hanging down. "All together now, let us lift him up gently." Occupied as they were with Berhoum, they forgot the machine which continued to run, chugging away, filling the shop with its noise.

Just as they started to lift him up, the lights went on. The security police and guards came running to the shop and stopped as soon as they heard the noise of the machine. Berhoum the Timid raised himself when the lights came on and understood that they had been discovered. Despite the intensity of his pain, he stood up on his good leg, pushed away his companions and said to them: "Flee . . . Leave me alone and flee! Go out the other side, you can escape by the small door . . . Save yourselves! Better that one be taken than four!"

All that night, Cherifa spent awake and waiting at home. Sleep had fled. She waited for her dear Berhoum to return and tell her all. She had prepared everything required for a cake of buttered bread to take with his coffee. But information came to her in different forms.

One told her: "Your husband repaired the boiler, then he went to report to the police in charge of economic sabotage who were assigned to the factory."

Another told her: "Berhoum repaired the boiler, but then fell in it after setting it going. It swallowed him up and spit out his blood."

There was also one who said: "After repairing the machine, he was captured and tortured. They wanted him to confess how he was able to climb up on the boiler without a ladder. But Berhoum did not divulge his secret."

One told her: "Berhoum has become the head of the factory! After having fixed the machine, he had an accident and is in the hospital in a coma."

One told her: "He is badly burned!"

One told her: "He broke several bones!"

One told her: "He was boiled alive!"

One told her: "He is lucky! If he dies, he will be hailed as a martyr for the cause!"

Cherifa rans to Si-Khelifa's house to demand his advice. She found his door shut. His neighbors said they had seen him leave early in the morning with someone from the neighborhood. He was in a hurry. He was cursing and swirling his stick. Cherifa put on her veil, took the buttered bread, and ran to the hospital.

THE ORDERLY: Don't be long. Let him rest.

SI-KHELIFA: Can I speak to him for a moment?

THE ORDERLY: You can if he regains consciousness. And even if he cannot answer, he can see you and hear you.

CHERIFA: Berhoum! I am your wife, Cherifa! God be thanked, you are safe and sound! You are out of danger now. The orderly says that you were in a coma.

BEKKOUCHE: His hand moved!

LAAREDJ: Are you sure that he is really Berhoum, son of Ayoub?

CHERIFA: Absolutely. This is him.

LAAREDJ: How can you recognize him when he is all wrapped up like a mummy from head to foot?

CHERIFA: I recognize him by the glint in his eyes and by his hands. I recognize him by the mole on his eyelid and by the tattoo on his hand.

FILALI: Did we give you enough blood?

THE ORDERLY: Enough for him . . . With some left over for us. He needed only this bottle.

FILALI: The workers were quick to come and give their blood. You will have all the provision you need!

THE ORDERLY: May the Almighty provide for you as you have provided for us.

LAAREDJ: Must he remain a long time with this plaster, these bottles, and these tubes?

THE ORDERLY: You must ask a doctor! He knows better than I. He can tell you . . .

CHERIFA: It must be a bad fracture, eh?

THE ORDERLY: It wasn't just a fracture! He had several of them, poor fellow! He had a blow to the head, wounds on the face . . . But you should ask the doctor, he will give you all the details.

SI-KHELIFA: The evil creatures! They did this with a joyful heart.

THE ORDERLY: Those who brought him here said that he suffered from an accident at work. Their report says that he was working on a machine, hanging four meters above the ground, and that he slipped and fell into the machinery.

BEKKOUCHE: He is moving his fingers! Look! Look! The poor fellow! He is trying to tell us something!

CHERIFA: Berhoum! Can you hear me? Do you want to speak? You cannot? They have closed your mouth! Who? Do you want to write? Do you have a paper and pencil here?

THE ORDERLY: I will go look for some . . . Don't touch him!

SI-KHELIFA: Try to control your pain, Berhoum! Courage! Hang on to life; we still need you!

CHERIFA: Don't worry about us! Your children are proud of you and all the people in the neighborhood speak only of you! The all admire you! Si-Ahmed, the spice merchant, poor man, thought you were dead. He came to our place with coffee and sugar, weeping. He said to me: "Your man, the Timid, was a man of stature! May God accept his soul! I will cover the costs of the funeral." As for Meriem . . .

SI-KHELIFA: Be quiet, woman. He is weeping! . . . The whole quarter is topsy turvy because of you! People promise that as soon as you are cured, they will march you out of the hospital with drums, trumpets, and flowers!

THE ORDERLY: Here, woman! But don't take too long! Don't overdo it!

CHERIFA: Berhoum! Here! Here is a pencil! I will hold the page for you.

BEKKOUCHE: A good deed, my sister . . . Please distribute the fruits that we brought to the sick.

CHERIFA: Even this buttered cake, share it among them. My God, bless your parents! . . . Gently, Berhoum . . . Tomorrow, God willing, I will bring you a cafe au lait and a bowl of soup. Look, Si-Khelifa! What has he written!

SI-KHELIFA: Look, Laaredj, read!

LAAREDJ: Give it to Filali, I . . .

FILALI: Me? I know how to count, certainly, but as for reading . . .

BEKKOUCHE: Alright! Read it yourself, Si-Ho Chi Minh!

SI-KHELIFA: Si-Khelifa's eyes are worn out . . . and he studied

Vietnamese.

THE ORDERLY: Let me see . . . "What do the workers say about Miss Steamer?"

FILALI: The factory is in a turmoil! In ferment! The workers are congratulating each other under the very windows of the administration. It is like the Festival of Ayed, when people embrace each other and beg each other's pardon! Half of the night shift refused to go home; they made a gift of four hours of work! They said it was to show solidarity with the son of Ghalem and to demonstrate their position. The union bureau is on our side. They say that they will send you a letter of official congratulations next week.

LAAREDJ: When the guards and security police carried you off, the boiler remained working for more than a quarter of an hour. All the workers stopped working to listen to its rumbling. They seemed to be observing a moment of silence! What a pity you were not there! A great ferment reigned this morning in the factory because of Miss Steamer! And the more the work areas celebrated the more torments the administration seemed to suffer! The workers laughed and the others ran; the workers shouted insults and the others fainted away!

BEKKOUCHE: Someone said to them: "If you want to sell the factory, it is now or never! Strike while the iron is hot . . . and before the dinar starts to fall!" Another said: "We should lend him to the Americans as a technical consultant; he will report their schemes to us!" Dark designs were brought to light as the boiler stirred up all the muck! Everything was breaking apart on all sides! In the offices it was extraordinary! "Let go of me if you want me to let go of you!—If you complain against me, I will unmask you! . . . " Some said, "It's sabotage!" and others, "It's a plan to create disorder!" and still others, "As you know, I have really sharp teeth, and I may swallow you up!"

FILALI: One administrative agent said: "The workers are opposed to the National Charter! They want to increase the production of paper, which will result in adding to the consumption of paper by the bureaucracy!"

THE ORDERLY: Let him rest . . . Tomorrow, God willing, you can tell him the rest. Excuse me, my sister, I must give him some medicine. The doctor will soon be here.

SI-KHELIFA: Just five more minutes with him and we will leave! Berhoum! You have given honor to us! Even if you are mutilated, your mission has been a good one. The workers are proud of you. Those who were about to receive their licenses thank you. Everyone knows what happened. They know that after the guards and security agents deposited you at the hospital, certain individuals came and beat you . . . Fear nothing! The workers will identify them one by one! They are determined!

THE ORDERLY: The doctor is coming! Be quiet! Be quiet or he will be angry with me . . . Go, my brothers, please. Let the sick man rest. Go, leave!

DOCTOR: Is this the patient's family?

CHERIFA: I am his wife. This is his neighbor and the others his fellow workers.

DOCTOR: He is saved now, God be thanked.

ALL: Thank you and may God preserve you!

DOCTOR: According to the report that we received, he says that he fell down and that then he was beaten and mutilated.

CHERIFA: How, mutilated?

DOCTOR: His nose was cut off.
ALL: God is great!

DOCTOR: Please follow me. I am going to make out a medical report. Perhaps you wish to file a complaint?

THE NARRATOR: Berhoum the Timid, son of Ayoub the Dry, spent more than a month in the hospital. Poor Cherifa put herself to much trouble. Every day she brought him food and fruits. She prepared for him only the most succulent offerings, and the money that they had saved up was all spent on them, so eager was she to confront the misfortune. She then said to her husband: "The important thing is that you were saved and that you are going to recover your health . . . Thanks be to God, it could have been much worse!" At the hospital, every two or three days a bit of plaster was removed from Berhoum. After two weeks he was able to get up from his bed and walk with crutches. He sympathized with his fellow patients in neighboring beds, and told them his story. One of them said to him: "I have a cudgel. The day you decide to avenge yourself, just let me know. I will be your companion." Another said to him: "I have a double-barreled pistol, from the war. It is hidden at my house. When you have decided, just tell me a day in advance and I will lend it to you, my brother." He also sympathized with the invalids and the hospital workers. Some called him "The Smooth One," others "The Engineer." During visiting hours, when people swarmed into the room, Berhoum slid under his covers with shame and put a covering over his face.

When Berhoum the Timid, son of Ayoub the Dry, left the hospital, he was accompanied by patients who wished him good-bye and overwhelmed him with their support.

One said to him: "Take them by treachery as they have taken you by treachery!"

One advised him: "Beat them over the head!"

One urged him: "Strike and flee!"

One recommended: "Cover your nose well if you don't want to catch cold!"

One suggested: "Offer food to the needy; God will repay you for what you have done."

He left the hospital, his face hidden, holding his balluchon in one hand and Cherifa with the other. They took a taxi home. On the way, Berhoum did not say a word. The driver, curing this time, never stopped teasing him and asking questions, and Cherifa did all she could to answer and to turn the conversation away from her husband.

— "Did he undergo some surgical operation?"

— "Yes," she answered.

— "These days, the doctors have only one idea in their head: operate! Operate! They are simply butchers!"

— "You remind me of butchers, may God remind you of the profession of faith! It seems that they want to increase the cost of butterfat?"

— "Everything keeps costing more, ma'am, and gets harder to find! Mint, snails, mushrooms, can you find them? Chick peas! You can look for them at the pharmacy if you don't find any! As for pepper . . . they say that it is going to be sold in jewelry stores!"

When they arrived, the taxi driver said to Cherifa: "In the car, I have some fresh honey still in the comb, excellent for wounds. I can give you a good price on it if you are interested . . . "

When Berhoum the Timid, son of Ayoub the Dry, arrived home, he found his children and Si-Khelifa awaiting him on the front step near the door. They wished him welcome and came in. After having drunk some tea and chatting a bit, Ho Chi Minh took Berhoum by his hand and said to Cherifa. "We are going out on the terrace; we must speak."

They opened the window of the room and sat on the mat facing the sea. Si-Khelifa placed his hand on his neighbor's knee and said: "Everything is for the best! A strike has broken out at the factory and Laaredj has been licensed. The direction has changed and the union office has been shaken up. Production has increased and the technical staff has taken the workers' side. Our friends are relying heavily on you during this period, since your moral authority is great thanks to the courageous attitude you have taken. The workers have complained. They have submitted a detailed report on your accident and on the factory to the regional authorities. They are calling on you to submit your own complaint, the sooner the better!"

— "No," responded Berhoum the Timid, son of Ayoub the Dry.

— Why no?"

— "I am not going back to the factory!"

— "But the working conditions are beginning to improve. The workers are thinking about a solution to the problem of pulp, and they need you at this moment."

—"No, oh Si-Khelifa, I am not going back. I cannot. Timidity! Timidity! My timidity has increased since this happened to me. The factory where my nose was cut off! I cannot go back there!"

—"You are mistaken, Berhoum! On the contrary, now is the moment to forge ahead. I have been mutilated several times in my life. My leg was shattered with bullets. Look at my ear; only half of it is left! And every time I received a wound I felt my faith confirmed and my experience deepen!"

—"But you have lived in other circumstances," said Berhoum. "You lived during a war, with people in arms! But I am facing a struggle too complicated for me, and my arms are very slight! Moreover, their resentment against me is very great."

They remained silent for a long time, observing the immensity of the sea.

—"You are therefore resolved?" asked Si-Khelifa.

—"Yes," answered Berhoum. "I thought about it a long time in the hospital and Cherifa agrees with me. She has begun to look for work . . . as a maid. She will soon begin to work while waiting for God to open up something for me."

—"Think again, Berhoum! Your comrades think of you as their leader! Put aside this timidity which is suffocating you! Don't abandon the common goal."

—"No."

—"What? You want to give up everything? And your complaint?"

—"I will submit a complaint. It's a question of principle. I am going today to register it with the police."

Berhoum the Timid, son of Ayoub the Dry, took his medical certificate and left his house. He went out stealthily with a white veil on his nose that Cherifa had sewed for him like those little veils that women wear and which was attached at the back of his head with a bit of lace. He went to the police headquarters carrying in his hand an empty box that he took to give himself a better appearance. Going through the neighborhood, he was followed by children. Some of them said to him: "Thanks be to God that you are safe and sound, uncle Berhoum!"

One of them said: "His face is as flat as the nape of his neck!"

Another said: "Uncle Berhoum, do you want to break the bank or are you protecting yourself from cholera?"

Another called him "Berhoum the bare-him!"

An old inhabitant who knew him called out to him in pity.

One among them said to him: "The people in the glass works are asking for you. They have a broken machine and would like you to repair it!"

Another said: "Ach! The police! They're making a raid! Be careful, they're just around the corner!"

Someone said: "Why don't you go by the flea market? Maybe you can find something better for you than that veil. Look for some of those glasses with a nose attached!"

Others applauded him, but from a distance.

Berhoum, son of Ayoub the Dry, left his neighborhood. He left a victim of dizziness and hiccuping. People's comments continued to go off in his ears like bombs: "His face is flat . . . the bare-him . . . the glassworks . . . the bank . . . the police, the cholera!" His chest was oppressed, his knees buckled. He sat on the sidewalk, put the box upside down over his head as if it were a hat, and opened his veil to breathe a little. Whoever passed near him was stunned. They detoured around him. They stopped a moment to look at him. They said: "May God protect you, they are getting more and more numerous!" They threw him a bit of money saying: "Bravo! Here is an original way to beg. Our people are creative!" They said: "His nose does him honor! Someone who has a clear political position and who is trying to say to us: the poor are all boxed in. A pity that I did not have a box; I would not have been nosed out!" They said: "You are the leader, we will be the followers!" They grumbled: "You have sold out the village! Ah, my brothers, just look at this scene: a blockhead in a box!" They said: "The more progress we make, the more the working class will suffer!" They said: "Write ECONOMIC CRISIS on the box!"

After taking a moment to rest and allow his dizziness to pass, the son of Dry's courage returned. He arose and resumed his walk among the people, his box still over his head, his arms through its handles. He said to himself within his own conscience: "I will go by the flea market first, just to see . . . You never know . . . Perhaps . . ."

He walked through the town and the words of those close to whom he passed echoed and resounded within the box. From time to time, he allowed himself to be distracted by the words and ran into a wall or a tree. He heard someone say to his beloved: "Ah, if it were only possible to leave the town to the people and to build us a town for ourselves, up there near the forest, so that we could breathe a little!" He heard a girl say to her friend: "Love, in this country? What sort of love? Red or black? Speak of love to your brother and you will have yellow eyes . . . or black!" He heard someone say to a companion: "How do you expect me to get any thinking done when I have now spent more than ten years concerned with housing! Habitation inhabits my brain. Here I am walking and talking with you, while my head is full of housing! Moreover, everyone you see has some such occupation. Just look at those passing by! You see that one over there, he has a Mercedes in his head . . . See that poor chap there, he's got two pepper pots in his head! And that one, a refrigerator! That other one has in his head Spain and a bit of smuggling! . . . There . . . There's the proof for you! Just look near yourself. That one has given up! He has gone to pieces and put a box over his head . . . Just see how that policeman is watching!

He heard a young man, chatting with a friend, say to him: "In the beginning, democracy had the upper hand. In the second round, violence discovered how to respond; it unleashed a terrible stomach punch that made it stagger, followed up with a series of left-rights, left-rights. In the third round . . ."

Berhoum the Timid became dizzy. The box was stifling him. He raised his head to breathe and look at the people about him, his veil attached to his neck and hanging down. Whoever caught sight of his face furrowed their brows and turned their head, while he, running with sweat, his eyes overflowing, blurred, felt as if he were gliding in the sky like a feather, rising and falling as he floated above people's heads . . . Then this town began to seem strange to him. Bizarre images appeared to him, as if he were no longer master of its spirits. He saw people standing in a line and reaching in each other's pockets as they cried out: "Justice!" He saw naked children running and carrying embers in their hands. He saw people in suits and ties brandishing arms and placards on which had been written "VORACIOUS TO THE DEATH," "DOWN WITH THE CONQUERED," "WHOEVER WILL NOT DANCE WITH THE

AMERICANS WILL BE BOOTED OUT." He saw packed buses rolling on two wheels and throwing out passengers into the street at every turn. He saw clocks running backward and flames bursting from administrative buildings. He saw fire leaping from balconies and windows, and snakes going up and down stairways, sliding along in a creepy way . . . He saw the sky swell up and the sun wink, emitting blue and red rays.

Berhoum the Timid, son of Ayoub the Dry, was frightened. He was frightened and began to run, his head in the box. When he was outside the town, his spirits revived. He took off the box and rested a moment. Then he put the veil back on his face and entered the flea market. He strolled about looking at things. He stopped before a heap of objects and debris of all sorts. The proprietor of the place came up to him and asked: "Are you looking for anything in particular? Surely you are able to speak, my brother! Whatever you are looking for, you can find it at my place! Truly, I have everything! Speak up my friend, this is the flea market! You need be ashamed of nothing! Even if you need a boat or an airplane, that can be managed for you!

—"I need a nose to cover up this hole," said Berhoum, "some sort of nose . . . "

—"A nose! That's rather difficult in a flea market . . . My neighbor has arms and legs of wood, but he is gone to luncyh. It seems to me, as God knows best, that I have seen in his shop things that looked like noses. I cannot tell you if they were made of ivory, porcelain, or plaster . . .

—"No," said Berhoum, "I would like a nose . . ."

—"You, you want a nose of flesh!" the man interrupted him. Then go to the barber who practices the art of bleeding there on the corner. He will cut off one and put it on you."

—"No . . ."

—"Yes! He's a devil of a man! Nothing is impossible for him! He can even take you along with him. You can make your choice at leisure and discuss prices with him!"

—"No."

—"No? Why not? I have explained it to you! Last Saturday, he removed a bilious vesicule from someone! He took it out while the man remained standing! Perfectly! People surrounded him and all saw it! . . Certainly he will take you with him. You can make your own choice and deal with him as you wish! Noses, they are not lacking today! Rather it is snuff which cannot be found! Noses, many people wear them today simply for decoration . . . Ah, I could not have said this in the old days! Pendants were hung from them, they were tattooed, mint leaves were put in them. But today . . . They are worn only so that their owners will not catch cold!

—"No . . ."

—"But as I have told you! Ah, if I had someone to take care of my shop I would go into town with you and you would see!"

—"What I want is a rubber nose . . ."

—"Ah, you should have told me! For that, you must go to the shop of Teigneux, the tooth-puller. He sells them! But be careful. He will sell you a nose with glasses and a half-dozen stockings as well! And he'll charge you a high price, the rogue!"

Berhoum, son of Dry, wandered among mounds of ironwork. He did not bargain nor did he buy. He left the flea market dragging his feet and returned to the city. There he directed his steps toward the police station. Arriving before the building, he spent a long moment thinking before going in. "I will go in. I won't go in. I will go in. I won't go in . . . " Finally, clasping the box to his breast to stifle his timidity, he plunged into the offices.

FIRST POLICEMAN: Look, my brother, look . . . Above all, don't shoot! . . . Look, my hands are raised!

BERHOUM: P . . . P . . . P . . . Pl . . .

FIRST POLICEMAN: I have no gun, my brother! The case is empty. See for yourself!

BERHOUM: No! No! You . . . You . . . te . . . tr . . .

FIRST POLICEMAN: I swear by God that I am telling you the truth! Look around and see for yourself! I am only here to welcome people and to register complaints . . .

BERHOUM: That is the reason . . .

FIRST POLICEMAN: I told them: "Don't leave me alone to face the public." I told them: "Our public is dangerous! Put someone with me!" I told them: "One of these days, I will have trouble!" I said this to them no later than yesterday! Ah, my brother, I am only a simple policeman, a God-fearing man. I have no money!

BERHOUM: Last month...

FIRST POLICEMAN: What happened last month? I know nothing about it, my brother!

BERHOUM: I was beaten . . . and today I come . . .

FIRST POLICEMAN: You come to avenge yourself! But I know nothing about it, my brother! I didn't beat you! I insult people, I spit in their faces, I put them in prison or injure them; but I never beat anyone! God pardon me! Lying is a sin. I did strike someone once. I slapped a woman, five years ago. I was overcome by evil! I thought she was an ordinary woman like you see everywhere, since she had breasts and long legs! I had to apologize and . . .

BERHOUM: No! It was at the factory! The paper factory . . .

FIRST POLICEMAN: But I have no connection with that factory, my dear brother! I have nothing to do with it! I am a simple policeman. My superiors are the ones who are concerned with factories, patrons, and big business. I just gather crumbs — a bit of coffee here, a few pounds of fish there, a watermelon here . . .

BERHOUM: In the name of my ancestors . . .

FIRST POLICEMAN: He fears only God! In the police hierarchy, I am on the very lowest rung. My salary is insignificant. I have told my colleagues that we should form a union and fight for our rights, but they didn't want to . . . I have seen people more highly placed than I who have shown the way. They have gone on the attack and triumphed! I have tried to follow in their footsteps, I don't deny it! Even at the central court house there are important magistrates who dip into funds . . . But I have nothing to do with all this, my brother! Ask anyone about me; consult my neighbors! There are those whom

I have helped take the holy pilgrimages. Others whose sons I have saved from taking the wrong path. I have protected some from punishment, even released them from prison! Some . . .

BERHOUM: Your hands! Your hands!

FIRST POLICEMAN: They are raised! What do you want of me, brother? You are playing with fire! What more do you want? I have told you everything, what can I add?

BERHOUM: But I want to speak of noses . . . of noses! . . .

FIRST POLICEMAN: I've stuck out my nose for my brother! I have defended my brother when he has been the victim of a denial of his rights. His mother and father-in-law beat him and threw him out of his own house, though he had seven children . . . I took out my pistol, only to frighten them . . . Thank God the business stopped there . . .

BERHOUM: In the name of your ancestors, my brother . . .

SECOND POLICEMAN: What's going on, Si-el-Hadj? Who is that person there?

BERHOUM: I . . . I came . . . I . . . I . . .

FIRST POLICEMAN: Get your hands in the air! He is armed! He has a grenade in the box!

SECOND POLICEMAN: There! There! I've done it, my brother! I've never seen the like in our country!

FIRST POLICEMAN: Confess! Admit what you have done! Purify yourself a little! He is here to avenge himself!

SECOND POLICEMAN: Me, a child of my country . . . Where can I begin?

BERHOUM: You are mistaken, my good men! I came here to

register a complaint about my nose and the box I am carrying is empty! Just look!

FIRST POLICEMAN: You came to make a complaint about your nose?

SECOND POLICEMAN: The rogue has come to complain. He is not armed! Lower your hands, Si-el-Hadj.

FIRST POLICEMAN: And why didn't you say this at the beginning?

BERHOUM: You never let me speak . . . and I was struggling with hiccups.

FIRST POLICEMAN: You drove us to distraction! Out of our minds! Every moment you invented something new!

SECOND POLICEMAN: Thanks be to God, Si-el-Hadj, you are safe and sound.

FIRST POLICEMAN: He burst in here, masked, his hand in a box! I said to myself: "Our hour has come." I thought he was going to blow up the police station.

SECOND POLICEMAN: Someone cut off your nose and you have come to complain?

BERHOUM: Yes.

FIRST POLICEMAN: The rascal gave me a real fright!

BERHOUM: I beg your pardon. It was a misunderstanding, that is all.

SECOND POLICEMAN: It's fatigue, Si-el-Hadj! Ask for a leave. You are exhausted.

FIRST POLICEMAN: He drove us crazy! He drove us crazy! He made us see all of it! All those days of thefts, of blows, of knives, of blood! The one who beats his family and then says his prayers. The one pursued by individuals armed with hatchets! The one going out for a walk who has his nose cut off! How can I be expected to have a peaceful spirit?

SECOND POLICEMAN: That film yesterday evening on television clearly affected you.

FIRST POLICEMAN: You say that someone mutilated you . . . in the middle of your face . . . Your identity card . . .

SECOND POLICEMAN: Si-el-Hadj, those two kids brought in for smuggling, someone up above has demanded their release. There was a call about them . . .

FIRST POLICEMAN: Here are the keys. Go turn them loose yourself. Here are their papers. They must sign here . . . You must go see a doctor to give them a certificate . . .

BERHOUM: There it is. That's the certificate of the doctor who treated me.

FIRST POLICEMAN: You bring to mind a story . . . A book that my son loaned me. It contained a strange tale about a nose. Somebody named Gogol wrote it. I think he is some African . . . Are you still at this address?

BERHOUM: Yes.

FIRST POLICEMAN: Is this your name? Berhoum? And this happened at the paper factory?

BERHOUM: Yes. And then, at the hosp . . .

FIRST POLICEMAN: No! Go sit over there. Wait a minute. I am going to see the inspector . . . I heard them talking about the paper factory yesterday.

SECOND POLICEMAN: Where is Si-el-Hadj? You have not driven

him off, I hope.

BERHOUM: He went to see the inspector . . . He said that he would only be a minute.

SECOND POLICEMAN: You have burnt out your throat with drink, haven't you?

BERHOUM: I know nothing about that.

SECOND POLICEMAN: Hard drinking, you know all about that! Your eyes are rolling in your head like billiard balls!

BERHOUM: Pardon me, but you are mistaken . . . I am a citizen . . .

SECOND POLICEMAN: What's that, I am mistaken? Are you trying to teach me my job? I recognize my man from his eyelashes alone! You all pretend to be timid when you come in here!

FIRST POLICEMAN: They're waiting for you inside . . . Come here. Stand right there!

INSPECTOR: You are the son of Ayoub?

BERHOUM: Yes.

FIRST POLICEMAN: Berhoum . . . That business with the boiler that they stole to cook with . . . at the paper factory . . .

SECOND POLICEMAN: Right! Berhoum! Is that Berhoum? I recognized his eyes!

INSPECTOR: We sent a delegation to your house this very morning. Didn't you leave the hospital today?

BERHOUM: Yes. I must have left my house before the delegation arrived.

INSPECTOR: After leaving your house, where did you go?

BERHOUM: I went through the village and took a turn through the flea market. I said to myself . . .

INSPECTOR: You said to yourself that maybe you would meet Laaredj . . . or one of the others?

BERHOUM: Laaredj? What does Laaredj have to do with the flea market?

INSPECTOR: A secret meeting. Some new plot. A strike, perhaps?

BERHOUM: A secret meeting? A strike? Pardon me. You are questioning me even though I have not yet said anything. Let me make my complaint and then question me.

INSPECTOR: Si-Berhoum, the boiler man, there is a warrant out for you and I am the official in charge of this investigation. I was the one who sent the delegation to your house. Your passport?

BERHOUM: I have no passport . . . I don't know anything about this business.

INSPECTOR: You will understand soon enough . . . What is your shoe size?

BERHOUM: Forty-three in winter and forty-two in summer. Also forty-three when I leave the steam baths.

INSPECTOR: Do you have a complete set of teeth? Have any of them been extracted?

BERHOUM: Half of them . . . I use the other half for chewing.

INSPECTOR: What are your relations with the union?

BERHOUM: I am a member . . . But sometimes I condemn them, sometimes I congratulate them . . . Let me repair your machine. There is a screw loose.

INSPECTOR: This machine never stops working! . . . Have you said your prayers?

BERHOUM: And have you said your prayers?

INSPECTOR: I'm asking the questions here!

BERHOUM: But this question should be left for the Judgement Day.

INSPECTOR: What are your political activities?

BERHOUM: A poor soul like me? . . . Most recently, I voted for deputies that I did not know; I voted entirely by chance.

INSPECTOR: Who visited you in the hospital?

BERHOUM: My children, my family, and people who cared for me.

INSPECTOR: Did Laaredj come to see you?

BERHOUM: He came to visit me, poor fellow, and gave me some of his blood. He also brought me some honey. He told me that he brought it from Kabylie.

INSPECTOR: Who wrote "A SOCIALIST ADMINISTRATION" on the boiler? With a question mark following it?

NARRATOR: Berhoum the Timid, son of Ayoub the Dry, suffered a good deal in his confrontation with the Inspector. The questioning lasted all afternoon. "What? How? How much? When? Who?" He was questioned about the workers, the factory, the boiler. He was also questioned about matters having no relationship with this subject, just to confuse him. Thus, he was asked if he had paid his rent, when he bought his bread, if any members of his family worked for the government, if he wanted to cooperate with the police, if he had a balcony, if his neighbor had books, if he believed in witchcraft, if his wife Cherifa bought henna in leaves or powder. He thus went from pillar to post, but always came back to the factory by another route to give depth to the search. Berhoum tried to slip between the questions from time to time, or to jump over them.

Finally the Inspector, after giving him a declaration to read and to sign, congratulated Berhoum and opened up to him. He said: "This evening, you will be our guest. We will keep you here to pass the night with us, and tomorrow morning, God willing, we will present you to the judge . . . with a number of charges." Oh, Si-Berhoum. Charged with disturbance, theft and sabotage in the paper factory! Charged with having pushed the workers to rise up and attack the supervisors! Charged with having distributed slanderous tracts about the administration of the factory and with having organized a strike, with the aid of Laaredj, from the hospital! "As for ourselves," added the Inspector, "we will retain for ourselves your identity card since your features are altered. We require you to furnish us with new identity photos, without a veil, and a ruling from a judge to the effect that we can create for you a new card and that we can put under the rubric 'Identifying marks,' that you are a person without a nose."

Berhoum the Timid, son of Ayoub the Dry, went to file a complaint and found himself in a hole. He spent the night in the police station, unable to close his eyes or eat. In the middle of the night, there were put into his cell a youth under the influence of drugs and two individuals living in another world, inebriated and happy, giving off a strong odor of vomit . . . One of the two drunks seized Berhoum, regarded him for a long time, pushed him away, and said to his companion. "Give me another one of the same and see if my sister, this veiled woman here, wants anything to drink!" Berhoum got rid of him by pushing him against the wall. The prisoners spent the night snoring and spitting while the unhappy Berhoum tried to digest what had happened to him while the noise of the typewriters of the Inspector filled his ears and rattled in his head. The odors in the tiny cell stifled him. He began to lack air, to hallucinate, and to see images. Ghostly figures called to him. He saw Si-Khelifa who smiled at him and said to him: "As soon as a man is born, he begins to struggle and continues until death. Rest a little and breathe the sea air. You still have a long way to go!" He saw El-Farzia, his mother, embracing Cherifa and saying "Berhoum, my little one, is a man, worthy son of his father. He has not flinched and has not denounced his friends."

In the morning, Berhoum the Timid was summoned before the magistrate. Before entering the court, and lagging a bit behind, he saw Cherifa, Si-Khelifa, and Laaredj, standing proudly in a line. The judge questioned him about his deposition. But Berhoum was oppressed and exhausted. Fear, panic, the lack of sleep, his hiccups and the odor of the cell all mingled in him. Then he broke free of his stupor and began to cry out, to complain, to demand justice: "I am innocent! I am innocent! Innocent! It is all a plot! You have organized a scheme against me! I am an honest worker. I sought only the good of my brothers who are working for the general good and for social justice! I, the plaintiff, the victim, I have become the accused!"

Berhoum the Timid was suddenly set free, like a flood! He was seized with rage and began to spew out a whole series of slogans like a machine. The courtroom was in confusion, in tumult. The peace was disturbed. The magistrate leaped up in rage. The police officers quickly seized the son of Dry and put him in handcuffs. An hour later, his clothing changed, his hair cut, he was locked up in the central prison. The factory workers got together and advocated for him from the first week. The prisoners provided an official opinion on his case, saying: "A difficult matter! Political!" The hearing was postponed several times. Berhoum the Timid began to regain his composure in prison. He made friends with the prisoners with whom he began to share provisions. The guards and the prisoners began to appreciate him and to consult with him. They called him the Man in the Iron Mask. He became very active in prison and from time to time lectured his companions with the words of Ho Chi Minh. Berhoum suffered in detention and great was his desire to return to his children and Cherifa. He had learned things. He had reflected on society and considered it. He had heard things that surpassed understanding.

THE GUARD: Inside! Inside! You have ten minutes to speak, no more, no less!

A VISITOR: She prepared a sheep's head for you; she didn't find enough guts for the stuffing.

A PRISONER: My friends, they are keeping me here for another two years. Has Rekia given birth?

A WOMAN VISITOR: The tracks for the new road go by our house. We have settled in the huts across the way so that we can keep the same address.

BERHOUM: They play games and study . . . I am among the best in the class.

A PRISONER: You know what was discovered in the soup. Use another trick. Next time put it in the cake.

A VISITOR: Melons are now in the market. If you like, I will bring you some apricots.

BERHOUM: I am proud of you. You are worth ten of me, Cherifa!

A PRISONER: If she gives birth to a girl, let her settle her affairs and go back to her mother!

A WOMAN VISITOR: We saw the seventh episode last evening . . . We all wept! The engineer was the cause of everything . . . But the doctor has returned and will marry her.

BERHOUM: My timidity is leaving, little by little! . . The constraint!

A PRISONER: That business has crushed me! And I told you not to invest in the private sector!

A VISITOR: A spring erupted in the house of our neighbor down below! God be thanked, we can get water there now!

BERHOUM: Tell Si-Khelifa that there is nothing better than prison for meditation!

A PRISONER: I must change lawyers! Nobody listens to him and he doesn't know how to lie!

A WOMAN VISITOR: Kheria went to the house of a fortuneteller who read his fortune. She told him that the moon was in the house of Mars.

BERHOUM: I miss you very much! Send me photos of the children!

A PRISONER: You don't cast pearls before swine! . . . He doesn't know where his feet are taking him, but he keeps going! We are angry here. Yesterday evening we got into a fight over a bit of sugar.

A VISITOR: Don't get into any trouble, you risk spending another six years here! You're doing well enough! You've gained weight. You don't lack anything! Close your eyes and it will be sunrise already!

BERHOUM: I wrote to the workers, to each one individually, to thank them.

A WOMAN VISITOR: I was given a quantity of it that Jarrila helped me carry, and I gave a sack of it to our neighbor Khadidja.

A PRISONER: As soon as I get out of prison, the demons who live there will flee as well.

BERHOUM: No, my brother, I am not speaking to you! I am speaking to my wife and I just told her "I love you." There's nothing wrong with that . . . !

A PRISONER: He no longer has any feeling! If he wishes to take his sister back, let him take her back, since he is also a judge!

A VISITOR: That's expensive! Twelve thousand a kilo! Did you like the plate of mallows?

BERHOUM: You have grown more beautiful, Cherifa! I wrote you a long letter.

A WOMAN VISITOR: Why did he get involved in politics? He has a sharp tongue and his wife always gets things muddled up! Besides, she loves gold!

A PRISONER: He is like a king. He lacks nothing. He has money! You have to grease his palm! Every day he is brought a basket of provisions!

BERHOUM: Tell them to answer me as quickly as possible . . . and with details. Tell Si-Khelifa that "they" are getting ready to send young people to El-Bayadh to get pulp.

A VISITOR: He has a blue tail, he brought it from Spain . . . But he has not yet begun to speak, the rogue! And he adores greens!

A PRISONER: No one is allowed to sleep in my room! Let them make other arrangements! Let them sleep in the hallway!

BERHOUM: All news comes through here! Official and unofficial!

A PRISONER: . . . A distant relationship! Not even a kissing cousin! The lawyer is the important thing! They say he can be bought . . .

A WOMAN VISITOR: A puzzle! A puzzle! Twenty-three souls in the father's house! In only two rooms!

A PRISONER: On top of the armoire, near the milk pot, this is a glass fish. That's where I put the key, in a little box.

A VISITOR: When they opened him up, they found in his kidney a stone as big as your fist!

A PRISONER: He has gotten into bad habits. Now, it is every day, every day!

A WOMAN VISITOR: He has brought me a car and is up to his ears in business . . . His brother died the other day.

A PRISONER: The semolina bread with aniseed pleased them. The stuffed eggplants drove them crazy!

BERHOUM: Don't worry about it. I am used to the food here.

A VISITOR: My bit of strife has hidden the honey under the cat . . . You will find it there.

A PRISONER: Great! Stop being alert for a moment and they will steal your teeth!

A WOMAN VISITOR: For three months we have not found it! Where would you look?

A PRISONER: After the hospital they brought me here . . . Tell him that the gray one has a bad navel and that the bear no longer knows the way to Mecca. He will understand.

A VISITOR: After the trip by car, I still had to go two kilometers by foot!

A PRISONER: But I tell you that they are eating as much as they can! It will be enough to draw them out!

A WOMAN VISITOR: Pepper, allspice, a liquorice stick and some mulberries . . . Is that it?

THE NARRATOR: A few months after, Berhoum, son of Ayoub, left the prison. No one was waiting for him at the door. He said to himself: "So much the better. I will surprise them and return without warning." He threw his cloak over his shoulder and set out. Immediately, he was frightened by the noise of the city and of the large highway. He was afraid to cross the street, as if he no longer knew how to conduct himself. A policeman had to help him cross to the other side. He took him by the arm and said: "Wouldn't it be better for you to stay over there, working and cultivating the ground! Where are you coming from with your cloak?" — "From the kingdom of the damned," answered Berhoum. Having come a little way from the prison, he turned back toward it to view it and say his good-byes. He made a gesture and traced out a quick little dance, two steps to one side and then a shake. Then he went on his way, at a rapid pace. He felt relieved, as if his timidity had left him. From time to time, he stopped before a store to look at the merchandise and to see himself in the glass. He walked rapidly and said to

himself: "Ah, perfumes, and I am going back to Cherifa whose
perfume I have forgotten . . . Good heavens! It that a coach or a car?
That one over there, he is going to find himself before long in the
clink! Good! They have restored that type? It's now the fashion . .
The kingdom of the damned . . .? This evening, God willing, a good
bath and then relax! I will stretch out and ask Cherifa to massage
my chest!" He walked along rapidly and sang:

> "Oh cock pigeon fly off on your trip
> Go to Aicha's house, take him the message
> That I fear the hunters, I fear their bloodshed."

He walked along rapidly, eager to see his children and to
draw them to his breast . . . Now, leave us! We have to speak in
private, Cherifa and I! You two, Larbi and Tayeb, see, I have bought
you a few roasted peanuts. Go on outside!"

Berhoum arrived home and rapped at the door. "Who is there?" said
a voice."—"Representatives of the electric company." They opened
the door and were stunned. The girls leaped to his neck and began
embracing him. The little ones jumped about. "Papa went away!
Papa has come back!" They surrounded him like a swarm of bees.
They took his cloak and made him sit down, took off his shoes,
carried to him cushions for him to relax on, prepared coffee for him.
Daouia said to him: "Blessings and health to you!" Halima said
"Have you succeeded in your studies, Papa?" El-Aounia said to him:
"Take a bath and change your clothes, Papa, we'll fatten you up!"
Larbi said to him: "Our team didn't lose, Papa! We won, last Friday!"

Cherifa returned home from work. The neighbors gave her
the news at the entry door. She climbed the stairway, crying out in
joy, and arriving home, dropped to her knees and drew her man up
to her, embracing him and kissing him on the face and neck. Her
arms around Berhoum, she rocked him, weeping. She said: "They
made the lord of my dwelling suffer even though he was innocent.
My cousin suffered injustice, although he was innocent!"

Berhoum told them about the prison and the astonishing
things that went on there. He noticed that half of the furniture was
missing. He said to Cherifa: "Our home is beginning to look like Si-
Khelifa's! It is beginning to become larger and more empty." They

passed a long time together talking and laughing. That evening, Si-Khelifa brought Berhoum an envelope containing a little money and a letter from the workers at the factory, in which they thanked him and told him about the the new rights that they had obtained and about the boiler. They told him that they had painted the boiler as green as a plant and had christened it "THE BERHOUMIAN MACHINE THAT REVEALS CRIMES."

After prison, all sorts of things happened to Berhoum the Timid, the son of Ayoub the Dry. He waited for a long time to get back to work. He changed his trade several times. He worked in the private sector for several different bosses, and each time he was discharged without reason. Wherever he went, the boiler matter followed him. And then the veil was an obstacle now. He attracted attention to himself and caused disturbances. On several occasions, he was brought in by the police during general sweeps and arrests. Little by little, Berhoum became possessed by melancholy. His spirit, it seemed, became more and more disturbed. His timidity returned, more intense than before. He spoke now less and less. He became suspicious, and it seemed to him that he was being watched and followed. He felt as if there were a string attached to his head, stretching from earth to heaven, so that wherever he went he felt it above him. He began to suspect even his neighbors and the people in the quarter. He began to wear his shoes backward in order to leave no trail. And if someone asked him a question, he responded in an obscure way or by symbols. Thus, if someone asked him: "What time is it?" he would reply "In what part of the world?" If someone said to him: "Where are you going, Si-Berhoum?" he would answer: "My ultimate goal is the grave: a few feet of soil." If someone said to him: "Some detergent has just arrived from Italy. Let's go buy some!" he would answer: "No, I am waiting from them to import some vinegar from America!"

The unhappy fellow imagined that he saw the ghost of his father, Ayoub the Dry. The specter appeared to him and spoke to him! His family believed him mad. They said: "He is possessed by demons!" Si-Khelifa spoke to him on several occasions. He neither inclined his head nor answered. Cherifa burned incense and wept. He neither noticed her nor spoke to her. It was as if he were living in another world.

Berhoum the Veiled hid in his house and let his hair grow.

He went out only at night. He left at night and wandered in distant suburbs. He walked at night in the poor quarters and believed that the ghost of his father Ayoub accompanied him, walking by his side. During these nocturnal ramblings, Berhoum met others like himself, men pursued by misfortune, mutilated by catastrophes, and excluded from society . . . Men humiliated like him, sunk into despair, having lost all hope and wandering in the lower depths of existence . . .

Berhoum felt a kinship with these people. Among them he found confidence, peace, and rest. He felt kinship with them and called them "the village phantoms." He learned of their secrets. Every night, they gathered in an agreed place near the cemetery or behind the flea market, above the waste heap or beyond the port. During these evenings, they organized meetings and discussed the individual, philosophy . . . they discussed society and studied together the means to break through it and find again a place for themselves. Berhoum was seduced by this atmosphere. He let himself go as if he were living in a dream and as if some magic power drew him. Berhoum the Timid, son of Ayoub the Dry, was no longer capable of living hidden in his home. He broke with his family. He sent them a letter to reassure them. Daouia, Si-Khelifa, and Cherifa gathered around the message. They read and re-read it but could make no sense of it. They folded it up, convinced that he had completely lost his mind and the ability to hide his thoughts. In it, he spoke of an ideal society, a village filled with flowers, a green and wooded fortress, an impregnable citadel . . . In it he spoke of its internal organization, of the liberty of expression and creation . . . He spoke of his friends "Seek-the-Peace," "Look for the Good," and "Live-as-She-Pleases." The inhabitants of the quarter heard about the letter from Berhoum. They were all sorrowful about it and prayed for his cure. They called this letter "The farewell epistle," and looked for him for a long time, but in vain. They said: "It is nothing, an absence, an attack of insociability . . ." The son of Ayoub and his companions were no longer mentioned. An inquiry into the "Phantoms of the City" was undertaken, and the police spoke of a "social curse, a grave danger threatening the inhabitants of the city," of a "group outside bounds and social relationships; we do not know how many of them there are nor how they live. We have no power over them. It is possible that they are supported by some foreign power."

A few weeks later, the young people of the quarter reported to Si-Khelifa some news. They told him: "The Christian cemetery is haunted! Ghosts leave it under cover of night! We have seen with our own eyes open caves from which light appeared!   We have heard singing and talking! . . ."

When night fell, Si-Khelifa, accompanied by Cherifa and several men from the quarter, went to the Christian cemetery. He said to them: "Be quick! The wooded fortress mentioned in the letter is the cemetery. Be quick! We must rescue them before the police fall on them!" They agreed upon a plan, and, arriving at the Christian cemetery, they walked around it. Then they cast a glance over the wall. All was dark, dim. They saw no light, nor did they hear anyone talking. Si-Khelifa said to Cherifa: "Now, come with me. We are going to climb over the wall and enter. We must remove all doubt. We are going to go in and be sure. As soon as we are over the wall, hold on to my belt and walk with me stepping in my tracks!"

CHERIFA: Oh, Si-Khelifa, I am dying of fear!

SI-KHELIFA: Quiet! Just listen! Walk on tiptoe! And be careful where you put your feet!

CHERIFA: Mt belly is in my throat I am so afraid! I have never entered the Christian cemetery! Oh Lord Protector, protect me!

SI-KHELIFA: Quiet! Look out! There is a pit there! Follow me closely!

CHERIFA: I am attached to you and my eyes are closed!

SI-KHELIFA: You're afraid, are you? You, that people say are so cool.

CHERIFA: I'm afraid of ghosts! In the name of Allah, the Almighty, the Merciful . . .

SI-KHELIFA: Quiet! Don't move anymore! I hear some human breathing!

CHERIFA: Ah . . . it's a woman's ghost!

SI-KHELIFA: Just be quiet! Ah! It's over here!

CHERIFA: It's not a human breathing! It's my lungs that are going to burst with fear!

SI-KHELIFA: Ah! The young people were right!

CHERIFA: I am fainting! What's that?

SI-KHELIFA: Open your eyes and see! There is a cave there, an open tomb, right under your feet!

CHERIFA: Oh, dear father! Are there dead bodies in it?

SI-KHELIFA: Of course! See the coffins piled up . . . Be quiet!

CHERIFA: What next? Ah, dear mother! Alas for Berhoum, oh, Si-Khelifa, alas for my unfortunate husband!

SI-KHELIFA: Hold your breath! Be quiet!

CHERIFA: Ah! Dear God! Dear God! Dear God!

SI-KHELIFA: Judging from the smell, I think that there are people all around us. Hold on fast to me!

CHERIFA: My hand is paralyzed! It is numb!

SI-KHELIFA: Change your hand and be quiet! . . . Is someone there?

BERHOUM: Yes, Si-Khelifa.

CHERIFA: Ah, Mama!

BERHOUM: Cherifa! Cherifa! She has fainted! Water!   Light the candles!

LIVE-AS-SHE-PLEASES: Get up! Cherifa! Cherifa! Arise!

CHERIFA: Si-Khelifa! . . . Si-Khelifa!

SI-KHELIFA: Get a hold of yourself! It's your husband!

BERHOUM: Cherifa!

SI-KHELIFA: You have terrified her, the poor creature!   She is trembling all over.

BERHOUM: And you, Si-Khelifa, were you afraid?

SI-KHELIFA: Of course I was afraid!   Afraid of being bitten by a snake! Afraid of getting beaten! If I had been alone, you would have really caught it from me!

CHERIFA: Why are you living in the cemetery, Berhoum! Now, come back home with me! Come on, leave this inferno! Death is penetrating me here . . . my body is freezing!

LIVE-AS-SHE-PLEASES: It's only water!

BERHOUM: Allow me to present my friends: Live-as-She-Pleases, Seek-the-Peace, Calm, and Look-for-the-Good. And of course, you know me, Deham!

SI-KHELIFA: You live here among the dead?

LIVE-AS-SHE-PLEASES: None of them see anything odd about it!

CHERIFA: These open caves are all full of dead bodies?

BERHOUM: Yes. But we have cleaned them out, limed them, and settled in them. We also have rooms above the caves.

CHERIFA: But then you are all ghosts, Deham!

BERHOUM: Yes. My head is together now. Without them, I would certainly have been lost.

SI-KHELIFA: You are living on the margins of society, in a cemetery, and you are satisfied with yourself?

LIVE-AS-SHE-PLEASES: That's Si-Khelifa the Indochinese, isn't it?
BERHOUM: Yes, it's him!

SI-KHELIFA: How do you know me?

LIVE-AS-SHE-PLEASES: Deham has told us much about you.

SI-KHELIFA: You live in holes and you claim to have your reason! If there had been a war, I could understand . . .

BERHOUM: But we have cleaned up the caves. We live in marble, Si-Khelifa! Who else does?

LOOK-FOR-THE-GOOD: It's better than blue stone!

SI-KHELIFA: I don't understand.

CALM: We gather dry herbs, plant flowers, and trim the trees!

BERHOUM: You hear this silence, Si-Khelifa? Smell the pine trees!

SI-KHELIFA: It's astonishing!

CHERIFA: What do you live on?

BERHOUM: Everybody works.

SEEK-THE-PEACE: Each one has a trade. Some work on their own account, here and there. Some work in the private sector, underground!

LOOK-FOR-THE-GOOD: We go from one job to another and have thus gotten into the way of migrant work.

LIVE-AS-SHE-PLEASES: Most of us have neither family nor dwelling.

BERHOUM: There are two youngsters with us. They are down there next to the cemetery. We gave them that section. Before they were sleeping in the Moorish baths... amid the heat and vermin!

SI-KHELILFA: No! I cannot get this into my head!

CALM: Explain, Si-Khelifa!

CHERIFA: All this means that you have taken over the property of others and that you have defied the law! You have not respected the dead and you have committed a sacrilege!

BERHOUM: No, Cherifa! The cemetery is built on Algerian land . . . our land! It was abandoned until now and we have taken it over in full knowledge of what we were doing. As for the dead . . . no one has touched them. We have improved their atmosphere and we have given this place a soul! Never, since independence, has the cemetery been as proper as it is now!

CHERIFA: So, do you want me to bring the children and come to live here with you?

BERHOUM: No . . .

A VOICE: Si-Khelifa! Si-Khelifa!

SI-KHELIFA: We are coming! Don't worry! We are speaking with the phantoms quite democratically on the tombstones!

CHERIFA: Speak, Berhoum! What do you plan to do?

BERHOUM: I will not be here long . . .

CHERIFA: What? You want to rest some more? The police will recapture you and you will go down again!

LIVE-AS-SHE-PLEASES: We must hurry up and end this experiment.

SI-KHELIFA: Is this only an experiment, then?

BERHOUM: Yes. These people live one month in a slum, one month in a Moorish bath, one month in a tent, one month under a tin roof . . . They want to experiment and at the same time have a little stability. In fact, each one wants to experiment in connection with his own problems. Me, to regain confidence in myself, to find again the moral force that would allow me to hook back up to life again, to cling to life, to conquer the humiliation that has taken possession of me, and to recover my dignity. This experiment has taught me that the individual carries in himself an ocean of energy, and that, whatever the circumstances—even if one is hurled to the bottom rung of the ladder of living beings—he can still find an opening, a way to climb back up again. He is capable of invincibility.

SI-KHELIFA: I will continue to ponder these words later; they are real philosophy! I will sit facing the sea and reflect deeply on this speech. But here I do not feel well.

CHERIFA: And your health, Berhoum?

BERHOUM: Thanks be to Allah! They say that my nose is growing back . . .

SI-KHELIFA; The workers in the factory call for you to resume your work. Laaredj has been taken back in and Bekkouche was voted in by the workers, elected to the governing council! They have a huge plan for water and pulp! They need you!

A VOICE: The police! Si-Khelifa, the police! We are going to disperse.

SI-KHELIFA: My stick! I told you! I told you I felt uneasy!

LIVE-AS-SHE-PLEASES: Don't be afraid! Come, follow me, Cherifa!

CHERIFA: No, my sister! I will remain with Deham! Wherever you go, I will go with you! I will not leave you!

SI-KHELIFA: Come with me! Don't be afraid! We'll go out the same way we came in! Let's go! Hang on to my belt! Si-Khelifa was at Dien Bien Phu! It will not be said that he was captured in a Christian cemetery!

SEEK-THE-PEACE: Don't be impatient! Take it easy, I pray you!

CHERIFA: Do you still find a cause for laughter, men without heart!

BERHOUM: Be quiet and follow us . . . Help me put back this marble plaque over the Fernandez tomb . . . Put out the candles. Everyone hold on to each other!

SI-KHELIFA: What! What is your plan?

BERHOUM: We have dug out tunnels that lead from the caves to the bridge behind the cemetery. We will come out near the river and from there we can follow the road to the seashore.

SI-KHELIFA: And what if they have brought dogs with them?

BERHOUM: They will spend the whole night in the cemetery scratching at the marble.

SI-KHELIFA: I finally begin to understand . . . You have given me proof! In Vietnam . . .

BERHOUM: After you, I beg . . . Come along and I will introduce you to the dead as we go.

CHERIFA: I am afraid, Deham my brother!

BERHOUM: Come along behind Si-Khelifa. Hold on to him. Here, take a candle. I am going to put this marble slab back into place and then will rejoin you. Tomorrow morning they will find the place neat and tidy.

A POLICEMAN'S VOICE; You are surrounded! You hae no choice but to come out and surrender! We know you all, every one! Berhoum! Moustache! Ringworm and Kheira-Chorba! You have just three minutes! After three minutes, we will set loose the dogs! Chorba! Your wife has filed a complaint against you! This cemetery is foreign land! This cemetery is covered by immunity! It is as if you had entered an embassy! You are going to create a diplomatic incident with France! This is a political matter!

END

Oran, July 13, 1987

Jalila Baccar

ARABERLIN

by Jalila Baccar

Translated by David Looseley

ARABERLIN

by Jalila Baccar
2002

Originally commissioned and staged by Horizon Theatre Rep

CHARACTERS

AÏDA, over forty. a German Palestinian and former actress

ULRICH, her German husband, the same age as his wife,
    a businessman and former sympathizer with the RAF
    (Red Army Faction)

KAÏS, their 17-year-old son, a high-school student

MOKHTAR, a young Lebanese Palestinian, AIDA's brother,
    an architecture student suspected of being a member of
    an Islamic terrorist organization

KATARINA, German, 26 years old, florist

MOKHTAR's girlfriend, member of a local choir

The choir members:
  KATARINA
  MARIANNE GROSS, a survivor of the former German Democratic
    Republic
  JÜRGEN, former gynecologist
  ANNICKA, cook
  DANIEL HERZOG, dog groomer, and, subsequently, dog killer

HANNAH SCHLICHT, member of a humanitarian organization

KARL KATZ, journalist for a popular daily

A PERSON OF NO FIXED ABODE, in the church

FEMALE POLICE CHIEF

TWO POLICE OFFICERS

The play was put on using five actors, each playing several parts. It was first staged in Berlin, at the Drama Festival, on September 17, 2002, directed by Fadhel Jaïbi, with Martina Kraul, Peter Knaack, Hurdem Riepmüller, Patricia Tiedke, and Karim Cherif.

SCENE 1

The Rehearsal

Characters in evening dress enter an empty space.
A footbridge running between two sets of tiered theatre seats, which face each other.
Sections of a gray concrete wall rise up on either side of the footbridge,
Obscuring or revealing the actors as they come and go
There are five of them: three women and two men
They cross the space and stand at the other side, in two rows
They stare at an invisible point in front of them
For a long moment, they stand silent and motionless.
Then their faces start to move
A mouth wide open
A silent cry
A tongue wandering sensually over the lips
Lips tight, almost invisible
A neck stretching
An arm raised in an ample, fleeting gesture
Eyes staring wide-open
A head swinging from right to left
A head thrown back
A body bent
Then sounds start issuing from their throats
Bursts of organic sound
Mumbling, singing exercises, various cries . . .
They leave the stage chaotically
Then return with musical scores
They open them
Get ready and start the first song
Perhaps a folk song
A hymn to the soil and the labor of peasants

Their voices are quiet at first,
Get louder and louder
Then end in a whisper
Only their heels beat out the rhythm
Scattered cries ring out every now and then
Now they start their second song
A religious song interspersed with animal noises
They sing together, then each separately, rising to a crescendo
They stop abruptly and frantically look for a score they can't find
Papers are scattered
Bags rummaged through
Pockets emptied
A male choir member then starts to burble timidly
Tripping over his words
Because they can't get out of his mouth clearly
The others look at him in surprise
They try to make out the tune
A second, female choir member recognizes it and starts singing
Followed by the third (male), then the fourth (female)
The voices rise up in unison, launching into a love song
Only one young female choir member remains silent, moved
She hangs her head, overcome by tears
She steps out of line and turns to face them
They stop singing and look at her, astonished
She tries to explain something to them
She moves forward, back, around in a circle
Her tears turn to laughter and vice versa
She burbles snatches of incomprehensible words
Gesticulates, gets frustrated, then stops abruptly
She looks at them in silence, her eyes full of tears
She stamps her feet and exits without a word.
A pause
A male choir member takes from his pocket a first piece of juicy fruit
He stuffs it into his mouth
He takes a second and a third piece of fruit
And eats them greedily
The juice running down his chin
The second male choir member is seized by a series of uncontrollable
    twitches

The third, who is female and the oldest, starts running through her scales
*   again, in a hoarse voice*
The fourth female exits to fetch a handkerchief
She methodically wipes her hands and armpits
Then turns to face the others
And starts conducting them
They sound cacophonous at first
But gradually they start to harmonize
As their colleague conducts them
Finally ending in a fine melody.
The lights slowly go down.

SCENE 2

The Separation

The young actor enters and stands against the wall
He looks straight ahead as if talking to somebody

MOKH: "I'm leaving
I have to leave
Please, ask me nothing
Say nothing
Let me see this through to the end
I have to leave
For this is my destiny
I should never have crossed your path
Never have loved you
People like me should not love"

Actress 2 enters and sits at the piano
She plays a melody suited to the narrative

ACTOR/MOKH: That evening,
As she was making a rose-petal tart,
He entered
In a fine, soft light, he stood
His fine dark face, he hid

For there on his unshaven cheek a warm tear he shed
And in his fine, husky voice, he said:
"I'm leaving"

Actress 1 appears
She presses herself against him and throws her arms around him

MOKH: "There's too much blood, too much violence.
Those who truly love justice have no right to love
They stand up straight, as I do, head held high, eyes front
How could there be a place for love in such proud hearts?
Love gently makes us bow our heads, Katy
My neck is not going to bend
I love my people
I love them with a love that's vast and expects nothing in return
A love that brings no happiness
I love them and I live far away from them.
Oh! Katy my love
I am not of this world
There's a warmth here that is not for me
Yes, that's my lot in life, a love that cannot be.
I shall do what I have to
And then, perhaps, there'll be peace for people like me"

Actress 2 exits
The actor addresses the audience

ACTOR/MOKH: Wasn't that just great?
It wasn't by him of course
He got it from a play by Albert Camus, called *The Just*
Otherwise, he'd have just come out with clichés
And their love deserved better than that
You see, he really does love Katy,
He loves her so much,
And he can't stand seeing her cry

Actress 2 sits at the piano again
She starts playing a lovely romantic melody as she speaks
The two young actors carry on kissing and cuddling

ACTRESS 2: The story of Mokhtar and Katarina
is a great love story
They met in her florist's shop
One rainy Saturday
It was thirty-three minutes after one in the afternoon
And he was wearing a white roll-necked sweater.
He had his nephew with him
He looked up at her and she swooned
He said hello and she dissolved
And she's never been the same since
He used to come to her place most evenings
Whole nights making love,
Fantasizing about their shared dream:
To build a garden city
He'd be the architect, she'd do the flowers and the gardens
She knew absolutely nothing about him
He'd never once asked her over to his place
But that didn't bother her
She loved him
She was happy
She was floating
But, sadly, even the greatest stories have to end
Otherwise, every writer and every hack
Of every age and every nation
would be out of business

She plays one last note
Then closes the piano lid
On the way out, she passes Actress 1 who takes over the story

ACTRESS 1: Now you mustn't hold this against her,
But Katy's the emotional kind
She hates big good-byes, she hates tears
And boy, were there tears that night!
Because, when she heard the tragic news,
Katy didn't say a thing
But the tears came rolling down
That lovely, rosy, Bavarian face
Tears that he wiped away

Tears that he kissed away as he left
But tears that would not stop
She tried consoling herself,
By telling herself it wasn't the first time
A guy had dumped her,
But it was no good
She just couldn't come to terms with losing him
That poor girl got through one pack of tissues
Then another
Then a third, the last she had.
So then she started on the toilet rolls
But the tears still wouldn't stop
So she was forced to use the sponge-wipes
Her old blouses
Her dresses, sheets, curtains, checkbooks
She even tried the ironing board
But those tears still wouldn't dry
She filled saucepans, cups, and jugs
The bathtub and the mugs
She watered the plants and she washed the rugs.
And then, worried that she and her nice quiet neighbors would be
    flooded out
By this deluge of lachrymosity,
Or that she might dissolve altogether —
Because in one day and night she'd lost forty pounds —
She made up her mind to throw herself in the Spree River
And let herself be dragged down, body and sobs,
Into its icy waters
So she heads for the door.
But just as she goes to open it
The phone rings,
Her mother tells her the dog's had puppies,
And the will to live wins the day.

Darkness

SCENE 3

The Search

Two actors — a man and a woman — enter
Each stands at either end of the space
They signal to each other with furtive gestures and expressions
A great complicity between them can be felt
Each invites the other to start speaking
From time to time they glance at the audience
As if apologizing for being unable to get started
Because they are speaking hesitantly and stammering

SHE: She was an actor
The man clowns around
And pretends to be acting
Well . . .
She *was* an actor *once*
But it's been a long time since she did any acting
He mimes everything she is saying
He was in computers
He continues to act everything out
That day
He was away on business
He bursts out laughing and mimes a frantic dance
Well, that's what he told her anyway.
Sure, he'd been traveling a lot lately
But up until now
She'd had no reason to be suspicious
They were happily married and . . .
She gets annoyed
Anyhow, who cares,
That's not the point of the story
He pretends to keep a low profile
It was four in the morning
And while *he* was snoring away in a Munich hotel
She was asleep in their nice Berlin apartment
Suddenly, there was a ring at the door
The actor knocks very loudly on the screen

She wakes up with a start, can't figure out what's happening
Has a quick look
In her son's room
Just to make sure he's still there
The knocking gets louder
So without even asking who's there
She opens the door

HE: And in rushes an army of cockroaches
How many would you say there were?

SHE: Hard to say
10, 20, 50, 150, 1,000 . . .
D'you know what fear feels like?

HE: What me? Nah!

SHE: Well, *she* did
The kind of fear that grabbed her in the gut and gave her stomach
    cramps
The kind of fear she'd been trying to forget
Ever since she left her birthplace in war-torn Beirut,
The kind of fear that gave her . . .
Sorry . . .

She exits, doubled up

HE (*aside*): Diarrhea . . .
Now, actually, that army of cockroaches
Was the highly respected Anti-Terrorist Brigade . . .
Showed up in the dead of the night . . . . unannounced . . . .,
With a proper search warrant
And all the trimmings.
The officer in charge —
Or maybe it was a judge —
Tells her they're looking for her brother
Mokhtar El-Kodsi
A Palestinian architecture student
Suspected of being active

In an Islamist terrorist organization

She returns

SHE: That isn't true, there's been a mistake
*She gets worked up and it's impossible to tell if it's the actor or the character
    speaking*
Her brother was never an Islamist
In fact, he was an atheist
And his parents were communists
His mother was Christian
And *she's* German
Sorry . . .
She rushes out

HE: Oh my, that diarrhea . . .
You'll have to excuse her,
It's so embarrassing,
Specially with all these men around
Turning the place over
For the slightest clue

She returns

SHE: Don't touch those!
They're manuscripts from the first century of the Hegira

HE: So what's the Hegira?

SHE: It's the Muslim calendar
Those texts have been in her family for centuries
They have no right to take them.

HE (*shouts, with irritation*): Sure they have the right
They have the right to do whatever the hell they like
I mean, what does she think this is?
A social call?
So they can all have a nice cup of mint tea?
Anything in Arabic was suspect

And so it was taken away

SHE: Why're you shouting?

HE: I'm being like them

SHE: But they didn't shout
They worked in total silence
Only the officer

HE: Or the judge . . .

SHE: Interrogated her
He had dark eyes, very dark and very big
He watched her the whole time,
Stared at her without ever blinking
He was good-looking
And she had diarrhea
Sorry . . .
She exits

HE: The questions were short and to the point
Why did she put her brother up
When he came to Germany?

She answers from behind the screen
SHE: He needed help getting settled in

HE: Like, for three years?

SHE: He was her brother
And, for people from the East,
Helping your own is a duty

HE: So why had he left?

SHE: He got a grant

HE: Who from?

SHE: Some foundation in Europe

HE: When was the last time he'd been here?

SHE: Two or three months back

HE: Did he phone sometimes?

SHE: Not often

HE: Strange, for people from the Middle East

She comes back

SHE: I'm German, she said, still weak in the knees

HE: Why had she applied for German nationality?

SHE: So she could have the same rights as you

HE: And the same duties?

SHE: . . .

HE: What's that chador doing in their apartment?

SHE: It belongs to her husband

HE: Oh yeah?
So where is he?

SHE: Who?

HE: The husband

SHE: Away on business

HE: Did he go away often?

SHE: Why?

HE: Did he get on OK with his brother-in-law?

SHE: Yes, she thinks so, why?

HE: And the son . . .

SHE: What about her son?
He's under age
They've got no right to interrogate him

HE: He's got the Koran in his room

SHE: He's got the Bible too

HE: It wasn't an accusation

SHE: I'm glad to hear it
She was really angry with herself
She was angry that she couldn't control herself
Couldn't concentrate on the questions
Couldn't answer the way she wanted
Cool, intelligent, witty
Like the heroine in some novel or film
Or one of the characters she'd have liked to play on stage
If she hadn't messed up her acting career

HE (*mockingly*): She kept stammering, getting her grammar wrong
Her Lebanese accent came back
And as well as everything else, she had . . .

He whispers the word "diarrhea"

SHE: She was afraid
Afraid for her brother
Afraid for her son
Afraid for her husband

HE (*aside*): Poor thing
She was worrying about her husband
While *he* was having an extremely good time
With a female co-worker in the hotel nightclub
And when, after the roaches—I mean, the cops—had gone,
She decided she'd give him a call,
He'd just started some particularly delicate negotiations
With that same co-worker in her bedroom

SHE: Still, he did jump into the first plane home

HE: He found her completely dehydrated
Rings under her eyes
And getting ready to go to Brigade's headquarters
For more questioning

The two actors go back into character
He tries to kiss her
She pulls away

ULRICH: You should have called me sooner

AÏDA: Your cell phone was off
And you weren't in your room

ULRICH: I was having a drink with some clients

AÏDA: At four in the morning?

ULRICH: Look, don't let's argue about this now
I'm calling a lawyer

AÏDA: I already have
He's expecting me.

ULRICH: I'll come with you

AÏDA: You better had
They asked me a whole load of questions about your past

ALRICH: What past?

AÏDA: Your Far-Left past

Darkness

SCENE 4

The Interrogation of the Florist

The actress who is a pianist enters and stands in front of the piano
She lifts the lid then slams it shut again
She does this two or three times
In the same rhythm
Then she strikes one key repeatedly, in a military fashion
Policeman 1 enters pushing Katy before him
Her head is covered with a black plastic bag
They cross the space and exit the other side
The female police chief appears
She has her hair up in a bun and she is wearing a severe-looking suit
She watches them exit, then disappears herself
The pianist continues to beat out a rhythm for the scene

THE PIANIST: Katarina, S . . . H. . . .
26 years old
Height 1m 78
Caucasian
Hair dark
Eyes dark
Good teeth, apart from one cavity that's been neglected
Divorced, no children
Politics none
Owner of a florist's shop
Inherited from her father, deceased
Mother, horticulturalist
Hospitalized for the last six months with a serious illness
Policeman 1 comes back during this speech, holding the black bag
His belt is undone
He slowly walks forward and is extremely agitated

He sniffs the bag, caresses his face with it
Then starts stuffing it into his mouth
Until it disappears completely
He chews on it frantically
Then he yells something
Once, twice
The third time Katy reappears, heavy-eyed
He gives her an order she does not understand
He gesticulates, she still can't understand
He opens his fly and drops his pants
She finally understands and starts doing the same
The lady in the suit comes back
Katy freezes
The agitated policeman turns around
Realizes he looks ridiculous
Hurriedly pulls up his pants
Takes the bag out of his mouth
Points an accusing finger at Katy

POLICEMAN 1: It was her, she started it
Temptress
Slut, spawn of the devil

He exits shouting
Katy stands frozen to the spot, stunned
The female police chief, smiling, gestures to her to pull up her pants
Then walks steadily toward her
And exits
A second policeman enters
He smiles at her fawningly
He reaches out a finger toward her, sticks it in her mouth
Licks it and exits
The agitated one returns, even more agitated
He gestures to her with his head
She doesn't understand
Which inflames him even more
He drops his pants
Your pants, your pants . . .
Katy drops her pants

Your top, your top
Quick, quick
He starts unbuttoning his shirt
But one button won't undo
He gets frustrated with it
Wriggles around
Under the amused gaze of the police chief who has been watching him for a
      while
He goes out yelling abuse at Katy, like the first time
The police chief steps forward a little
Katy tries to pull up her pants

POLICE CHIEF: No, leave them
Spread your legs
Thank you

She goes up to her
Twists her head around toward the back
Sticks a photo on her forehead and presses her forehead against the wall
And exits, replaced by the fawning cop

POLICEMAN 2: Tea or coffee?

KATY: What?

POLICEMAN 2: Would you like tea or coffee?
Or maybe both?

KATY: Just water please

He goes out
The agitated one runs back in, with no pants on
He stands in the middle of the space and lets out a yell

KATY: The restroom!

POLICEMAN 1: No!
Quick, quick, we don't have time
She's right behind me

Katy takes off her shoes and drops her pants
Quick, quick
Over here

Katy goes over to him and the police chief enters
The agitated one exits, still blaming the poor florist

POLICE CHIEF: Where's the photo?
You dropped it
Pick it up.
Katy obeys
Recognize him?

KATY: No

POLICE CHIEF: How about in this one? Still don't recognize him?
He's with your fiancé in his apartment
You didn't take the photo yourself?

KATY: No I didn't

The police chief continues showing her photos and throwing them on the
  ground

POLICE CHIEF: Pick them up
And tell me if you recognize a face or a location
Come on, don't stop
Run, run, faster . . .

Katy picks up the photos and runs and runs
Obstructed by the pants around her ankles
She tries to take them off but the police chief, with the help of the
pianist, who is really the one setting the pace of the scene either on
the piano or by making noises,
Won't let her stop running
The police chief disappears
And the fawning cop returns with a glass of water
He hands it to Katy

POLICEMAN 2: Would you like to call someone?

KATY: My lawyer

POLICEMAN 2: Would you like to eat something?
You must be hungry

As soon as she stops running so she can drink,
He goes out and gets her a second glass
Then a third
And a fourth
Then a bottle . . .
He forces her to drink
But Katy can't drink any more
The police chief comes back and orders her to run even faster
The pianist plays louder and louder
Faster and faster
And Katy runs faster and faster
With two glasses in her hand and her pants down
She collapses, panting
Policeman 1 comes back with the black plastic bag full of water
And pours it over her head
A pause . . .
She comes around
They start the interrogation
With Katy now dripping wet and panting, her pants half torn
and a look of alarm in her eyes

POLICE CHIEF: Where'd you first meet him?

KATY: Who?

POLICEMAN 2: Mokhtar

KATY: My place

POLICEMAN 1: At home?

KATY: At the shop

POLICEMAN 2: When?

KATY: Eight months ago

POLICEMAN 1: What day was it?

KATY: A Friday

POLICEMAN 2: What time?

KATY: Thirty-three minutes after one in the afternoon

POLICE CHIEF: What was he wearing?

KATY: A white sweater

POLICEMAN 1: How about his underpants?

KATY: Black

POLICEMAN 1: You screwed straightaway?

KATY: No!

POLICEMAN 2: So what about the underpants?

KATY: I don't know

POLICE CHIEF: You said black

KATY: His pants were black

POLICEMAN 1: He a good lay?

KATY: That's none of your business

POLICEMAN 2 (*yelling*): Did he wash before or after?

KATY: After what?

POLICEMAN 1: After the screwing

KATY: I don't know

POLICEMAN 2: Did he like blowjobs?

POLICEMAN 1: Sodomy?

POLICE CHIEF: Did he pray?

KATY: At my place, no

POLICEMAN 1: How about at his place?

KATY: I don't know

POLICEMAN 2: Yes you do!
You said: "At my place, no"
So that meant, at his place, yes
Otherwise, you'd have said no
And then we'd have known you meant not at your place or his place

KATY: I don't know
I never went to his place

POLICE CHIEF: You know his address?

KATY: He told me he shared digs with a student friend

POLICEMAN 1: You know him?

KATY: No, he never introduced me to his friends

POLICEMAN 2: Why not?

KATY: I don't know

POLICE CHIEF: Why did you throw away the photo?

KATY: What photo?

POLICE CHIEF: The one of Ali Abdallah

KATY: I don't know who he is

POLICE CHIEF: So why did you throw away his photo?

KATY: I didn't throw it away
It fell down

POLICEMAN 1: Who pays when you go to a restaurant?

KATY: Him, me, I don't know, it depends

POLICEMAN 2: On what?

KATY: I don't know
I don't know any more
I'm tired

POLICE CHIEF: So are we

POLICEMAN 1: I'm not
I really don't mind staying with her, if that's OK with you

POLICEMAN 2: Did he drink?

KATY: No

POLICEMAN 2: Did he eat pork?

KATY: No
Neither do I

POLICEMAN 1: Why not?

KATY: We're both vegetarian

POLICE CHIEF (*ironically*): I told you, this girl is a saint
Not only does she live amid the flowers
But she also doesn't smoke, doesn't drink, doesn't eat meat . . .

POLICEMAN 1: Yeah, but she screws

POLICE CHIEF (*angrily*): You think we're stupid?

POLICEMAN 2: Were you there when he took his photos?

KATY: Some of them

POLICEMAN 1: Which ones?

KATY: I don't remember
He never went anywhere without his camera

POLICEMAN 2: Why all these shots of the Reichstag?

KATY: I don't kn . . .

POLICEMAN 2: Why?

KATY: Because he liked the dome, I guess

POLICE CHIEF: What did you talk about?

POLICEMAN 1: And don't say "flowers" either

KATY: But we did

POLICEMAN 2: Did you talk about the attacks? 9/11?

KATY: No

POLICEMAN 1: Politics?

KATY: No

POLICEMAN 2: Islam?

KATY: Sometimes

POLICEMAN 1: The Arabs, Israel?

POLICEMAN 2: The Americans?

POLICE CHIEF: Did he have any special marks on his body? Tattoos, scars?

KATY: Yes, yes

POLICEMEN 1 and 2: What, where?

KATY: He'd had surgery for appendicitis

The pianist plays a few last notes
Closes the piano
And joins them, holding a blanket that she puts around Katy's shoulders
She wipes the floor with a floorcloth that she moves around with her foot

PIANIST: That's enough now!
You've been playing the cops as caricatures
Shows you've never been arrested or questioned before
They're not that sadistic
They can even be really nice
She addresses the audience
All the same, it is part of the job
I mean, they're not going to treat gangsters
Terrorists and assassins with kid gloves
They're only doing their duty, protecting the law-abiding citizen

She exits
The three actors/policemen apologize
And tiptoe out
Katy takes off the blanket and addresses the audience

ACTRESS/KATY: Poor Katy is totally confused
She just can't figure out
What she's being accused of
Being in love with a man?
Going to bed with him
Without trying to find out every tiny detail about him?
Is it a crime to be so romantic?
Looks like it is
Even her mother had said it
She was furious, the mother,
She just couldn't see how
Anyone could fall in love with a man
Who wasn't the spitting image of her own husband
"You mark my words, Katy, one day you'll be sorry"
Could it be that day has come?
Was Mokhtar really a killer of the innocent?
Was she that blind?
It was true she knew next to nothing about him
But she'd only known him eight months
It was true he'd not introduced her to any of his friends
But she did know his nephew
It was true she had no idea about his political views
But he had talked to her about his dream of being an architect
About light and fresh air
About schools
Where love would be the main subject on the program
He talked about everything but death and destruction
Here or anywhere else.
Did all these fine speeches really hide
A Machiavellian mind, full of hate and the will to destroy?
NO!
She'd have sensed it
She'd have seen it in his eyes
He'd have given himself away
She was convinced: Mokh is innocent!
And he'll prove it.

Darkness

SCENE 5

Everyone's talking about it

The oldest actress enters, nimble and twirling around. She greets the audience

MARIANNE: Hello there!
Welcome to my home
Let me introduce myself: I'm Marianne Gross
That's with "ss" at the end
This space is mine, you know
OK, I don't exactly *own* it
But it's my patch, it's my creation
I am the soul and the spirit of the place
I deal with it all here
From the coffee to the program
And I'm proud of that
I was a dancer once, under the old regime
But there was an incident . . .
Well, let's say there was an accident which . . .
Her mood darkens, she goes quiet and pensive
After a moment's silence
She picks up her story again, becoming increasingly upbeat,
As she chases a bug across the floor
Which she frantically squashes
I'm not going to rake over painful memories
I like to think *positive*
So, I used to be a dancer, and now I'm a concierge
That's life
Who knows what's around the corner.
I have so much energy in me!
So many ideas!
So much imagination!
So much love!
I'm an artist, you see, through and through
I cannot live without creation
It's not the art form that matters, it's the Art
So, adieu dance, hello music and song.

When I took the destiny of this building in hand
As the concierge, it was a wretched, dismal place
I put flowers everywhere, I brightened it up
I even persuaded the owner
To change the color scheme.
To say thank you he lent me this space
So I could devote myself to my art: the art of singing
Not just any old singing, mind you,
Here we sing only of love
The love of God
The love of your neighbor
"Love and kindness," that's our motto
Now don't get the idea it was easy
To get it all going
A choir isn't just about voices
It's about the people behind the voices
Human beings with stories, problems
Dramas, tragedies even
And I know what I'm talking about
I had to track down these model citizens of mine
Motivate them
Channel their energies and turn them into choir members
And what a choir!
Believe me, I'm proud of them
So proud
Ladies and gentlemen, I give you
Jürgen
Jürgen makes his entrance
She looks at him, moved
Oh Jürgen, Jürgen, Jürgen
He's so kind, so gentle, so thoughtful
He's my favorite
And yet—poor man—he's suffered so in his life
He's widowed like me
Used to be a doctor

Jürgen is moving forward
Limping across the space, without saying a word

MARIANNE: Gynecologist,
Had his license taken away
He exits
Such an injustice!
He suffered so, when his wife died
She killed herself, you see, and without so much as a word of
    explanation
Left him locked in despair, the poor man
And then that Jezebel came along
Tried to lure him in
But he resisted and she persisted
She hounded him and he held out to the end,
Decent man that he is
So, to get her revenge, she accused him of the worst crime of all:
Rape
Not of raping her, oh no, too clever for that, the she-devil,
But her fifteen-year-old daughter
Who went to see him about going on the pill—
At fifteen, would you believe that?
Like mother, like daughter, I say—
The case caused such a stir
He was totally traumatized
Practically suicidal
The choir saved his life, did you know that?

Jürgen returns, goes up to her and puts his arms around her

JÜRGEN: She's so kind, Marianne
But so talkative
So nosy
So indiscreet
So intrusive
That even her late husband was happier getting shot on the Berlin
    Wall
Than living with her for the rest of his days
In the 1970s, it was . . .
Riddled with bullets . . .
The man he was with surrendered as soon as the guards shouted the
    first warning

But he just yelled out
"Marianne, even death is sweeter than the sound of your voice"
Alleluia! Alleluia!

He exits
She continues

MARIANNE: He was so cast down by such infamy
That he wasn't able to defend himself
Lucky for him I was around
I read about it in the papers
And I decided to save him through song
Alleluia! Alleluia!

Annicka makes her entrance
She constantly rubs her hands and wipes them on her skirt

ANNICKA: Did you call, Marianne?

MARIANNE: Annicka, a cook by trade
Lovely voice!
But the smell is sometimes unbearable

ANNICKA: I do my best to spare you
Look, I've just bought a new deodorant
And some lemon-scented soap
She takes the deodorant and soap from her bag
And shows them to her
It's the garlic and onions that do it
She exits

MARIANNE: No it isn't, it's her armpits
And yet, it's strange, there's no African in her . . .
I was in a crowded bus once, I was sitting next to a Black man
I tell you, it was sheer torture
Not that I'm a racist of course . . .
I'm going to let you into a secret
Just between us
The cook there, she's not German

Well, she is, she has a German passport
But she's not pure
She's got other roots she likes to keep to herself
But I found out
I mean, your identity has nothing to do with your passport, I'm sure
    you agree.
Especially not today

Annicka returns with her score

ANNICKA: I've had a wash
We can start now if you like

MARIANNE: We're waiting for the others

ANNICKA: What others?

MARIANNE: Hanna, Willy, Katarina, Daniel, Martina

ANNICKA: Marianne, stop being silly
Most of them left ages ago
And if you carry on talking instead of singing
You're going to end up on your own with just Jürgen

MARIANNE (*to the audience*): Can't you smell it?
(*to Annicka*) Go and have another wash. Please
Or I'll be forced to let you go

ANNICKA (*to the audience*): She couldn't afford to, they need me too
    much
I'm the only one around here whose voice
Doesn't sound like a foghorn
I could actually make a career for myself in a good choir
If it wasn't for this damned smell following me around
She exits

MARIANNE: See? I rule them with a rod of iron.
I can hear footsteps
It must be the lovely Martina arriving

Ladies and gentlemen, I give you our youngest member, the lovely
    Mart . . .
A young man enters
You're not Martina

DANIEL: No, I'm Daniel, Daniel Herzog

MARIANNE: Oh yes, the dog killer

DANIEL: Best dog groomer of all time
Since I was fiteen
I've been washing them, clipping them, perfuming them, filing their
    nails, doing their hair
Every size and every breed
German shepherds, greyhounds, boxers, dalmatians
Fox terriers, poodles
Ungrateful, the lot of them
You stroke them, they piss on you
You make a fuss of them, they scratch you —
Look at my hands, they used to be so soft, white, delicate —
So I started hating them, loathing them in secret
Torturing them, methodically
You might even say artistically
Without anyone noticing
It was exciting, it was intoxicating
Until the day that damned Chihuahua showed up
He started screaming blue murder
So I ripped his tongue out
That was all

He tells his story as he crosses the space
He exits

MARIANNE: No it wasn't all
He spent a year in a psychiatric hospital
That's where I got him from

Daniel returns

DANIEL: And what exactly were *you* doing there?

MARIANNE: I was visiting

DANIEL: Visiting who?

MARIANNE: A relative

DANIEL: Who?

MARIANNE: None of your business

DANIEL: It was her son
She's got a son who's schizophrenic
She hides him away 'cause she's ashamed of him
She won't face up to it
Bad dog, Marianne!

MARIANNE: I never wanted him . . .
Daniel, I mean
But it take all sorts to make a choir, isn't that right?

ANNICKA: Right
So can we start now?
It's getting late and I've got my evening shift

MARIANNE: I'm waiting for Katarina

ANNICKA: Katarina?
But she can't make it
I saw her yesterday on TV
They said she was a terrorist
At least, I think they did
I switched over to see *Inspector Derrick*
MARIANNE: Idiot
She's not the terrorist
It's her boyfriend

DANIEL: In the paper it said

He was going to plant bombs
In all the public places in Berlin
To punish the Germans

ANNICKA: What for?

MARIANNE: Idiot
He's an Arab

ANNICKA: So what?

MARIANNE: The Arabs detest the Jews

ANNICKA: But the Germans aren't all Jewish, are they?

MARIANNE: Idiot
Don't you know your history?

ANNICKA: What history?

DANIEL: The history of Germany

MARIANNE: See what I mean?
You don't get an identity from a passport.

ANNICKA: I don't understand any of this history
If he's an Arab and he hates Jews
Why doesn't he plant his bombs in Israel
That's where the Jews are, isn't it?

DANIEL: They showed a documentary on TV about the terrorist
    attacks
There was blood everywhere
An arm sitting in a tree like a bird
A nice shapely leg standing upright in fishnet tights
A head in a helmet
A . . .

MARIANNE: Stop it

Katy has nothing to do with any of that
She's a respectable member of the community
Her only mistake was trusting a foreigner
She should have been on her guard
Rather than opening up her home to just anyone

DANIEL: Yeah, but the papers say
She's not as nice as all that
Her mother says she hasn't seen her for five years
And she doesn't even visit for Christmas
Her ex has spilled the beans about why they divorced
Seems she preferred her wieners circumcised
At the time she'd taken in some Kurd,
She claimed he was an illegal alien and homeless

MARIANNE: I know
I read the papers too
I even started a file on it all
She takes a book of press cuttings from her bag
Look
All the articles are there
I've been in touch with a journalist too
I'm giving him an interview so I can set the record straight
No one knows Katy better than I do

ANNICKA: But I thought you'd only known her two months

MARIANNE: So what?
It doesn't take me long to get through to someone's inner self,
Their soul

JÜRGEN: Plus, of course, you wouldn't mind seeing your picture in
     the paper, would you, my dear?

ANNICKA: Would they come and hear us sing?
Could be good publicity

They turn around
Katarina is there

MARIANNE: My dear, dear Katarina
We're with you all the way
We're so worried about you

She rushes over to her, puts her arms around her and hugs her very tight

Darkness

SCENE 6

The Mayonnaise

Two actors in a square of light
Each one occupies one end of the square
They are wearing indoor clothes
The woman is holding a bottle of olive oil
And the man a bowl, with a spoon in it
They look at each other
He blows her a kiss
She gives him a sad smile

ULRICH: I love you

AÏDA: I love you too

ULRICH: Thanks

AÏDA: It'll be something else for me to think about too

They both move into the center of the space
And kiss each other politely
Then they address the audience as actors

ACTOR: Ten days after the brother's disappearance

ACTRESS: After the shock of the police raid on their home

ACTOR: After the hours of questioning
And the pages of testimony they'd had to sign

ACTRESS: After the media harassment
And the dozens of poisonous, biased articles
About them

ACTOR: Life is quietly getting back to normal

ACTRESS: Tonight, they're entertaining

ACTOR: They're having a dinner party for friends and colleagues
He would rather have taken them to a restaurant, naturally
But she refuses to go out . . . Too risky

ACTRESS: She'd either have to wear an Islamic head scarf
So as not to be recognized
Or put up with being hounded by the paparazzi

ACTOR: So instead they've invited four sets of friends over
Unfortunately two of the couples have declined

ACTRESS: And by an odd coincidence, for the same reason
The wives both have toothaches

ACTOR: This dinner is very important to him
For ten days he's been neglecting his work

ACTRESS: What with the police, the lawyers
His wife's anxiety attacks
And the nightmares she keeps having

ACTOR: And the hundreds of calls he gets every day

ACTRESS: There was just no time
For any business contacts

ACTOR: From this evening on, he's getting on top of things again
That's definite

ACTRESS: It's not strictly speaking a business dinner

But there's no harm in kicking a few ideas around

ACTOR: Get the feel of his associates . . .
See how far they're behind him
In his current difficulties
And he's determined not to lose a single cent more

ACTRESS: He's got to win them over

ACTOR: And tonight he's got a great trump card
His wife's a real cordon bleu cook

ACTRESS: Cooking has always been a kind of therapy for her

ACTOR: Once she gets into the herbs and spices, she forgets about
    everything else

ACTRESS: Tonight, though, it'll be hard to concentrate
She keeps thinking about her brother
She misses him, she's afraid for him
And she secretly longs to hold him in her arms
Kiss him
And protect him, like she did in Beirut in '82

ACTOR: As a matter of fact, tonight's menu is Lebanese French.
Everything's ready
Except the mayonnaise

ACTRESS: For them, this is practically a love ritual
They always make the mayonnaise together
He beats the eggs, she pours in the oil
Cute, huh?

ACTOR: Especially when it's Tunisian olive oil
Best there is, she says

They are now in the middle of the space
Standing face to face
They go back to being their characters

And start preparing the mayonnaise
He reaches out and strokes her face

ULRICH: You've still got a slight temperature

AÏDA: No, I'm OK
Just a little dehydrated

ULRICH: That's normal when you've had diarrhea for a week

AÏDA: I don't want to talk about it
It's revolting

Their son Kaïs crosses the space on his skateboard
He pays no attention to them and is looking at the sky
They don't even notice him go by

Mrs. Gerhard slammed the door in my face
I said hello
And she deliberately slammed the door in my face

ULRICH: Sweetie, Mrs. Gerhard never did like you
She hates foreigners
And *you*'ve always laughed at her for it

AÏDA: I'm not a foreigner
I'm German
And I shouldn't have laughed at her
I should've thrown boiling water over her
He has stopped beating the mayonnaise
Do it harder!
Don't be limp-wristed about it

ULRICH: Now you just watch what you're saying here
I'm as macho as they come
And he leans over to kiss her
She avoids him
What's up?
I'm sensing you're mad at me

AÏDA: I'm mad at the whole world
Not at anyone in particular

ULRICH: OK, so give me a kiss
He leans over again to kiss her
The phone rings (a voice offstage imitates the sound of ringing)
He hands her the bowl and goes out to answer it
She beats the eggs frantically
The son goes by still looking up at the sky
He stops on the other side of the space, listening
ULRICH returns and picks up the bottle of oil without speaking
A pause

ULRICH: Wrong number

AÏDA: What did they say?

ULRICH: A wrong numb . . .

AÏDA: What did they say?

ULRICH: Just nonsense

AÏDA: Like what?

ULRICH: "Dirty terrorists"

AÏDA: And?

ULRICH: "We're gonna get you"

AÏDA: And?
Kaïs continues from where his father left off
He calmly pours forth abuse
as if intending it for himself

KAÏS: "Dirty Arabs"
"Mad dogs"
"Murderers"

"Ignorant savages"
"Hairy-faced fleabags" . . .

He exits

ULRICH: You shouldn't let him answer the phone
I want him to stay out of all this

AÏDA: You think that's possible?
We don't live in a cocoon
He has to find out what kind of world he's living in

ULRICH: Those stupid bastards don't represent German society

AÏDA: I'm glad to hear it!
But they exist and we have to deal with it
I hear them out to the very end
Till they've emptied out all their venom
Spat out their hatred
Till they run out of steam and hang up first
Then you know they'll leave you alone for a while
And anyway it gives a little entertainment
To the poor cop who's tapping the phone
Can you imagine what he has to write in his report?
If he's the conscientious kind
I guess he must have to dissect every insult and analyze it
Just in case there's a coded message in one of them
Careful of the oil, you're spilling it

ULRICH: I'll wipe it up

AÏDA: It's not the mess I'm worried about, it's the oil
That's my last bottle

ULRICH: Who cares!
I don't give a shit about the oil
And I don't give a shit about the mayonnaise either
You're the one I care about
I want you to be calm, mellow

And I want you to kiss your gorgeous husband who loves you madly!

The phone rings again

AÏDA: I'll go . . . mellow
She exits
Her voice can be heard from behind the wall
Hello?
Oh, hi!
Long silence
Yes, I quite understand
No, no, don't worry about it
Of course I will
Thanks for letting us know
Bye
She comes back, with a strange smile on her face
That was the Schoüls
They're not coming
Guess why

ULRICH: . . .

AÏDA: The Patricks went to pick them up
But Eva didn't feel well
And as it's her first child, she panicked
So Katia has to stay with her for support
Gets you right there, doesn't it?

ULRICH: But she's not in the ninth month, is she?

AÏDA: No, fifth or sixth, I think

ULRICH: Which hospital have they taken her to?

AÏDA: They haven't gone to the hospital
They're all having a nice little drink all together
And they don't want us there
Haven't you got it yet?

And stop beating that damned mayonnaise
No one's going to eat it

ULRICH: You're crazy, d'you know that?
Totally paranoid
You want me to start doubting my friends now?
No one's even allowed to have a problem anymore
No glitches, no obstacles
No coincidences
Or Madam's going to think it's a conspiracy against her

Aïda loses her temper

AÏDA: Oh no!
I'm not the one imagining conspiracies
It's those so-called friends of yours
Who've been avoiding me like the plague
Since I became the sister of a terrorist
It's the kind neighbors who look away when they see me
And slip abusive, threatening letters under the door
It's the good-hearted butcher who makes me wait
While he serves everyone else first
It's those upright citizens who disguise their voices
And shower me with insults down the phone
It's those scrupulous journalists who hound me day and night
The eager cops who watch us and tail us
And it's you, my darling husband, even you think there's a
    conspiracy

ULRICH: Paranoid, totally paranoid

AÏDA: You think so?
In the ten days since this nightmare began
Not once have you said what you think of the charges

ULRICH: Because I don't want to get in a state over nothing

AÏDA: You call my brother's disappearance
And the charges against him nothing?

ULRICH: The investigation's ongoing
And I don't have enough evidence to form a view

AÏDA: Well that neutrality does you credit, my darling
Except that there's one important detail you're forgetting
This fugitive, this Public Enemy Number One, is Mokhtar
My brother, your protégé
Your "eldest son" as you used to call him
Mokhtar, whom you introduced to the great philosophical,
Humanist ideas of the West
Whom you spent whole days with
Helping him exorcise his fears and anxieties
His frustration at being the son of refugees driven out of their
     homeland
Who always came back happy, with a spring in his step, from those
     cathartic walks you used to have
And who liked to call you one of the Just

ULRICH: You know, I just can't figure this out
Exactly what are you accusing me of?

AÏDA: Of questionable neutrality

ULRICH: Meaning?

AÏDA: You're not defending Mokhtar

ULRICH: . . .

AÏDA: Do you believe he's capable of killing?

ULRICH: I don't know

AÏDA: Well that's good to know

She picks up the bottle of oil and the bowl and exits
She passes her son on his roller boots
He crosses the space without even looking at his father
He stops, facing backward at the other end of the space

Ulrich takes a step toward Kaïs
He goes to say something to him
Gives up and then exits in turn

Darkness

SCENE 7

Civil Society

The two actresses playing Aïda and Katy are facing the audience

ACTRESS/AÏDA: Aïda and Katy were not left to cope on their own
With their detractors, accusers
Persecutors, not to say their torturers

ACTRESS/KATY: It would be unfair of us to claim they were

ACTRESS/AÏDA: Some societies produce their own antibodies
To stop themselves sinking into barbarism

ACTRESS/KATY: Isn't that what distinguishes a democratic regime?

ACTRESS/AÏDA: Well, we think it is

ACTRESS/KATY: Honestly, we do . . .

ACTRESS/AÏDA: The two women were assisted, supported, even taken care of by various voluntary bodies,

ACTRESS/KATY: NGOs, clubs of all kinds
The weekly press, journalists, pastors, artists, intellectuals

ACTRESS/AÏDA: Hawkers, some homeless people

ACTRESS/KATY: Not with the same motives, admittedly
Not for the same reasons
But both women, once the first distressing days had passed

Found a network of support
And selfless encouragement
Which was balm to their soul

ACTRESS/AÏDA: It didn't bring Mokhtar back of course

ACTRESS/KATY: And it didn't stop the police constantly questioning them

ACTRESS/AÏDA: But still, it was good not to feel alone

ACTRESS/KATY: Even though some of the harm done couldn't be put right
Especially not for Katy who had to close her shop

ACTRESS/AÏDA speaks to her friend:

ACTRESS/AÏDA: You shouldn't confuse the material issues with the moral ones

ACTRESS/KATY: I'm not confusing them
But they do make a difference, don't they?

ACTRESS/AÏDA: But Katy's not exactly dying of hunger, is she?

ACTRESS/KATY: No

ACTRESS/AÏDA: Well then, you shouldn't mention them
That's not what we're talking about
She turns back to face the audience
So they were invited on lots of radio shows
To talk about themselves and Mokhtar

ACTRESS/KATY: About their childhood, their parents
About their ideological convictions and their political views
About war, about peace

ACTRESS/AÏDA: About the effect of gamma rays on Arabian cacti

ACTRESS/KATY: And about the problem of violence against women across the world

ACTRESS/AÏDA: Aïda was in demand for TV debates
As the token guest
On political or geopolitical shows
On talk shows and variety shows aplenty

ACTRESS/KATY: So was Katy

ACTRESS/AÏDA: Shows where Islam, Muslims, Arabs and Islamists
Became the hot topic
For an hour or so
In front of a dozen other guests
She had to explain certain ambiguous suras of the Koran

ACTRESS/KATY: So did Katy

ACTRESS/AÏDA: Or interpret certain passages of Arafat's latest speech
ACTRESS/KATY: So did Katy

ACTRESS/AÏDA, irritated, turns to the other actress

ACTRESS/AÏDA: What d'you mean, so did Katy?
How could Katy explain the Koran
Or interpret Arafat's speeches?
She's totally nonpolitical
And doesn't know a thing about Islam

ACTRESS/KATY: Yes but people still asked her the questions

ACTRESS/AÏDA: Oh yes? So what did she answer?

ACTRESS/KATY: That going out with a Palestinian Muslim
Didn't necessarily mean knowing anything about Islam
Or becoming an expert on the Palestinian issue
Katy is well aware of her own limits

But she did justify the wearing of the kurba
By Afghan women even after the Taliban left

ACTRESS/AÏDA: Burka, not kurba
How on earth can she justify a thing like that?

ACTRESS/KATY: Because women have been wearing the kurba

ACTRESS/AÏDA: Burka

ACTRESS/KATY: The burka for centuries
It needs time, a change of attitude,
It needs development at a social and cultural level
For things to start moving and evolving
That kind of thing isn't going to happen overnight
Just because the West wants it to
Isn't that so?

ACTRESS/AÏDA: For someone who's nonpolitical, that Katy does
    pretty well

ACTRESS/KATY: Just because you're not political doesn't mean
    you've got no common sense

ACTRESS/AÏDA takes the point and turns back to face the audience

ACTRESS/AÏDA: So Aïda was there to bring out the contradictions
    in what the other guests said

ACTRESS/KATY: So was Katy

ACTRESS/AÏDA: To point out that not all Arabs are Muslims

ACTRESS/KATY: And not all Muslims are Arabs

ACTRESS/AÏDA: To respond to their worries

ACTRESS/KATY: And above all to reassure them that Muslims
    weren't all barbarians

Bloodthirsty, uneducated and dirty

ACTRESS/AÏDA: Or oil barons
With palaces and harems
All over the world

ACTRESS/KATY: She had to argue
Find the right words
Stay calm when provoked
And smile for the cameras

ACTRESS/AÏDA: Aïda played along for a time
And even became quite famous

ACTRESS/KATY: So did Katy

ACTRESS/AÏDA: On TV, there was a repeat of a film she'd had a
small part in

ACTRESS/KATY: Same with Katy

ACTRESS/AÏDA gets irritated

ACTRESS/AÏDA: Don't tell me she was an actress too!

ACTRESS/KATY: No it was an advertisement for plant fertilizer
She was ten at the time, she weighed one hundred pounds and had
long hair
What part did Aïda have?

ACTRESS/AÏDA: She played a Palestinian terrorist who hijacks a
plane
And takes the passengers hostage
She gets shot by the heroine, a young German Jewess
Whose parents had survived the Nazi concentration camps

ACTRESS/KATY: Was it a German film?

ACTRESS/AÏDA: No, American, but shot in Berlin

ACTRESS/KATY: And why did she accept the role?

ACTRESS/AÏDA: She's an actor
When you have to earn a living, you can't always be particular

They turn to face the audience

ACTRESS/KATY: One month on, the two women were exhausted,
    washed out,
But there was no change in the Mokhtar case
As other news stories took its place

ACTRESS/AÏDA: They even became aware that certain debates,
Triggered off by some statement or other,
Were taking them a long way from the matter in hand

ACTRESS/KATY: So, by mutual consent, they decided

ACTRESS/AÏDA: To stop playing this game, a democratic game
    certainly

ACTRESS/KATY: And maybe a necessary one

ACTRESS/AÏDA: But it was just not enough

ACTRESS/KATY exits
ACTRESS/HANNAH enters from the other side
She too addresses the audience

ACTRESS/HANNAH: Hannah saw Aïda on TV
She was being totally manipulated by media people
Hannah decided to help her
She called her
But Aïda systematically put the phone down
So one day she went up to her in the street
Aïda walks quickly across the space
Hannah calls over to her

HANNAH: Mrs. Berg, Mrs. Berg!

Please! Listen to me
I'm Hannah Schlicht
From the organization called Justice for All

AÏDA: Go to hell, you and your justice
I don't need anyone
I don't trust anyone anymore

HANNAH: You're quite right to be suspicious
But our organization is very keen to help

AÏDA: I want to fight my own battles

She goes to leave
But Hannah stops her

HANNAH: You won't be able to
You have no experience
You need support, politically
And even psychologically
You look exhausted

AÏDA: Leave me alone!
You're just vultures circling a carcass

She moves away
Hannah falls in beside her

HANNAH: Wait!
Take my card, it has my private number on it
Don't hesitate to call me
Any time
I'll be there for you
She hands her the card
Aïda refuses to take it
Hannah puts it on the ground
Anyway, my organization is already working on the case
The charges brought against your brother have no basis
The photos they found at his place and yours,

The phone number of the prime suspect,
Ali Ahmed Abdallah,
The two trips to Cairo and Afghanistan the police say he made
None of this adds up to any kind
Of evidence to justify charging him
Think about it and call me

Aïda hesitates, picks up the card and turns to the audience

ACTRESS/AÏDA: She called her the next day
She was determined not to let any opportunity
To solve the mystery of her brother's disappearance
Slip through her fingers
So a crisis center was set up
To collect, sift and dissect
All the information gathered by the organization's networks
In Europe and across the world
A machine was finally set in motion
And it helped Aïda feel hopeful again

Darkness

SCENE 8

The Church

The actress/pianist enters and sits at the piano
Madame Gross also appears, with a scarf over her head
[Editor's note: Mrs. Gross was called Marianne earlier in the script.
    This shift is in the original text.]
We are in a church
She dips her fingers in an invisible font
Crosses herself then kneels
The sound of church bells rises from the piano
Madame Gross crawls to the middle of the space
She lies on the floor, her arms forming a cross,
And she prays
She looks up, filled with intense emotion
Tears roll down her face

She takes off her scarf, ties a knot in one end
And starts to flagellate herself

MRS. GROSS: Oh Lord!
Almighty Lord, help me
Have pity on my soul
And guide me to the paths of righteousness
Lord! Sweet Lord!
I come to make my confession to you
I am in darkness
And have need of your light to show me the way
Mea culpa, mea culpa
Jesus! Oh sweet Jesus!
Forgive me
For I am wicked
I have sinned

She hears a man's voice, amplified by a loudspeaker

VOICE: Who comes here to trouble me in my retreat?
Who calls me?

Mrs. Gross, staggered, looks up
And looks for the source of the voice

MRS. GROSS: Who's there?

VOICE: Guess

MRS. GROSS: Jesus?

VOICE: In person

MRS. GROSS: Jesus? What, my Jesus?

VOICE: Not just your Jesus
Don't be selfish, my child
And who might you be?

MRS. GROSS: A lost sheep who comes to implore your forgiveness

VOICE: What is your name?

MRS. GROSS: Gross, Lord, Marianne Gross!

VOICE: What do you want of me?

MRS. GROSS: I want you to help me purify my soul
You are the only one I can open my heart to
To relieve my torment

VOICE: What have you done, my child?
Confess your sins

MRS. GROSS: I am wicked
Vain and hypocritical, Lord
I have lied
I may have done harm to
Someone who I actually like a lot

VOICE: Of whom do you speak, poor wretch?

MRS. GROSS: Katarina, Lord

VOICE: Ah! The famous florist

MRS. GROSS: So you know her too?

VOICE: I know everyone, my child!
What have you done to this Katarina?

MRS. GROSS: I spoke to the press
I told them so many things
I deliberately mixed facts
With lies
I went through her bag
Stole her address book and photocopied it
I phoned her in the middle of the night, disguising my voice

So I could insult her
I threatened everyone whose name was in her book
If they carried on seeing her
Or using her shop
I watched her, spied on her, hounded her, isolated her
But I didn't cure her
Oh Lord!

VOICE: Cure her of what?

MRS. GROSS: Why, of her love for that abominable assassin
Whatever I did
I did it for her own good

VOICE: If your acts were guided by love
There is no sin
Just don't overdo it, that's all
Madame Gross says nothing and cries even more
She beats herself even harder
What's the matter, my child
Are you perhaps keeping something from me, something more
    serious perhaps?

MRS. GROSS: Yes, oh yes I am!
Hate, Lord
I'm filled with hate
It runs through my veins
I try to punish myself
To scourge myself
To pray and to sing your praises
But it's no good, sweet Jesus!
It's just no good
Lord!
You who are love
Show me the way
The way of love
The way of tolerance
The way of sharing

VOICE: But who is it you hate so much, my child?

MRS. GROSS: Foreigners
I loathe them
Their smell drives me crazy
I hate seeing them on our streets
In our cafés
Our markets
Our schools
Our factories
They invade our space
They steal our air
They make us dirty
They rob us
They rape our women
And deprave our young people
They're coming for us, even in our own lands
They plant their bombs
They murder your followers
They want to force their rituals on us
They're barbarians who don't believe in you
Oh Lord,
I want them dead, exterminated

VOICE: If they're so wicked
Not loving them isn't so very grave a sin

MRS. GROSS: But Lord
You are Love
You teach us to love and share
And I don't want to share anything with them
I want them out
I want them out
I want them out

VOICE: All of them?

MRS. GROSS: Yes, all of them
The Muslims

The Turks
The Kurds
The Arabs
The Portuguese
The Albanians
The Indians
The Buddhists
The homosexuals
The young
And, and . . .
The others

VOICE: Others? What others?

Mrs. Gross whispers:
MRS. GROSS: You know!
The OTHERS

VOICE: What OTHERS, tell me

MRS. GROSS: The Jews, Lord

VOICE: But I'm a Jew myself, Marianne
And young
And foreign
I come from Palestine

MRS. GROSS: Yes, but you're our Savior
Our purifier
Our guide
Our Messiah
Our beloved Jesus
The Son of God
I love you
I love you
Will you forgive me my hateful thoughts, Lord?

VOICE: I'm not sure yet
I'll have to think about it

Check with my staff

MRS. GROSS: You don't decide for yourself then?

VOICE: Well of course I don't
We have democracy up here too, you know
You *are* a Democrat, aren't you?

MRS. GROSS: Of course I am
What a question!

VOICE: Are you sure you're not a Communist?

MRS. GROSS: No, God, no!
I was once, I had no choice, I was forced into it
But that's all finished with now
Communism took my man away from me
It shot him down on that horrible Wall of shame

VOICE: So you're a nationalist then?

MRS. GROSS: Oh yes!
Oh yes!

VOICE: And a National-Socialist maybe?

MRS. GROSS: . . .

VOICE: Marianne?

MRS. GROSS: Lord

VOICE: I'm waiting . . .

MRS. GROSS: Yes I am
But only in theory and out of conviction
I believe that only the National-Socialists, with your help
Can root out Evil
The Evil that's undermining our country

And making me so unhappy

VOICE: Why are you so unhappy, unhappy one?

MRS. GROSS: I'm lonely, sweet Jesus
Other than you
And my poodle Belle
Who's so old and tired now
I don't have anyone
I lost my family during the war because of the Jews
I lost my husband because of the Communists
And now I'm losing my country
Because of all these foreigners
And my security because of the Islamists
The only thing I have left is resistance
And this hate that's eating me up inside
Oh Lord,
If it's right for me to shoulder this hate
Give me the courage to make it burst forth
Help me be less hypocritical
Help me shout what I believe from the rooftops
Without being scared or afraid of anyone
And if my heart must be cleansed of this hate
If you order me to learn to share with them
And to accept to mix with them
I'll do it, for your sake
But it's going to be very, very hard
And very, very slow
So be patient with me and show unto me the path of salvation

A strange-looking individual appears. almost naked
Wearing dirty white underpants
He holds a loudspeaker between his legs and a microphone in his hand
He flattens himself against the wall
And spreads his arms in the form of a cross
She is speechless at the sight

MAN: MARIANNE GROSS
Do not renounce what is in thee

For thou art as God, the father, made thee
Do not deny thy good qualities
Thou art honest and true
And honest and true shalt thou remain by the will of God
Accept what thou art and thou shalt feel lighter
Take up thy bed and walk
Thou art light, so light
Lift up thy arms to make the cross and float
Thou fliest, fliest like a bird without a brain
Cheep-cheep, cheep-cheep, cheep-cheep . . .

Mrs. Gross runs and jumps across the whole length of the space
She is in a trance
Kaïs has been on stage for a while and is watching the scene, taken aback
He is wearing a bulletproof jacket and a helmet

KAÏS: You making a movie in here?
Addressing the man
Who are you?

MAN: I'm Jesus! Doesn't it show?

KAÏS: Well, if you're Jesus
I'm Mohammed

And he throws him out
Mrs. Gross lets fly at Kaïs
Hitting him with her scarf

MRS. GROSS: Get out, get out
You even persecute me in the House of God, you barbarian
Jesus, my Jesus

She exits looking for her vanished Messiah
Left alone, Kaïs stares ahead for a moment
A long silence
Then he slowly looks up to heaven
And in an all-powerful voice, he cries out
KAÏS: God, can you hear me?

In your name, people hate each other
In your name, they kill each other
And you watch them doing it without moving a muscle
GOD
If you exist, then I pray for one thing only
JUST LEAVE US ALONE

Darkness

SCENE 9

The Expulsion

The Actress/Aïda appears
A scarf round her head and clutching a bound book
The Actor/Kaïs enters
He glides slowly on his skateboard
And goes and stands in front of the wall, next to her
Aïda looks at him for a long time
The Actor/Ulrich enters carrying a travel bag
He stands next to them
The three of them are facing the audience
Each unfolding his or her own narrative . . .

ACTRESS/ AÏDA: They were gliding past her
Hand in hand

ACTOR/ KAÏS: He started striking out

ACTOR/ ULRICH: He was on the Frankfurt-to-Berlin train

ACTRESS/ AÏDA: Her brother and her son
Coming toward her side by side
Melting into one body
Then separating into two distinct forms

ACTOR/ KAÏS: He didn't say anything
He just hit out hard, very hard

ACTOR/ULRICH: He'd been away for three days
Business, nothing but business
He'd had to work very hard, these last few days

ACTRESS/AÏDA: The ground was frozen
Dazzling white
They could walk on it without difficulty
There was no noise
Nothing, no sound
Not even the twittering of a distant bird
The landscape had an unreal beauty

ACTOR/KAÏS: He couldn't hear anything anymore
Couldn't feel anything
Couldn't see anything
Just a big fat mouth sniggering
And he had to make it shut up

ACTOR/ULRICH: He really did want to be around more,
To support his wife,
Keep an eye on his son
But the firm was in trouble
Two of his associates had dumped him
When the Mokhtar affair had flared up
And now he had to handle some hard-nosed clients alone

ACTRESS/AÏDA: Suddenly the ice beneath Mokhtar cracked
And he started sinking
Kaïs reached out to catch him
But the force of the water was stronger than he was
And was dragging them both down
She, Aïda, by some miracle, found herself on a rock
She cried out but no sound came

ACTOR/KAÏS: He had to make that big fat mouth shut up,
That gaping hole full of fangs
And that slimy viper squirming around inside it
He had to smash it
He had to hit out, out, out

ACTOR/ULRICH: His reputation had taken a beating
In the media
His brother-in-law was a suspected terrorist
Who'd been given shelter in his house
And he himself had once been a Leftist
And was now exposed as an unfaithful husband
By the malicious confessions of his former mistress
It was a reputation he had to get rid of whatever the cost

ACTRESS/AÏDA: She felt ice-cold moisture breaking out all over
her body
She stretched out an arm like a tentacle to catch her son
Who was struggling to get back to his uncle
She was pulling, pulling with all her might
And when she had finally dragged him out of the water
Mokhtar was drifting away
Into a vast expanse of pure white

ACTOR/KAÏS: When he came to
He was lying on the ground
Hands tied behind his back
And dozens of eyes staring at him like he was a wild animal
His hands were painful
He hurt, hurt all over
And then he felt a warm, salty liquid on his face
Oh no! He wasn't going to start blubbing in front of them
He mustn't give them the satisfaction
He had to keep it in
But the heart is stronger than the head
And, to his horror, he heard himself sobbing like a kid

Kaïs huddles into his mother's arms
She holds him very tightly
For a brief moment
Then he pushes her away and skates across the space in the other direction
He disappears behind the opposite wall
As if swallowed up by it
Aïda tries to stop him
But he is much too fast for her

She turns back to the audience

ACTRESS/AÏDA: Nightmares, constant nightmares
She was having them day and night
The unexplained disappearance of her brother
The accusations
The lack of news
And now Kaïs's trouble at school
She was waking up in the middle of the night
Soaked in sweat
And her husband never there
When she needed him

ACTOR/ULRICH: Why was life getting so complicated all of a
    sudden?
The little white lies were turning into betrayals
The little business trips into parental negligence
The little rows into marital crises
And yet he loves his little family
Maybe he's not a model husband
Or a perfect father
But still, he loves them
And he's going to prove it to them
He mimes the action of ringing the bell
Ring ring!
He has his key with him
But he likes it when they open the door for him
Take his bag, give him a kiss, make a fuss of him
Ring ring!

AÏDA: He has his key with him
He can open it himself

Ulrich goes over and kisses her
She offers him her cheek

ULRICH: You OK?

AÏDA: I'm fine

ULRICH: What're you reading?

AÏDA: The phone book, why?

ULRICH: Have you had dinner?

AÏDA: No

ULRICH: What're we eating?

AÏDA: Nothing

ULRICH: Shall I get something?

AÏDA: I haven't done the shopping

ULRICH: OK!
So, I'll take a shower
And I'll take you out to eat

AÏDA: No

ULRICH: Why not?
What's the matter now?

AÏDA: I called you on your cell phone
It was off

ULRICH: Do you have some news?

AÏDA: Yes

ULRICH: Mokhtar?

AÏDA: No, Kaïs

ULRICH: Kaïs?
What about Kaïs?
What's wrong with him?

Where is he?
He panics
Calls his son
Kaïs! Kaïs!!
Kaïs appears
He skates over to the other side of the space and out of sight
What's wrong with him?

AÏDA: That all you can say?

ULRICH: Stop trying to make me feel guilty and answer the question

AÏDA: He beat up someone at school

ULRICH: Come on! That's not his style

AÏDA: And what exactly *is* his style, in your view?

ULRICH: Will you answer me, for Christ's sake?

AÏDA: He smashed a schoolmate's face in

ULRICH: And I'm a monkey's uncle

AÏDA: The kid's in the hospital
And we've just got back from the police station

ULRICH: You've got to be kidding!
What is all this?
Why was he fighting?
What was the reason?
Kaïs! Kaïs!

AÏDA: You're wasting your time
He won't tell you
And it wasn't a fight
It was a proper beating

Ulrich suddenly raises his head
A trickle of red is coming from his nose
He takes a handkerchief from his pocket and presses it to his face
It is obvious that he is used to having nosebleeds

ULRICH: Why?

AÏDA: He wouldn't say
The school called me
I found him in the principal's office
His hands were tied behind his back
The other boy's parents called the police
And their lawyer joined us at the police station

ULRICH: They filed a complaint?

AÏDA: Wouldn't you?
He broke his nose and two of his teeth

ULRICH: What in God's name is happening to me?
I mean, what is happening?
I've got a brother-in-law who plants bombs
And a son who's a trainee assassin
Is this something in your genes or what?

AÏDA does not react but answers with an icy smile

AÏDA: No, it's a cultural thing
As everyone in this country knows
We belong to a civilization that's inferior to yours
And no good has ever come out of it
Our men folk are just dumb brutes
Who can't take defeat and humiliation
So they take it out on you poor Westerners
It's awful for you, my darling
But that's what you get for marrying an Arab

ULRICH: Please stop playing games with me like this
I don't feel like arguing

AÏDA: Me neither
I'm going to bed

She goes to leave
He grabs her by the arm

ULRICH: We have to talk
Work something out
Draw up an action plan

She tries to break free

AÏDA: It's your son we're talking about here,
Not a business deal or a sale
And please let go of my arm, you're hurting me

ULRICH: I'll let go
But you're not going to bed
Nobody's getting any sleep tonight until we've talked this through
He calls out
Kaïs, bring me the vinegar and some cotton-wool
I've got a nosebleed
I want to know,
I want to know what started all this

AÏDA: Can't you guess?

ULRICH: I don't like guessing games

AÏDA: He must have insulted him
Called him a dirty Arab or something

ULRICH: But he's not an Arab

AÏDA: Oh right! I'm so sorry!
Dirty Kraut, then

ULRICH: Kaïs, the vinegar!

Kaïs enters with a bottle in his hand
He gives it to his father
Ulrich grabs hold of his hand
Why did you hit him?
Kaïs looks his father straight in the eye
Violently snatches his hand away and exits
Leaving the father taken aback
Ulrich soaks two pieces of cotton wool and puts them in his nostrils

A pause

He's changed, he's completely different
The look in his eyes isn't the same

AÏDA: Hardly surprising, with everything he's going through

ULRICH: OK I know it's not easy for him
But we mustn't panic
We'll work something out
Everything'll go back to normal, I know it will
Even for your brother
If he's done nothing wrong like you're sure he hasn't
Nobody's going to hurt him

AÏDA: I'm not the one who needs to be sure

ULRICH: I know that
But please stop poisoning your life with it
And poisoning your son's mind too

AÏDA: Well maybe you should be around more
And get him to talk to you

ULRICH: You know perfectly well that he's not exactly talkative

AÏDA: No, he's not talkative but he's very eloquent
He used to spend hours chatting to Mokhtar

ULRICH: Yes and look where it got him

He's been well and truly brainwashed
And you let it happen,
With your stupid identity crisis

AÏDA: I just tried to answer certain questions
I didn't avoid the issue!

ULRICH: OK, you're the perfect mother
And your brother's a saint
Stop preaching at me
Kaïs is my son too
I'm going to help him get out of this with as little harm as possible
And find a way forward

At that moment, Kaïs comes charging on stage
Lying on his back on his skateboard
He speeds across the space and out of sight
As his parents look on

Darkness

SCENE 10

The Journalist

Aïda enters and sits at the piano
She plays a few notes
Katarina appears behind her
She is dressed in a bathrobe
They look at each other
Aïda plays and talks at the same time

AÏDA: Dry thy tears and smile
Vanquish thy disgust
And forget thy pride
Hatred and desire are now but one
Beautiful art thou
Welcoming shalt thou be
Thou shalt not cry

Thou shalt not laugh
Thou shalt smile
Thou shalt not fix him with a stare
Thou shalt not touch him
With thy robe alone shalt thou brush against him
Thou shalt seduce him
But to his charms thou shalt not succumb
Alcohol shalt thou serve him
But none shalt thou drink
For it will make thee vulnerable
and thy vigilance will weaken
From the corner of thine eye shalt thou watch him
His gestures and expressions study
And accordingly act
Should he remain lucid
Patient shalt thou be
Should he be aggressive
Calm shalt thou remain
Should he be forward
Panic shalt thou not
Never from thy goal shalt thou err
The web has been spun
And for this one time, the spider is thee
Do not release thy grip
Attack at the right moment
Surprise me
Surprise thyself
I am behind thee, do not forget
Shouldst thou know weakness or doubt, call out to me
Breathe deeply
Relax
He is coming
I hear him
He is early
He is impatient
He climbs the stairs
Two more steps and he will ring

Katy makes a movement to go and open the door

Aïda stops her with a cry
No!
Do not go!
Let him wait
Make him languish
It will excite him
Or irritate him
And in either case
It will make him vulnerable

An actor appears
He is carrying a bag
And chewing gum
It's the journalist Katy is waiting for

JOURNALIST: Ring, ring!
Come on, open up, you slut
What're you waiting for?
Whore! Whore! Whore!
If she stands me up, I'm gonna demolish her
She wouldn't dare, the stupid bitch
Crazy fucking job, this,
Having to listen to the confessions of some slut first thing in the
     morning!
He turns to face the public
He's Karl Katz, the terror
Also known as Kaka
Because of his liking for scatological swearwords
He's a journalist on a very, very downmarker newspaper.
Not so long ago,
He was a top freelance reporter
And the most reputable, best-known papers
Were fighting over his articles and paying him a fortune
But booze and women got the better of him
His wife left him
His children disowned him
And the work just vanished
He goes back into character
Ring, ring!

If she doesn't open up
I won't be poking my finger on this goddam bell
I'll be sticking it up her shitty asshole

He spits out his gum
Just as Katy opens the door

KATY: Oh, it's you?

KARL: No, it's the garbage man

KATY: It's a real mess in here
Sorry, I was taking a bath

KARL: In my honor?
He moves up closer
You smell good

She moves away, glancing back at him wantonly
The game of seduction has begun

KATY: Come in
Make yourself at home
What d'you want me to call you
Mr Katz? Karl?
Or Kaka?

KARL: Kaka at your service, lovely Katy

KATY: OK, but for now *I'm* at *your* service. Tea? Coffee?

KARL: You kidding me, right? I want a long cold beer

KATY: At nine in the morning?

KARL: Why not?
I'm thirsty. I'm always thirsty.

KATY: Take a seat

I'll be right back
She exits
He doesn't move from where he is standing
But carefully looks all around
She returns with the bottle of beer
Hands it to him
He looks her over, still without moving
Come in
I don't bite, you know

KARL: Close the blinds
I can't stand daylight

KATY: Since I became famous I've stopped closing the blinds
There's nothing left to hide

KARL: It's a fucking pigsty in here

KATY: Sorry about the mess
I'm moving out in a few days

KARL: Why's that?
He finally puts down his bag
And takes out his camera

KATY: Can't you guess?
I need a bigger apartment now, with more light
And a smarter neighborhood
Thanks to you
I'm famous
This dump's ninety years old, it's not right for me anymore
It was my grandmother's
Look
That's her with my grandfather
And that's my parents
You'll recognize my mother, you've already interviewed her
This furniture was all theirs
Every little ornament has a story to it
I was suffocating

But now, thanks to you,
I'm finally going to get rid of this old stuff
and get everything brand new

While she's talking, he is taking photos of the place
Clicking away with his highly sophisticated camera
He doesn't miss a single detail
She fetches another bottle of beer
And gives it to him

KARL: You not drinking?

KATY: I have to get changed first

KARL: You look great like that
No need to change

KATY: You don't know what I'm going to put on
You'll like it even more, promise

KARL: There's just one thing I'd like right now
He moves up close to her
Tries to put his arms around her
She moves away
He takes photos of her
She lets him, even adopting suggestive poses
Why d'you invite me here?

KATY: To say thanks for making me see myself
Today, Kaka my dear, I'm a chrysalis
You know, despite all the things you wrote about me
My life was dull, sickeningly ordinary
I've always been average, depressingly average, at everything
My old grade-school teacher told you that, I guess?

KARL: She did.
So?

KATY: But that wasn't what you wrote

You wrote about a girl who was much more cunning
Intelligent, determined, manipulative even
Right?

KARL: I did.
So?

KATY: So I love it!
My ex used to think I was stupid
And about as sexy as a broom stick,
Well, he describes me now as the classiest girl he's ever met
You've turned me into a femme fatale
The heroine of a picture book or a TV show
You said it yourself
Next to me, Mata-Hari was a choir girl
I love that image
I've stopped being colorless, odorless, flavorless
Like people always said I was
I'm a woman who's determined and sure of herself,
Who knows where she's going and above all what she's got to do
You're my Pygmalion, Kaka

KARL: Pygmalion my ass
Let's go into the bedroom
The crap you talk makes me puke

KATY: Let's save the bedroom for later

KARL: I'm not talking about screwing, you slut
I'm talking about work
With a nude photo we could make a packet
Take that lousy robe off
You look like your grandmother
And show me some place nice and dirty
So we can take this fucking photo
And stop yapping, will you,
Your voice is doing my head in

KATY: I thought you wanted to interview me?

KARL: You know, you're even more fucking stupid than I thought
You think I need your whining
To write my piece, bitch?
And gimme something stronger to drink
Than this cat's piss

For a moment Katarina is nonplussed
She doesn't know what to do
The pianist reminds her of the job in hand
Low notes wake her from her lethargy
Give her a kick-start and get her back on full charge

KATY: What do you want?

KARL: Double whisky, tramp

KATY: This isn't a bar, shitface

KARL: You getting wet, asshole?

KATY: I got a hard-on, pussycat

KARL: Ouch!
The tigress's showing her claws
What a boner!
I'm keeping these photos
To jerk off with

He takes photo after photo
She lets him do it, adopting suggestive poses
They are in the middle of the space
They circle each other like two wild beasts in an arena

KATY: So you can still manage a hard-on
Kaka, you little shit
You impotent, dirty old man

KARL: Yeah, thanks to whores like you
And now, shut your mouth

And let me work
Or else I'll stick this chair leg up your pussy
To keep you quiet, you horny bitch

Suddenly she changes tone

KATY: Yeah, and a rabid bitch at that
You come near me and I'll bite that limp dick of yours clean off
And stuff it up your ass
Make you pay for what you did to my mother
Shit stirrer
My ex-husband, the loudmouth drunk
My grade-school teacher, the sadistic old hag
My ex-employee, the thief who got caught
Those poor bastards in the choir who took your bait—
None of them were enough for you were they?
You had to persecute my mother too
On her hospital bed,
A sad old paraplegic,
Tell her a load of filth about her daughter
Getting her in such a state
That now she's in intensive care
And all of that for a caption under a dirty picture
"Paraplegic mother of florist Katarina reveals:
No, my daughter hasn't visited me since she met that guy"
What a headline!
What a scoop!
What talent!
Congratulations! When's the Pulitzer due?
You manipulative little shit
You get pleasure out of destroying people
You harassed me, you slandered me
You twisted what the people closest to me said about me
You made Mokhtar out to be a monster
But the real monster is you

KARL: That reminds me, how's our would-be martyr doing?
Any news?
You can tell dear old Kaka everything, you know that!

Hey, did he promise you paradise?

KATY: My life with him was paradise

KARL: So, you planning to convert to Islam?

KATY: I'll discuss it with him when he gets back.
That answer OK for you,
Or you want to hear something else?

KARL: What are your views on suicide bombers?

KATY: What are yours?

KARL: I'm the journalist around here.

KATY: You want an ideological discussion?
Where I stand on the Palestinian issue?
On German foreign policy?
On immigration?
Or do you just want to crack the mystery of the terrorist's girlfriend?
Find out her favorite color
The dish she cooks best
Or how many orgasms she can have in an hour?

KARL: You're not the only slut I write about, bitch

KATY: But I could be the last, little peepee Kaka,
Because I'm going to get you
You destructive animal

KARL: You got that right, slut
Bull's eye
I am destructive
Unlike that crappy architect of yours.
I'm just a predator on the human race
And, trust me, as a race, us bipeds are not nice at all
I know that race better than most because I've studied it
I've caught every tiny detail in my viewfinder

In another life
When I was that poor, idealistic bastard
Who traveled the world searching out the TRUTH,
And tracking down the horror
As the bombs fell and the massacres started
From Lebanon to Rwanda
Afghanistan to Iraq
Not forgetting the squabbles in Latin America
Or the little local trouble in the Balkans
I saw the true face of man
And it's ugly, cruel, horrible
He has no pity for anyone
I hung around with death too
I saw her, with my own two eyes
And she laughed in my face
She touched me but she didn't take me
She said: "I'm too beautiful for you
You don't deserve me
Still, I'm just going to leave you with a little souvenir
A sliver of shrapnel
Just a little bitty piece
Right there in your head
That'll make you think of me
And long for me even more"
He touches his head, behind the ear
It's in there, right there
They couldn't remove it
And the pain's enough to make an elephant scream
And you expect me to be nice to you
And your old dying mother?
Fuck you, asshole,
You and your lousy truth
The only reason I'm interested in you
Is that you fill my bank account
You, your mother,
The mistresses of politicians
The gigolos of picture-postcard princesses
The bimbos on TV with their stupid scandals,
Anything that gets the ink flowing

Or a few short-lived tears,
That's MY TRUTH
It's truer than truth
And it's the only light I've got
In my apartment, the curtains are always closed
I live in the shade
That's how I manage to survive
Take it from me, you little innocent,
He who gets by in the dark
Gets by and prospers in the light
That's what life has taught me
In Lebanon with its divisions
In Afghanistan with its veils
In Iraq with its arrogance
In war and all its truth
All its fucking truth
War that smothers the world.
I don't want to suffer for a living anymore
And no one's going to change my way of seeing things
Mark my words, bitch
Even if *I* go easy on you, the others won't
Even if I don't write about you, they will
I have to get in first
So I can earn a crust
And prepare for a golden retirement
On some desert island, with not a living soul in sight

KATY: You want me to clap or something?
Strange, you talking about the world like that
When you can't even look people in the eye
With those glasses of yours, you're more veiled than an Islamic
    woman
You hide behind them
She snatches off his glasses and recoils in disgust
Ugh, disgusting eyes!

KARL: My eyes are disgusting because they've only seen disgusting
    things
My eyes are made in the image of the world around me

They just reflect that truth
YOUR TRUTH
You want me to write about a nice florist
Who opens her nice shop at eight in the morning
Who has a nice way of welcoming her nice customers
And closes up at eight at night to meet her nice Arab
And dream about building a nice garden city
Where everyone will be good-looking and nice.
It's so touching, I could die.
Well, no thank you
I write what I want to, by my own standards
And the laws of the free market
It's called the "freedom of the press"
And there's nothing you can do about it
Even if you take into your head to file a complaint
I couldn't give a shit
Going to court would be one more thing
To push up sales
We'll all be winners
Right, I'm out of here
A pleasure chewing the fat, doll

KATY: Hand over the film

KARL: You're kidding me, right?

KATY: You're not leaving here until you've handed over the film

KARL: Oooh Mommy, I'm so scared!
He goes to leave

KATY: The door's locked

KARL: What you gonna do, rape me?
Help!

KATY: And I warn you
If you happen to write about me or my family
Or about Mokhtar and his family

I'll smash you and your reputation

KARL: My reputation?
You think I still got a reputation to protect?
You know, honey, your stupidity is beyond belief

KATY: You think so?
Aïda!

Aïda appears

AÏDA: Hello, Mr. Kaka
Remember me?
I'm the terrorist's sister
Now look over there
And there
Two movie cameras set up by some trusted friends of ours
They wanted to beat you to a pulp
To teach you a lesson
But I said no
You see, we've stopped being bloodthirsty barbarians
We have much more sophisticated methods now
Like these cameras, wired to a truck outside
Everything's been recorded
It'd be fun selling those juicy revelations
To another shitty little paper like yours
With an amazing headline
"Kaka disabled, exposed as pathetic war casualty,
He went over to the gutter press
When a piece of shrapnel turned him into a birdbrain,
Now he smells so bad even death turned him down"
Not bad, huh?

He hands over the film
And leaves without a word
They burst out laughing

KATY: He's so dirty I want to purify myself

AÏDA: Where d'you get all that filthy language?
I nearly passed out

KATY: I stole it from San Antonio

AÏDA: You mean there's a saint who speaks like that?

KATY: He's not a saint
He's a character created by a crime writer,
Frédéric Dard, he's French
But how about you, what was all that about a truck
And trusted friends?

AÏDA: You're not the only one who watches American TV shows

Darkness

SCENE 11

The Bomb in a Bag

Jürgen and Marianne Gross are walking up and down the stage
Learning their song
Katy appears
She takes her place

KATY: Can we start?
Daniel then appears
And takes his place
Annicka arrives, in a rush

ANNICKA: There's a bag outside
She disappears into the cloakroom and comes back
She heads for her piano
Stops
There's a blue bag outside the door
Whose is it?
Nobody answers
They all look at each other, intrigued

Jürgen goes out and brings in the bag
He holds it gingerly
Feels its weight
And slowly puts it down in the middle of the space

DANIEL: It's a bomb

MRS. GROSS: A bomb?

DANIEL: A bomb!

Jürgen runs and hides in the cloakroom followed by Daniel
Then comes back for Katy
Mrs Gross finds herself alone
A moment of panic, then she rejoices, almost in a trance

MRS. GROSS: It would be magnificent if it was really a bomb
BANG!
A blast that could be heard on the other side of the country
A huge explosion that would shatter everything
Into a million specks of dust
Atomizing everything that ever was
Nothing, no one can resist it
There'll be nothing but a great big hole
A black crater they'll come and look at
And film a few months later
It'll be so wonderful to all go together!
Alleluia, alleluia!

The others come back from the dressing rooms and look at her, hypnotized
Everyone holds their breath

JÜRGEN: Ten
Nine
Eight
Seven
Six
Five
Four

Three
Two
One
Zero

A long silence
Nothing happens

MRS. GROSS: It hasn't gone off
She grabs wildly at the bag
Daniel runs over and gets it back, then hides it in the dressing room
Annicka is indignant
A strange sound rises from her throat
A cry of anger or relief
Of distress or happiness
Nobody will ever know
Not even her
The cry gets louder, changes into an operatic melody
Which makes her veins stand out and her face go pink
The others watch her, enthralled
Then the cry stops abruptly

ANNICKA: Can we start?
I really don't have time to waste
I start work again in exactly one hour

Mrs. Gross is still standing there in the middle of the space
Her face deathly pale

JÜRGEN: Mrs. Gross?

MRS. GROSS: Yes?

JÜRGEN: Can we start?

MRS. GROSS: I thought it was a bomb

The others look at her, stunned

JÜRGEN: A real bomb?
You know, you people really are crazy in this choir
He points a finger at Daniel
And you, you little shit
Don't leave your bag lying around
A bomb is a serious matter
I could have called the police
They'd have soon taught you a lesson

DANIEL: I'm the one who should be teaching you a lesson
Next time, it'll be a real bomb
If you're not very careful
If you carry on letting just anyone in
Don't you read the papers?
Don't you watch the news?
The whole world's afraid
The whole world's standing shoulder to shoulder
To fight the Axis of Evil.
The men with the beards and the blood lust,
They're everywhere
They're recruiting everywhere, I know they are
And you people, not only do you stick your heads in the sand
But you let one of their whores stay in the choir
Who says she's not in it with them?
Just because the police haven't got anything on her, doesn't mean
    she's innocent
And now she's walking around with a gun
It's in the papers
Well I'm keeping *my* eyes open
And I move we kick her out
What do you say?

Katy walks menacingly toward him

KATY: Kick *who* out?
DANIEL: You

KATY: Oh yes?
And why's that?

Mrs. Gross goes up to Katy

MRS. GROSS: Katy darling
You mustn't think we're plotting behind your back
But we've given it a lot of thought
You should take a vacation
Have a rest
You look dreadful

KATY: But I'm not tired
And I don't need a vacation
I relax when I'm here
So, shall we start?

She crosses the space
And takes her place
Only Jürgen follows her
The others watch her without moving

KATY: Shall we start?

DANIEL: Are you deaf or what?
We don't want you here
You're out

KATY: Out?
Why's that?

DANIEL: Why?
That's a good one, that is!
Now she's playing all innocent
You've made this choir dirty
You got in with a filthy Arab
And you showed him around Berlin
So he could find targets for his attacks

KATY: If that were true, the police wouldn't have let me go

DANIEL: But they haven't let you go

You're on parole, sweetie
The police have got their eye on you
They're using you as bait
And you're using our choir as cover
But we're not going to let you get away with it

KATY: You speak for yourself
Annicka?

ANNICKA: I like you a lot, I really do
But I don't know a thing about politics
All I know is that my husband is furious
His name's been in the paper
And the guys at work tease him unmercifully
They call him James Bond
So he told me I mustn't come here anymore

MRS. GROSS: Katy darling
Be magnanimous
Prove you love us as much as we love you
There are fewer and fewer of us because of you

KATY: Are you sure it's because of me?
You don't think it's more to do with the standard
Of the singing?

MRS. GROSS: Don't stoop to insults, Katarina
Leave with your head high

KATY: What if I don't leave?
Are you going to drag me out by my hair?

DANIEL: Out, bitch!

He turns nasty
Jürgen stops him

JÜRGEN: Hey, hey!
Calm down, hoodlum

What is this, a lynching?
Why should I throw her out?
She's never stopped me singing
You're the one stirring the shit here, dog killer

DANIEL: You trying to get laid, doc?
She prefers them circumcised
Want me to snip off the end of your wiener?

Jürgen leaps on him to hit him
Mrs. Gross intervenes
Getting between them to separate them

MRS. GROSS: Now don't let's get carried away
Let's stay calm
Let's not allow one ungrateful person to sow discord among us

DANIEL: If she stays, I go

JÜRGEN: If she goes, I go

Mrs. Gross loses her temper

MRS. GROSS: Stop it, don't say that
I'm the boss around here
I make the decisions
Let's have a democratic vote
Who wants her to go?
Daniel and Mrs. Gross raise a hand
Annicka hesitates
Annicka, make up your mind

ANNICKA: I don't know
My husband usually votes for me
But in this case I can't ask his advice
He doesn't know that . . .

Mrs. Gross interrupts her

MRS. GROSS: Raise your hand

Annicka raises her hand
Katy smiles
She remains calm
Fetches her bag
And heads for the exit

KATY: First. I'm going to learn Arabic,
Then I'm going to Mecca to become a real Muslim
After that I'll learn how to make bombs
And come back and blow you all to hell

MRS. GROSS: I'm sorry for you

KATY: Maâssalama

She leaves with panache
Silence
Jürgen throws down his score
Mrs. Gross stops him with a cry

MRS. GROSS: Jürgen! No!

JÜRGEN: BE QUIET!

He exits
Daniel picks up his bag

DANIEL: See you tomorrow
I don't want to miss the news
It's just so exciting!

He exits
ANNICKA: Marianne, I wanted . . .

MRS. GROSS: Go and wash, you smell

ANNICKA: It's my husband, you see . . .

He's very jealous
And I don't think I can . . .

MRS. GROSS: SHUT UP!
Be quiet, be quiet
Annicka wipes her armpits with a tissue and exits
Leaving Mrs. Gross alone and downcast
Then, little by little, her smile returns
She addresses the audience
I told you it was very hard
Leading a choir is a tricky business
But I never let myself get cast down
I like to think positive
Next week, we're having our annual concert
At the psychiatric hospital
It's an important booking that must not be missed
I have to do something, fast
She turns to the audience
And calls out to them
Who wants to sing in my choir?
Sing "Aaah!"
You? . . . You?
Come up and have a try
Come on . . .

Darkness

SCENE 12

The Just

Aïda is at the piano
She plays nervously while reciting a poem by Rumi

AÏDA: "What am I to do, Oh Muslims?
I know not who I am
I am not Christian, nor Jew, nor Persian
Nor Muslim either
I am of neither East nor West

Of neither continent nor ocean
I come not from the breast of the Earth
Nor from the light of the Sky
I am of neither yesterday nor today
Neither Rizwan, nor Eden, nor Hell
Are lands I know
Any more than this world, or the one beyond,
Neither the face of Adam nor the face of Eve
My homeland is where there is no homeland
My sign is without trace
Neither body, nor soul
I am but a splinter of HIS light
I have renounced duality
In two worlds I have seen but ONE
I am searching, I only know and call to HIM
Until the extinction of mine eye"

*After a moment, she gets up, holding a book
And continues reciting the poem, eyes closed.
At the other end of the space, a skateboard appears
It moves toward her as if it were remote-controlled
She stops it with her foot
Stands on it, slips and falls
She tries again
Until she finds an unstable balance
Kaïs appears
He watches what she's doing
Then goes over to her
He gets her to roll along on it
Faster and faster
She screams, laughs, clings on to him
They fall
Pause
Kaïs gets up, a different look appears in his eyes*

KAÏS: "I want to sacrifice myself"
*Aïda stiffens
She looks at him for a long moment
Not grasping the meaning of the phrase*

"We kill to build a world
Where no one will kill again!
We accept to be guilty
So that the world will one day be innocent"

AÏDA: And what if it were not so?

KAÏS: Don't say that,, you know very well that's impossible
And it would be to spit in the face of beauty
For a month now, I have been thinking of nothing else
This is the moment I have been living for until now
And I know now that I want to die in the act
Shed my blood to the last drop
Or go up in flames
In the fires of the explosion
Leaving nothing behind me
To die for an idea
Is the only way to be worthy of the idea
It justifies it

AÏDA: I desire that death too

KAÏS: Yes, it's a happiness one can yearn for
At night sometimes, I turn over in bed
Tormented by one thought: they have made us assassins
But then I realize that I too will die
And I feel at peace again
I smile, you know, and go back to sleep again, like a child

AÏDA: I would still like to help you. But . . .

KAÏS: But?

AÏDA: No, I'm being silly

KAÏS: You don't trust me?

AÏDA: "Oh no, my darling, I don't trust *myself*"
Shit, I've forgotten it

My mind's gone blank
She bursts out laughing
I didn't know you knew Camus's *The Just*
Did you know I played Dora at the Conservatoire?

She hugs him very tight
He lets her for a brief moment
Then breaks away

KAÏS: He gave me the book as a present a few months back

AÏDA: Who, Mokh? What was the occasion?

KAÏS: The umpteenth bomb attack in Jerusalem
Particularly bloody
I told him there must be other ways of fighting
Than killing civilians or blowing yourself up.

AÏDA: What did he say?

KAÏS: That it takes two to make a peace

AÏDA: Do you miss him?

KAÏS: Do you?

AÏDA: I spend my days hoping and waiting
For a phone call
A letter
Another police raid
A bullet in the stomach
News of his arrest
Or a steel coffin

KAÏS: Do you think he's part of a cell?

AÏDA: I don't know anymore

KAÏS: If he did call you, would you help him?

Break the law for him?

AÏDA: I'd give my life for him

KAÏS: That's easy to say
But it's just a phrase

AÏDA: Are you questioning my love for my brother?

KAÏS: I'm questioning everything
I've got fifty thousand questions crashing around in my head
Where does Good lie?
Where does Evil lie?
What does justice mean, or fairness?

AÏDA: There are philosophers who can answer those kinds of
     questions

KAÏS: But there's one question only you can answer
Why haven't you done anything to help your brother?

AÏDA: What d'you mean?
That's crazy
I'm moving heaven and earth for him
Lawyers, voluntary organizations, the police
The television, the press

KAÏS: You're doing all that for yourself
You're afraid of being rejected,
Treated like him
You're defending YOUR image
The well integrated Arab, the brand-new German
You flash your passport with so much pride
It makes me feel sick

AÏDA: What else should I have done, in your opinion?

KAÏS: Explain to them the rage he had inside him, the pain,
The injustice he felt, an injustice so tangible,

So physical you could cut it with a knife
AÏDA: Is that what you used to talk about, the two of you?

KAÏS: When he was living here
I woke up one night with a start
Mokh was pressed up against the window, panting, covered in sweat
His heart was beating really fast
He said to me: "I need light
Just a little light
Even the tiniest speck of light would do"
I have a feeling that today
He doesn't need artificial light anymore

AÏDA: What makes you say that?

KAÏS: Last time I saw him, he wasn't wearing his medal

AÏDA: What medal?

KAÏS: The one that saved his life during the war in Lebanon
The one that had deflected a bullet
He threw it away

AÏDA: Did he tell you that?

KAÏS: Yes!
He said: "I'm under God's protection
And whatever happens to me it'll be by the will of God
We are only his servants"

AÏDA: You never told me that

KAÏS: You never asked me

AÏDA: So what did *you* say?

KAÏS: Nothing

AÏDA: Well what do you think of it now?

KAÏS: That when you can't turn to human justice
You take refuge in divine justice
That faith in a God, whoever He might be,
Can ease the pain that humans endure
And inflict on each other.

She shouts

AÏDA: But no God can tolerate the death of innocent people

He shouts louder than her

KAÏS: Who said anything about the death of innocent people?
I'm talking about faith
Rediscovering your faith doesn't have to mean becoming a terrorist
He regains his composure
You see? Even you end up lumping the two together
He exits
She remains dumbfounded
Pause
He comes back, smiling strangely
What are we eating tonight?

She takes time to answer

AÏDA: What would you like?

KAÏS: Curried rice

She smiles

AÏDA: His favorite meal

Darkness

SCENE 13

The News of Mokhtar

Actress/Aïda is playing the piano
Hannah is at the other end of the stage
Holding her shoes
She addresses Aïda in a gentle voice

HANNAH: Aïda, Aïda!
Stop moping around
It's a beautiful day
You mustn't let yourself go
Come on!
Let's go for a nice walk
Forget your problems for a while
Come on . . .
Aïda gets up
Takes a few steps forward, but staggers
She has gone dizzy
Hannah rushes over to her
Are you OK?

AÏDA: I'm fine, it's nothing

HANNAH: Have you seen a doctor?

AÏDA: I just felt faint for a moment

They walk

HANNAH: I'm glad you're here
What about your son, how's he?

AÏDA: I don't know
He's always glued to his computer
and he's not saying much, as usual
But he's angry at us for not doing enough for his uncle
He's impatient

He wants results
It's his age, I guess

HANNAH: How about the new school, is he settling in?

AÏDA: He doesn't talk about it but at least he goes
And I think he chats to your psychologist friend
I've heard them talking on the phone
Hannah?

HANNAH: Yes?

AÏDA: Why do you do all this?
Where do you find the time
And the energy to deal with so many cases
Travel all over the world
And be there for people like me?

HANNAH: Well for a start, I'm not alone
There's a whole army of volunteers like me
And you really mustn't think
We're exceptional
She kisses her
They walk together in silence
Pause
Aïda!
Do you remember our first work session?
You wanted concrete answers to your questions
And I couldn't give them to you
But I asked you to trust us
And I told you we were moving forward on shifting sands
. . .
We have some news

Aïda stops

AÏDA: He's dead!

HANNAH: No!

He's alive

AÏDA: He's been arrested by the Americans!

HANNAH: No!
A pause . . .
Aïda holds her face in her hands
She swoons, falls, and gets up again
Hannah hasn't moved
OK?

AÏDA: It's the emotion
Go on, I'm listening
How is he?
Where is he?
Is he going to be able to come back?
When?

HANNAH: . . .

AÏDA: What? What's the matter?
Are you hiding something?

HANNAH: No!
I just can't answer your questions
He's alive, that's all
There's nothing else to say

AÏDA: Oh no!
You're not getting out of it like that
You've got to tell me more, Hannah!
You've got to

HANNAH: No Aïda, I won't tell you anymore
Because I don't know any more
It's a very confidential piece of information
I shouldn't have told you
It could be dangerous for him

AÏDA: But why?
He hasn't done anything

HANNAH: Are you quite sure of that?

They look at each other for a long time

AÏDA: If Mokhtar was arrested and found guilty
What would you do?
Would you wash your hands of him or carry on supporting him?

HANNAH: We'll check the evidence first
And if it's irrefutable
We'll do all we can to make sure he gets a fair trial
And if he goes to prison, we'll do all we can
To make sure his detention conforms to international law
Aïda gives a slight smile
Are you disappointed by my answer?

AÏDA: Disappointed, no
But my answer is slightly different
First I'd try to find out
Who decided this was a terrorist organization
If it was the U.S. State Department, I'd be suspicious
Whenever Islam and Arabs are involved
They lose all judgment
Then I'd try to find out where the attacks had taken place
If it was outside Palestine
I'd condemn them with every ounce of my strength
But if it was in Palestine, I could understand them . . . and I could
    justify them
Even though I too am horrified by violence
And believe me, I know what I'm talking about
Aïda rummages in her bag
And pulls out a newspaper, that she reads from
"I have moulded future terrorists with my own hands. I can't blame
    young men of eighteen years old for wanting revenge for their
    ruined houses. By forcibly entering their homeland, I have
    provided them with the ultimate reason for turning on me and

mine. As a soldier of the Israeli Defense Forces, I have provided them with the reason for blowing themselves up"
Ran Mendelssohn, Israeli soldier

HANNAH: You see, the just exist everywhere

AÏDA: But their voices aren't heard by the masters of the universe
She leaves then returns
Hannah!

HANNAH: Yes?

AÏDA: When he was a child, Mokhtar loved playing hide-and-seek
He was very good at it
Sometimes we'd spend hours looking for him, my mother and I,
And when he realized he'd made us very angry
He'd get us to forgive him by giving us a great big hug
Hannah, please,
If you make contact with him
Tell him his sister's waiting for a big hug

She stops, choked with emotion
They look at each other for a long time
Then leave the stage on opposite sides

Darkness

SCENE 14

The Splintered Family

Kaïs is in the middle of the space
Ulrich appears in shirtsleeves, tie undone
Holding his jacket and his travel bag
He seems in quite a hurry
He goes over to his son

ULRICH: Can you do a knot?

KAÏS: Dad?

ULRICH: Yes?

KAÏS: Can I talk to you?

ULRICH: You've got three minutes
I've got a train to catch

Kaïs answers without taking his eyes off the tie

KAÏS: Your hair

ULRICH: What's wrong with my hair?
Dandruff?

KAÏS: I prefer you with long hair
And with no tie
Ulrich Berg, known as the Red Monk

ULRICH: That's all garbage
I thought we'd agreed we wouldn't read trashy newspapers

KAÏS: Why did you change?

ULRICH: Because the world moves on and we move with it
But this really isn't the time
For an existentialist discussion
Bye, I'm going to miss my train
He heads for the door

KAÏS: You don't think it's weird
Going from the Church to the Red Army Faction
And ending up a businessman devoted to the free market economy?

ULRICH: What is all this?
I've never been a monk
Or a member of the Red Army Faction
And even less an extreme marketeer

KAÏS: What were you then?

ULRICH: An agent of the STASI!
Look, seriously
I can't discuss it in two minutes
When I get back, we'll have a long talk, if you like
I'll tell you everything, with some juicy details thrown in
Promise

KAÏS: I don't believe your promises

Ulrich puts down his bag

ULRICH: Why, have I ever lied to you?

KAÏS: Not to me, no
But you went back on the values you used to believe in

ULRICH: Oh, sure, right!

KAÏS: Did you justify the RAF's terrorist attacks?

ULRICH: I'm against violence

KAÏS: Is that what you think now
Or what you thought then?

ULRICH: The political situation was different then

KAÏS: You're not answering the question

ULRICH: It's true that I used to believe the RAF's struggle was
    justified
We wanted to change the world
Create a new social order based on more justice
We were attacking the structures of power, its institutions
But we didn't blow ourselves up in a market
Or on a bus, or in a café packed with kids
Nothing can justify the death of innocent civilians
KAÏS: And what do you call innocent civilians?

Reservists in a Tel-Aviv café?
The children of Jenine refugee camp?
The thousands of Americans killed in 9/11?
The thousands of dead Iraqis?
Who deserves to be called innocent?
Can you tell me that?

ULRICH: No, it's too complicated
All I know is that here we're not at war

KAÏS: You're not bothered about other people's wars anymore?
Aren't there any more Vietnams to defend today?

ULRICH: Yes, of course there are
But you can't take on
The misfortunes of the whole of humanity
You'll understand when you're older

KAÏS: Like you did

ULRICH: Yes, like I did

KAÏS: No thanks!
I don't want to end up like you

ULRICH: That's what I said to my father

KAÏS: And what did he reply?

ULRICH: He threw me out
And that's what'll happen to you
If you carry on talking to me in that tone of voice
You can go straight out and get a job
He puts his tie around Kaïs's neck
Pushes him toward the door
And throws him his own bag and jacket
If my money's so dirty
You're not forced to spend it, you know
Go out and earn a living instead of living on handouts

Aïda has been present for a while
At the other end of the space
Silently following the scene
Ulrich sees her and addresses her
He is increasingly irritated
I've missed my train
I thought he needed to talk to me
Man to man
And what do I get for the last five minutes?
Insults
According to him I'm an opportunist
A quitter
A deserter
He goes over to his son
Can you explain exactly why you resent me so much?
Because I've stopped being a revolutionary idealist?
Because I cut my hair?
Because I've stopped smoking pot?
Because I work like crazy
So we can send you to the best schools
And you can beat up a classmate
And get yourself kicked out, like the fool you are?
What *do* you plan to be exactly?

KAÏS: Pilot

A pause

ULRICH: Very funny

KAÏS: I took lessons on the Internet

Father and son are face to face

ULRICH: Why do you resent me so much?

KAÏS: I resent you for bowing down before the Master of the Earth
I resent you because the world's ugly
And because you do nothing to make it more bearable for me

I resent you because my heart's bleeding
And because you do nothing to stem the flow.
I resent you, Dad,
I resent you because I love you
But can't admire you

ULRICH: You have no right to judge me
I don't know what your uncle told you
But watch out, Kaïs
Don't forget you're in Germany
And the reality here is very different

Kaïs pushes his father

KAÏS: Leave my uncle out of this
At least he holds his head up high

ULRICH: Buries it in the sand, more like
Like all criminals on the run

Aïda intervenes from the other side of the stage

AÏDA: Mokhtar is not a criminal

ULRICH: And you, just shut up
And leave us alone!

AÏDA: I'll shut up if you stop insulting my brother

ULRICH: Your brother plants bombs and kills children

AÏDA: He is not guilty of any of the things he's accused of

ULRICH: If he wasn't guilty, he wouldn't be on the run

KAÏS: The brave don't run
He's on a mission

ULRICH: What mission?

What do you know about it?
Has he been in touch with you?
If you know something you have to tell the police
Kaïs turns his back on his father and disappears
Ulrich turns to Aïda
Do you know where your brother's hiding?
Has he contacted you
Or sent someone, or a message?
How do I know who you see
Or what you could be getting up to behind my back?
And you dare drag your son into this too,
Put his life in danger!
I trusted you!
What a fool I've been!
He goes toward her accusingly
 How do I know you're not part
Of a sleeper cell
Who are you, Aïda, who are you?

She answers him, smiling

AÏDA: Aïda Elkodsi
Daughter of Hassan Elkodsi of Jerusalem
And Marie Matrane of Jaffa
And . . . would-be terrorist
That answer your question?

They look each other up and down, as if seeing each other for the first time

ULRICH: This thing that's happening to us . . . it's horrible
I look at you and I think
This isn't the woman I was in love with
Your eyes are hard, cold

AÏDA: You said that to me on 9/11 too

ULRICH: Yes I did, because you were totally unmoved by the horror
   of it

AÏDA: I was not, I cried

ULRICH: Tears of revenge maybe, but there was nothing human in
them

AÏDA: There was something human in them
Because, like love or pity,
Resentment is profoundly human

ULRICH: You're wrong, Aïda
No distress, no injustice, no cause
Could ever justify the horror of 9/11
To my mind those were premeditated murders
Carried out in cold blood
Those terrorists are nothing less than assassins
Their leaders are gangsters of the worst kind
And their sympathizers are would-be accomplices
And if your brother is one of them
I will never defend him
That's what I should have said to you a long time ago
So that things were clear between us
Your son resents me because he thinks I'm neutral
Well, I'm not!

He adjusts his jacket and hair
Picks up his bag and heads for the exit

AÏDA: Ulrich!
He stops
I may not be here when you get back

ULRICH: You're leaving?

AÏDA: Yes

ULRICH: Where?

AÏDA: Beirut

ULRICH: How long for?

AÏDA: I don't know
But before I go I'd just like to remind you of something very obvious
I'm not religious, I'm the daughter of a Muslim and a Christian
And I'm married to a non-Muslim
In an Islamic fundamentalist regime, I'd be hanged
Which means that if Mokhtar was a fundamentalist
He'd have disowned me long ago.
And I need to tell you this too
I refuse anyone the right to lecture me about humanity
Just as I refuse to be a sacrificial victim
I fight for my rights
And for my people's rights
There!
If you think that sounds suspicious
You can always denounce me

ULRICH: Well, that's good to know

He goes out
She turns around. Kaïs is there

Darkness

SCENE 15

The Latest News

Katy is in the center of the space
In front of her is a metal bucket
And a pile of papers
Letters
Photos
And press articles
That she is tearing up and throwing in the bucket
Then she takes a letter out of her blouse and reads

KATY: "Cursed be the day I met you
Cursed be the day I touched you
Cursed be the day I felt you
Cursed be the day I kissed you
A pact stronger than all the hate and all the wars put together
Was sealed between us"
Katy starts tearing up the letter
Slowly and rhythmically
But she continuing to recite it from memory
Tears rolling down her cheeks
"I love you despite all the boundaries
And all the walls that stand between us
I love you and I curse myself for having made you suffer
I love you and I beg you to forget me
Expect nothing of me
Do not wait for me
My life is not my own
If it did not belong to my people
It would be in your hands
This letter will be the only one you will receive
By writing to you, today, I am endangering my own life
And my comrades'
It must leave no trace
Burn it . . .
And burn all that remains of me
Yours until death
Mokhtar"

She strikes a match and throws it in the bucket

ACTRESS/KATY: She found it in the morning, slipped under her
    door
In an envelope with no address, and no postmark
He was asking her to start a new life
She has already
Not with a man
But with her cause
She's dedicated herself to finding out, to understanding
And to taking action

So that justice returns
And peace is restored

A pause
Kaïs appears before her
He gets on his skateboard
She gives him a gentle push from behind
And exits
Kaïs slowly crosses the space
He addresses the public almost in a whisper

KAÏS: The air is my element
The air that everyone breathes
But no one owns
The air that recognizes no nation and no religion
No skin, no race
Absolute generosity
Universal donor
Air . . .
You who tear each other to pieces to have your place on Earth
Wake up!
Denounce the hoax! Take a long, hard look at this Earth.
The Earth!
A sphere, adored
By Earth-dwellers, who are drawn to her but never loved
Earth the enchantress
The sorceress
Earth the ogress
Devouring those
Who are chained to her
Who live off her
And are buried in her
Earth the miser
Taking all and giving nothing
From the sun, she demands light
From the sky, showers
From the air, oxygen
And from men, submission
She is said to be generous

Benevolent, nurturing
But in fact she is nothing
Dust among the dust
A sphere, hollow and conceited,
What would she be without the sky that brings her water?
Parched, cracked and sterile
What would she be without the sun that brings her light?
A black, lifeless ball
Earth, fickle and indulged
Never replete
Often angered
Spilling her guts
Vomiting her scalding lava
Bursting her swollen veins
Turning wildly in a dance of death
To swallow humans in their thousands
In a demonic feast
Earth-dwellers, it's you she feeds on
Wake up!
Free yourselves!
And make heaven your destination.

He crosses the space in one movement and disappears

Darkness

SCENE 16

The Departure

ULRICH appears in sportswear
He runs
Does a complete circuit
Looks behind him
Doubles back
And shouts

ULRICH: Jessy!

Come on, here girl!
He taps his thigh
Whistles
Then starts running again
After a time, Aïda appears
She is also in sportswear
She watches him
Then follows him as he runs
They cast furtive glances at each other
She stops briefly to catch her breath
Then starts running again more slowly
He, on the other hand, accelerates
And does a sprint
Aïda, panting, stretches out on the ground
He stops too
Tired?

AÏDA: A little
I knew I'd find you here
I didn't want to go without saying good-bye

She sits up
He massages her neck

ULRICH: Haven't changed your mind?

She shakes her head

AÏDA: I've discussed it a lot with Kaïs
I've tried to explain my decision
He's been very understanding
We've promised to call each other often

ULRICH: I'm sorry about what's happening to us
I really am!

AÏDA: Not as much as I am

She gets up and starts walking

He follows her
Whistling for the dog every now and then

ULRICH: Where are you going?

AÏDA: To hell

ULRICH: Alright then, I'll go with you

AÏDA: But we wouldn't be on the same side of this new wall

ULRICH: Are you going to Ramallah?

AÏDA: No, not yet
First, I'm going to Lebanon
For a while
After that, I don't know

ULRICH: Are you going for long?

AÏDA: I don't know

ULRICH: So what about me?
She turns toward him
What am I going to do without you?

AÏDA: It'll be a relief
You can finally spend some time on those contracts
Start seeing your friends again
Or make new ones, who knows?
You blamed me because you'd been in quarantine
You said the papers were more interested in you
Than your friends were
Everything will go back to normal now

He suddenly leaves her again
And does another sprint
He runs and runs
Then stops suddenly

And shouts at her

ULRICH: You're going to meet up with him, right?
He's in Lebanon
And this is all an excuse to go and see him
Isn't it?
Why should you care about a husband, a son, a home?
You're throwing it all away
Running off to hold your darling brother in your arms

She carries on walking and replies calmly

AÏDA: Hannah called
Ali Ahmed was arrested yesterday, in Brussels
They found weapons in his apartment

He stops

ULRICH: What about Mokhtar?

AÏDA: Still nothing

ULRICH: Is that why you're leaving?

AÏDA: No!
I'd already made up my mind
She carries on walking at the same pace
He watches her for a moment
Then starts running again with short strides
He overtakes her
Whistles for his dog once again

ULRICH: I bet she's digging up a bone somewhere
He disappears
Aïda also starts running again
And disappears in turn
Ulrich returns and panics at not finding her
He sprints over to the other side of the space
Just as Aïda returns

I don't want you to go
I'll take a few days off
We could take a trip
And talk it all over quietly
We've got to find each other again, Aïda

AÏDA: That's not possible anymore

ULRICH: But why not?
We've always worked things out before

AÏDA: We're not on the same side anymore
We're not looking in the same direction anymore
You have to face that

ULRICH: You don't love me anymore

AÏDA: Love's got nothing to do with any of this
You're still the love of my life and you always will be
She smiles at him
Come on, we're not going to start blubbing
Look, here are the keys
She hands him a bunch of keys
One for the office
One for the cellar
One for the garage
And this one's mine
She pulls one key out
And stuffs it in her pocket
That's for my mother's house in Jaffa
I have to get back now
I've still got a few phone calls to make

ULRICH: One last circuit?
They start running again
Then stop
He takes her in his arms and holds her for a long time
She pulls away from him and walks away without looking back
He watches her go

A pause
He calls his dog
Jessy! . . . Jessy!
And exits on the other side

Darkness

Fatima Gallaire

HOUSE OF WIVES

by Fatima Gallaire

Translated by

Carolyn and Tom Shread

HOUSE OF WIVES

by Fatima Gallaire
1990

First performed in the University of Massachusetts Curtain Theatre
in November, 2000
© January 2000 by Carolyn and Tom Shread

CHARACTERS

DRISS (*a common Arabic name; "idrissa" means immortal*), the husband

NAHNOUHA (*"busy body" in Arabic*), Driss's mother

TAOS (*popular Berber name meaning "peacock"*), Driss's first wife

MIMIA (*"nice" or "gentle" in Berber*), Driss's second wife

SIRÉNA (*"serene" in Arabic*), Driss's third wife

CHEMS (*"sun" in Arabic*), Driss and Mimia's eldest daughter

THE ANCESTOR, the grandmother

DRIFA & DRAIFA (*"kind" and "gentle" in Arabic; not usually used as names*), twin servants

AZOUZA (*"dear" in Arabic*), the midwife

TAOS'S MOTHER

MIMIA'S MOTHER

ACT 1
Scene 1

An oriental living room. The furnishings are modest but comfortable. An ottoman. A brazier. In a dim corner sits the aged ancestor: still, blind witness to all joys and depravities. She might represent the conscience of Nahnouha, an otherwise forceful character. For now, the ancestor counts her beads in mute prayer. All is silent. The regular ticking of an old-fashioned alarm clock might emphasize the silence. In another corner stands a traditional handloom.

VOICE OF A MAN APPROACHING: Scram and stop bothering me! Ahhhh! You two pests are always in my way! Why can't you give me some space and leave me alone for once? *(A man's footsteps. A young man enters with an axe. He throws it in a corner and collapses onto the ottoman. A sigh of relief. He turns to the grandmother.)*

DRISS: So Ancestor, is it clear today?

THE ANCESTOR: It's vague my child, only vague. A mere glimmering . . .

DRISS: Well, you won't be cold this winter. I've cut some wood for you. It's not a task I enjoy, but it's a man's work.

THE ANCESTOR: Man's work. *(pause)* I can't hear your wife any more. She told me she was leaving.

DRISS: She has left.

THE ANCESTOR: May God protect her.

DRISS: Ancestor, are you trying to tell me something?

THE ANCESTOR: I no longer have the right to speak. Time has buried me these past years. Your mother lives in the light, she can speak . . .

DRISS: She's on her way over. Apparently we need to talk.

THE ANCESTOR: If only you knew what these dead eyes can see, you who see no further than the surface of things, you'd be terrified. Do you sometimes feel how close the air becomes?

(*Enter two young girls, running and giggling. They place some logs in a corner. Enter Driss.*)

DRISS: Will you have tea with me, instead of rambling on?

THE ANCESTOR: Never say no to a little heaven on earth.

DRISS: Hey, you little bastards! Hurry up with my tea! And serve the Ancestor too. (*The girls obey. They arrange a low table before Driss, with a tea urn, and a glass that they fill. They serve the grandmother, then leave.*) Aaaahhhh! My carefree days are over. These days I'm a very unhappy man. . . . It seems only yesterday I was a boy, now I don't feel so young anymore. What do you think Grandmother, am I old already?

ANCESTOR: No. You've hardly begun to turn the wheel of life.

DRISS: But I'm already so tired . . .

THE ANCESTOR: That's because you're afraid . . . Your will is suffering because it can't do what it wants. Our tradition is just as harsh on men as it is on women.

DRISS (*moved*): How do you know that? You've no more value or rights than a cow. How do you know, when you don't even have the right to think?

THE ANCESTOR: Because I never gave up thinking . . or watching or listening . . . This tea is a sweet gift; it warms me inside and brings me back to life. Why is the light fading?

DRISS: It's a storm, Ancestor, there's a storm coming . . .

Darkness

Scene 2

Lights. Nahnouha sits opposite Driss.

NAHNOUHA: Son, leave it to me to judge the world. A man who raises someone else's children is a cuckold, whatever way you look at it.

DRISS: Well . . . I thought we were supposed to be talking about us. We'll get nowhere if I start upsetting you.

NAHNOUHA: At last you've come to your senses.

DRISS: It wasn't easy sending my wife off to her mother's house so we could have this talk. So can we talk now . . . about this problem that's keeping me awake all night? It won't be so easy next time. She's already suspicious.

NAHNOUHA: What use is a man who talks like this? Don't you see? That woman's worth nothing. Her womb is a graveyard. It won't produce a single living thing. I don't care what she says. She'll be happy if we just keep her.

DRISS (*taking the tea his mother hands him and slurping noisily*): Oh! Mother! Let's be fair. She's a good housekeeper and never says a word out of place.

NAHNOUHA: Well, there is that to be thankful for. But that woman, that so-called wife of yours, what is she for you? A dog? Not even that! Even a bitch can have pups, which is more than she can do! Or is it some pups you want to adopt?

DRISS: Ah! As father always said, "If you have something to say, say it." We're not talking about dogs here!

NAHNOUHA: Well, then, so what's that useless cuckold been saying?

DRISS: Mother, I'd prefer you to call him the Cyclist, like everyone else does. He might sell bicycles now, but he was a champion in his time.

NAHNOUHA: Oh, that's no dishonor.

DRISS: It's thanks to him I know how to ride a bicycle. You know, when I had that weak leg, it really helped me.

NAHNOUHA: I know son. But that's not my question.

DRISS: I need to see a doctor. He's been telling me for months. I absolutely must see a doctor.

NAHNOUHA: God Almighty, why are cuckolds so absolutely meddling all of a sudden? I'm simply too old to understand. Why see a doctor when the solution is obvious? It's stupid! And the old ways, what does your friend have to say about those? This is the most idiotic thing I've ever heard from the mouth of a man!

DRISS: From the mouth of your son, you mean.

NAHNOUHA: If you still consider yourself a man, yes.

DRISS: We were talking about the Cyclist. He's always given me good advice. And he mentioned a doctor, so yes I've been thinking about it! But I'm not sure about actually seeing one.

NAHNOUHA: Oh? But you're thinking about it?

DRISS: Yes, I am.

NAHNOUHA: And what about your mother's advice?

DRISS: I'm listening!

NAHNOUHA: Good, then I won't die of grief, which is what your hopeless father wanted. What do you want a doctor for?

DRISS: Well . . . um . . . God forgive me for raising the subject . . .

NAHNOUHA: God will forgive you; it's me who's asking.

DRISS: . . . raising the subject before your noble face . . . so . . . uh, well, he told me that when a husband and wife are childless, people immediately assume it's the woman's fault. They say she's barren and her belly's dead, that she's cursed. In a word, she's sterile. They forget that the husband might also be afflicted or incapable, I mean . . . he might not sow his seed.

NAHNOUHA: I can't listen to this anymore! My poor heart won't take it!

DRISS: It concerns us. We have to talk about it.

NAHNOUHA: Yes, but we don't need to talk about the ravings of a common cuckold!

DRISS: Look, if you'd prefer not to . . .

NAHNOUHA: My life of sacrifice began before I was twelve years old, the day your pitiful father came to take me to his home and harangue me with his talk about freedom for the people. Oh! He could certainly put on a show for the Resistance. The underground, he loved every minute! A model leader he was, a magnificent hero. But I knew him better. I soon brought him to heel when he came back home. But as the years went by, I bore witness to nine painful burials — nine sons — and I did it with dignity, I never shed a tear, I never once lost my mind. I'm beyond all suffering now and you're my tenth son, so speak, I can listen.

DRISS: Forgive me for bringing such pain to your heart, it's not my intention. Look, the neighbors are having their afternoon sleep, the courtyard's empty now with all this summer heat, no one can hear us . . . Let's speak the honest truth, even though it might hurt. I'm an unhappy man, but I'm not an imbecile. You're from an older and wiser generation so explain to me this great indignity: how can God let a man live his life without ever having children?

NAHNOUHA: An infertile man? Impossible! I've never heard such blasphemy! It's the woman who's either fertile or barren; she alone brings honor or disgrace.

DRISS: That's not what the doctors say. When they examined the Cyclist they told him his semen was clear as spring water, nothing in it to impregnate a woman. Forgive me for shocking you with scientific facts, but that's what he said.

NAHNOUHA: Quiet! Or the sky will fall on our heads. Rid your mind of these filthy thoughts!

DRISS: I'm talking about the Cyclist, Mother. It was a double blow for him that could have driven him to despair. Did you know, in some countries when people become desperate, they even commit suicide?

NAHNOUHA: So you want me dead now?

DRISS: Of course not, let me finish. His wife couldn't have children either so his misfortune was doubled. But they didn't hesitate, they looked for children where they could find them. His wife is still sterile, by the way.

NAHNOUHA: That I can understand. Sterility and pregnancy are the concerns of women. What do men know about them? They only sow, they don't reap.

DRISS: You know the story as well as I do. At the time it surprised us all. Some people were upset, but eventually they were praised for accepting God's will and adopting two orphans. Two brothers, born of the same womb. Remember, during the French Occupation? The Cyclist even gave them his name. He couldn't do that today.

NAHNOUHA: Why do you remind me of all this stupidity? It doesn't surprise me in the least that the French allow such decadence. Giving your name to a bastard!

DRISS (*searching for words*): You asked me what he said and I'm telling you what he said.

NAHNOUHA: I wanted to know if he said anything worthwhile.

DRISS: Of course he did. He talked about Cadi's daughter.

NAHNOUHA: I thought as much.

DRISS: . . . who was supposed to be sterile, and adopted a child, but then became pregnant.

NAHNOUHA: Quiet!

DRISS: . . . and then had more children, but she kept and cared for her adopted son, the one who brought her happiness.

NAHNOUHA: Enough, child . . .

DRISS: You tell me to speak and then you want me to be quiet. What do you want me to do? How can I speak and keep quiet at the same time?

NAHNOUHA: Speak! But only if you have something worth saying, so I won't die of grief.

DRISS: Mother, don't get yourself in a state. I'll keep quiet if you want.

NAHNOUHA: You're a very bad son. You're making me angry and anger is great suffering.

DRISS: Forgive me. Do you forgive me?

NAHNOUHA: NO.

DRISS: Mother!

NAHNOUHA: Not if you keep ranting on!

DRISS: I rant no more.

NAHNOUHA: Good. I'll do the talking. (*She gets up and walks over to her son, wagging her finger at him.*) You listen to me now, son of your father!

DRISS (*Somewhat worried*): Yes, Mother dear.

NAHNOUHA: Are you listening?

DRISS: That's all I ever do!

NAHNOUHA: Alright. I'll count it out on my fingers. You've been married for three years. Now, your wife should have had a child at least two years ago. We've had the patience of angels, that's what people say: other people . . . yes . .. public opinion . . . And you know public opinion can make or break a reputation. Sometimes a good reputation is lost for nothing, for a little too much patience for example. So, let's try to stay on the right side of the line, on the side of those who judge. Not with the herd of the condemned. Up until now our tolerance has been admired by the crowd, but there's a limit. They've admired our patience and indulgence . . . but soon it'll be cause for condemnation.   What are you doing sitting there slurping your tea while your reputation is collapsing? Son of mine, what do you think you're doing? Your duty as a man commands you to carry my life into the eternal future through your countless offspring. And what are you doing about it?

DRISS: Nothing.

NAHNOUHA: If this situation continues, we'll be dragged through the mud. Remember this when I'm gone and there's no one here to advise you: a lost reputation is never regained. Like a woman's beauty, it's gone forever.

DRISS (*getting up and pointing at his moustache proudly*): And what do you think this is? Grass? Parsley? No. It's a man's moustache! A man's dignity!

NAHNOUHA: Save all this donkey talk for your next wife, you'll need it to seduce her. And may God help her believe you . . . So, let's see . . . there are two weeks to go before the new moon, and that's the month of Ramadan when no one is married—not even men waiting for children, like you yourself. So two weeks and a month, that's a month and a half . . . then the fasting will end and we'll have the celebrations . . . add another week. Let's be generous and call it two months. If we act quickly and ask for the hand of your future bride, say this evening or tomorrow . . . in two months time you'll be married.

DRISS: You mean re-married.

NAHNOUHA: That's what I mean.

DRISS: Mother, two months is not a long time to organize a ceremony.

NAHNOUHA: You need a ceremony to do a man's work? Is that what you're saying? Incredible! That sterile wife of yours will keep ruining your reputation unless we act fast and relegate her to the status of mere furniture. No one expects furniture to have children. Do you understand?

DRISS: But what about the dowry? What about the trousseau? Is the government going to pay for all that?

NAHNOUHA: Oh! Your noble heart is bleeding child! Is that what you're worried about? We're honoring this young woman by asking for her hand. What more could she want?

DRISS: What custom dictates: a dowry and a trousseau!

NAHNOUHA: No! She'll want our family's name and reputation, two priceless treasures.

DRISS: We have nothing. Nothing to sell and nothing to buy. Let's put some money aside for a while, that'll give us time to think.

NAHNOUHA: What with? That chick pea brain of yours? And save from that meager salary you receive for wasting your life away in a dusty old office?

DRISS: Um . . . That's not exactly true . . .

NAHNOUHA: Quiet! I'm speaking! But there's still one problem: your present wife—Taos. And she won't be that for much longer unless she keeps a low profile. I'll handle this. You say she's gone to visit her mother? Excellent! And you convinced her to go? Even better! And she's already suspicious? Perfect! So I won't have to beat about the bush to tell her what she already knows. I'll explain how lucky she is to belong to an important family like ours, and instead of disowning her, we'll give her the choice . . .

DRISS: Choice? What choice?

NAHNOUHA: Of leaving or staying.

DRISS: But she'll want to stay! She'll want another chance.

NAHNOUHA: Meaning?

DRISS: Um . . . one more year.

NAHNOUHA: Never! . . . Well . . . God help us, do you love her?

DRISS: To be honest, yes.

NAHNOUHA: Yes, you didn't sound very enthusiastic . . . Ah! You're the bane of my life! Here you are defying me and standing up for your wife. Stabbing me in the back while I'm fighting for you. Stupid boy!

DRISS: You're the best mother in the world, and you're looking after my interests, so it's not for me to have an opinion.

NAHNOUHA: Why not, so long as your opinion's the same as mine?

DRISS: Well, this is how I see it. I'm a man of honor, because you raised me properly. In this village, there aren't many men of any age who can boast a flawless reputation. I'm a man of honor and an honorable man never betrays.

NAHNOUHA: Betrays? Betrays who?

DRISS: My wife.

NAHNOUHA: Your wife doesn't count. She's just livestock, one of your belongings. You could sell her any day of the year and no one could say a thing.

DRISS: Well, that custom is unjust. There are laws now.

NAHNOUHA: Are you telling me I was spared the pain of your burial, only to suffer the pain of your defiance?

DRISS: I'm only saying that if something new is going to happen in this house, first I'd like to inform my wife. Even if I do have the right to walk all over her, I'll do no such thing!

NAHNOUHA: I can't believe what you're saying! Thank God there are no witnesses to repeat it. Who cares about a woman who can't even fill a house with the laughter and tears of children, or the joyful sound of their tiny feet? I'm telling you, if this madness persists, you won't be walking out of here with your head held high for much longer.

DRISS: Are you saying honesty is madness? You know, she wouldn't betray me either.

NAHNOUHA: Who says? Where's the proof? Have you forgotten the duplicity of women and their shameful intercourse with the devil? Didn't you learn anything from the proverbs I taught you? You've been bewitched by the very first woman you met. You're lucky I'm watching out for you. I don't trust anyone. Certainly not a woman.

DRISS: So what are you then, Mother?

NAHNOUHA: I'm above everyone, and I judge everyone.

DRISS: You're very hard on this woman . . .

NAHNOUHA: This childless woman!!!

DRISS: . . . who loves, admires, and respects you.

NAHNOUHA: As she should.

DRISS: Well, I have the right to talk to her and perhaps this evening I'll do just that.

NAHNOUHA: Since when have you had rights? You can't even tell a good woman from a bad one. In my view, all you have are duties.

DRISS: Mother, this conversation isn't easy. Can't we give it a rest for today?

NAHNOUHA (*Incensed, she leaps up, as if to hit her son, but is stricken by a sudden pain. Driss jumps up to help, catches his moaning mother in his arms, and with affectionate care leads her over to the ottoman to sit her down*): Oh! I always knew . . . I would die by your hand . . . Unworthy son . . . Oh! My poor heart . . . Your father gave me hell on earth, but he didn't manage to kill me . . . Oh! No. But I didn't . . . love him . . . as much . . . as much . . . as I love you . . . All my dead children . . . you took all my love . . . You took it all . . . I gave you everything, you're the only light I have left now, you're the light of my aging eyes. I only see because of you. Jewels? They're trifles compared to life. The garden is full of them. Buried deep in the ground. Bracelets, pendants, gems, precious beads, a thousand and one rings, enough for a thousand women, all you could wish for, enough to fill my old age with babbling babies. I gave nothing to the Revolution. Ah! A fine lie. All it took was a few conversations . . . private talk . . . and false news . . . spread around the village . . . and even further. You're richer than you ever dreamt . . . Your father . . . he never knew how well-off we were . . . He was never interested. But keep the secret, keep the legend of our treasure chest alive, and beware of thieves. If . . . if I die, remember the game you played when you were a boy, alone in the garden . . . Play it one more time, count out the steps again . . . You'll find everything. If I die before I'm a grandmother . . .

DRISS: Mother dear . . . there . . . there . . . none of this matters . . . Is this my doing?

NAHNOUHA: I want . . . my granddaughters to wear my belts of amber and gold. I can see them now . . . Belts of gold coins made for women. Keep the finest for your favorite. Even the prophet had a favorite wife. The treasure is safe. I hid it from every government that came along. And I would have taken up arms to defend it — me, a woman!

DRISS: That's the mother I know and love . . .

NAHNOUHA: Boys have no right to gold. There's plenty in silver and gemstones to keep them satisfied. Do you understand?

DRISS: Perfectly! I don't want you suffering anymore. I'll take three or four wives immediately. A harem, it's like livestock, isn't it? Better to have several head to ensure the future.

NAHNOUHA: Now that's my son talking.

DRISS: But time's moving on, my break is over. I must go back to work . . . if you're feeling better.

NAHNOUHA: Help me up now . . . there. That's better. You go back to work and I'll stay here to greet your wife. Once I've explained everything, she'll be eternally grateful.

DRISS: You'd make a great lawyer.

NAHNOUHA: I am one. I defend what's right and proper. Taos is a simple woman from a poor background. If we join with a rich family in a second marriage, the honor will reflect on her. I'll explain it, she'll understand.

DRISS: Alright.

NAHNOUHA: Tonight show her some courtesy and respect, so she'll know her place in this house is secure. After all, if one day you have lots of children, she'll make an excellent nurse . . . Sterile women love children, they often have more patience than busy mothers. So, the fate of your first wife is decided. As for the second, it will be a privilege and her destiny to produce a line of noble descendants. A highly sought after honor that her father will be more than happy to pay for. He'll see to the wedding costs. You know the family I'm talking about. Those merchants have only ever had one reference and that's money.

DRISS: I know, Mother, I know . . .

NAHNOUHA: Aaaaaahhhhhh! I feel better already. You may be a man now, but you'll always be my little boy. You'll never seem bigger than the child I bore. How strange . . . Everything's fine now. You may go.

DRISS: Alright Mother. I'll make my way back to work, and tonight I'll have dinner with my eldest cousin, he always lays the best table. I'll come home late and I'll show some courtesy to this woman about to embark on a life of suffering . . .

NAHNOUHA: Who's talking about suffering? We're talking about honor.

DRISS: May I leave you now? The office doesn't approve lateness. (*Driss kisses his mother and walks to the door.*)

NAHNOUHA: You forgot one thing.

DRISS (*coming back, somewhat surprised*): Yes, Mother, what?

NAHNOUHA (*standing tall, she gives him a magnificent slap, screaming*): THIS! YOU FORGOT THIS!!! That's what you get for disobeying your mother!

DRISS (*keeping his dignity in the affront*): Alright, Mother. So long as I know what you think.

NAHNOUHA: Don't be insolent! Get out!

DRISS: Now, now, Mother.   The neighbors are awake.

NAHNOUHA: Ah! That's true. Go to the door so everyone can hear me.

DRISS: Good-bye.

NAHNOUHA: Ah? Is that you going to work son? (*Louder*) Yes, go now . . . it's a very difficult job . . . only those who can read can do it . . . Good-bye . . . May God be with you. (*Exit Driss. Nahnouha sighs with relief. She is happy, savoring her victory. She sits down on the ottoman.*) That's better . . . Now I've put the world back in place, I think I deserve a rest.

She slumps down on the ottoman with a relaxed sigh.

Darkness

Scene 3

Enter the daughter-in-law, Taos, returning from her mother's house. Taos is humble and unassuming, but efficient.   She stoops to embrace her mother-in-law, then swiftly removes her veil, which she folds and places in a corner. She sits down at the loom and works in nervous silence.

NAHNOUHA (*sitting down):* How's that wrinkled old mother of yours?

TAOS: Not too bad. May God bless you.

NAHNOUHA: Better than last time?

TAOS: No, but better than the time before.

NAHNOUHA: She's had one foot in the grave for years, if I don't watch out she'll be burying me.

TAOS: Why do you speak ill of the afflicted?

NAHNOUHA: Are you being insolent?

TAOS (*stopping still*): In God's name, no.

NAHNOUHA: Do I have to keep an eye on you too? You raise your head too often, for no good reason. Get back to work!

TAOS (*frantically returning to her weaving*): Have I ever shown disrespect in this house?

NAHNOUHA: I'm beyond a daughter-in-law's disrespect. I didn't live to be this old, to see all the people who knew me when I was a child pass away, who knew me when I was young and beautiful and then mature and beautiful and now when I'm old, I didn't live to be this old to concern myself with a little bastard's disrespect.

TAOS: Such words from the mouth of my God given second mother!

NAHNOUHA: What do you expect? You never had a father.

TAOS: He left to earn our daily bread when I was born, and then exile took him away forever.

NAHNOUHA (*strutting about*): Never forget that I bore many, many children, and you'll never be able to measure up to me. (*Silence.*) Did you hear me?

TAOS: Yes.

NAHNOUHA: And what do you say?

TAOS: It's the will of God.

NAHNOUHA (*suspiciously*): Or is it God's punishment that you're barren, because you've sinned in some way? (*Taos cries silently, working but not answering.*) Answer me!

TAOS: God is good and I trust in his mercy. I will wait . . .

NAHNOUHA: Well I won't! We gave you the honor of our name and you've betrayed us. I chose you myself, you were in good health and a hard worker. Healthy as a mare and ready to be mounted, ready to breed. What's left of you now, after three years of marriage? What's left of us? We're on the brink of shame!

TAOS: Mother of men and sorrow, for pity's sake, listen to me!

NAHNOUHA: No! I won't listen to a sterile woman.

TAOS: What are you saying? Listen to yourself! Don't unleash your demons on me! They might harm your descendants.

NAHNOUHA: There are no descendants! That's what I'm saying: you're sterile.

TAOS: It's the will of God, I tell you. You're an old witness in this life and you've seen other tragedies like mine. Some of these stories have had happy endings when there's been someone with the wisdom to wait when everyone else has given up. Some women are said to be sterile, but with one last chance, the chance of time, eventually they do have children. If they keep their faith, they bear children.

NAHNOUHA: Listen, fatherless and childless daughter. Listen to me closely!

TAOS: As always my hands are working, but I am listening.

NAHNOUHA: When all is said and done, no one can take your place in this house. You're a good worker and I won't replace you.

TAOS: So, you haven't forgotten I am your son's wife, and this is my home?

NAHNOUHA: Nothing will change that.

TAOS: Thank God for hearing my prayers.

NAHNOUHA: You can thank me. Let me continue. It's never simple to say the obvious. But the fact is that when a man and woman meet, it's not long before she's with child . . .

TAOS: In marriage . . .

NAHNOUHA: Unfortunately not, not always in marriage . . . Some shameless girls don't wait that long.

TAOS: Nor do some men.

NAHNOUHA: Hold your tongue, childless woman!

TAOS: I was just adding to what you said . . .

NAHNOUHA: What I say is enough. When I speak, it's the truth. You're trying my patience. Do you want to make me angry now?

TAOS: Do I?

NAHNOUHA: Well. Earlier my son was talking about seeing a doctor.

TAOS: He's a just man.

NAHNOUHA: You've changed him since he's been more your husband than my son. He speaks a strange language. See a doctor? He might as well walk around with his trousers down! He might lose face that way, but he wouldn't lose his honor!

TAOS: You raised him and he's a good man, don't forget that.

NAHNOUHA: I brought him up and I know he's a weakling. And you . . . you . . . you're . . . you're nothing!

TAOS (*crying softly and moaning*): Me, I'm just a wretched orphan . . .

NAHNOUHA: That's right. Since the time that your worthless father long ago abandoned you and your mother to a life of poverty, he must surely have died. Dead and gone, an infidel, run off to the land of infidels, where alcohol flows and where — God forgive me — women even show their knees!

TAOS (*crying but still working*): I'm an abandoned orphan . . .

NAHNOUHA: Will you ever stop tempting misfortune? (*Taos still sniffing. Nahnouha, looking at the brazier*) If you don't stop now I'll throw these hot coals at your head, that'll bring you to your senses!

TAOS (*calming down*): I'm sorry . . . Forgive me for troubling you.

NAHNOUHA: And not before time. Now, if you have some remnant of intelligence left in that cheese curd brain of yours, I'll sum up the situation and you'll see how it's to your advantage.

TAOS (*stopping her work*): With respect, I'm listening.

NAHNOUHA: As God is my witness, I can't deny your qualities. He hears me and He reads my heart. It's by His will— His will for justice— that I'm talking to you now. Like so many mothers-in-law, I could have said nothing and sent you away to rest for a few days at your mother's house. When you came back, there'd be another woman here in your place . . . Some may act that way, but not me. I'm as good as gold, a precious pearl, a pearl that generations of divers have given their life's breath for . . . I expect honesty and I despise betrayal. Even if one day there are three or four wives here, I want you to keep the upper hand in running this house. See how I place all my trust in you? You're my first daughter-in-law. Your heart is just, but I don't believe you'll ever have children; so you'll never be tempted to favor yours over others. Anyone listening knows how much I value you. Besides, when you have a poor dying mother, what else can you do except love your mother-in-law?

VOICE IN THE COURTYARD: Taos! Taos!

NAHNOUHA (*outraged*): Who's that?

TAOS: Just a neighbor. She comes to see me from time to time.

NAHNOUHA: Who?

TAOS: The girl who works at the post office.

NAHNOUHA: That braying mare? I don't want to see her! Send her away!

(*Taos stands up quickly; she goes out and we hear whispers. She returns and sits back at the loom.*)

NAHNOUHA (*suspiciously*): What did she want?

TAOS: She wanted to show me a book.

NAHNOUHA: A book? You can't even read, what do you want with books?

TAOS: She can read.

NAHNOUHA: So why does she come round here showing you books?

TAOS: Because they tell beautiful stories, and terrible stories, and because they tell about life. My sweet neighbor, Siréna, reads so well, it really is God's miracle. When I see those strange marks on the pages, they mean nothing to me, but when she reads them, they become so beautiful, so alive, and sometimes so sad.

NAHNOUHA: Very strange. It's as if that girl has cast a spell on you. I hope she doesn't tell you any improper stories.

TAOS (*returning to her work*): What do you mean? Stories God would condemn? No, nothing like that. She doesn't tell me that kind of story.

NAHNOUHA: Well, I don't want her coming here anymore. You don't need all those stories corrupting your mind. She's no friend. And besides, she works!

TAOS: Yes, she's valuable. She earns money.

NAHNOUHA: She's a public woman, she goes out unveiled and exposes her body to the desires of men. I wouldn't want her for a daughter-in-law if I were given her weight in gold. Ah! That girl irritates me. She's made me forget the most important thing.

TAOS: What important thing?

NAHNOUHA: I've known your mother a long time: she's a strong, fertile woman. She brought a generation of strapping young men into this world, just as I did, except all her sons are still alive. But they've all gone now, following in the footsteps of their father. Your father. Your mother did the work of a harem and I pay her my respects, even if I'm sometimes carried away and call her a good for nothing.

TAOS: I might not look like her, but I'm a strong woman too.

NAHNOUHA: A strong woman? That remains to be seen. Which brings us back to the subject, our misfortune, and your sterility!

TAOS: If that were true, the misfortune would be mine first of all.

NAHNOUHA: You don't count.

TAOS: I feel normal, and I'm in good health—believe me!

NAHNOUHA: That's enough! Next you'll be claiming my son is . . . uh . . . impotent . . . That he has water in his works or that he's cursed by his ancestors. I won't accept such insolence! (*Taos resigns to silence*) I've decided. Tomorrow, I'll take one of my finest gold bracelets, one of the rare and priceless ones that can't be bought or sold anywhere. I'll go and look for a second wife for my son. A fertile wife. In about two months, you'll have one more person to cook for. So keep your head high. (*Silence. Taos works more slowly.*) I'm asking you from the goodness of my own heart, do you understand?

TAOS (*softly*): If I had sons, young men, good little boys, I'd teach them to respect their wives as much as their mothers.

NAHNOUHA (*rising heavily to her feet*): But you don't have any sons! So be quiet!

TAOS: I'll be quiet.

NAHNOUHA: Good. So now you've been warned. You have a fine future of hard work ahead of you. Don't compromise it. There's never a shortage of hardworking women. Where did I put my veil? (*Taos stands up, hurries to give it to her and helps her put it on.*) You're a good girl, I've always thought so. But you have a way of thinking for yourself that's tiresome. You always want to be in charge, and I think you'll make a good nurse. Do as I do and pray that your co-wife is fertile and ready to prove it. Otherwise we'll all be miserable. Now I leave you in peace.

(*They embrace.*)

TAOS: May peace go with you.

(*Nahnouha leaves.*)

Darkness

Scene 4

Slowly Taos returns to her loom and gradually returns to her work. Her actions become increasingly uneven, rude, and rough on the wool she is weaving. She moans like a wounded animal, at first softly, then louder. This crescendo of violence occurs in both her actions and her voice. Then, as if her mind is made up, Taos sticks her reed in the wool and gets to her feet. Her eyes are haggard, filled with pain, which she expresses in words and gestures.

TAOS Ohhhh! Why me? Why am I a wretched orphan? Abandoned by my father and now it seems by my husband, if that's what she's saying. I was hardly born before I knew the pain of neglect. One of the worst injustices. And here I am rejected again and I've hardly begun my life as a woman! Help me God! Save me from a doubtful future. I had so many brothers they could have been an army, but never did they once come to my defense. They all left me. I've always been obedient, but this world treats me unfairly.

I've always kept my silence when I wanted to speak, I've always accepted when I wanted to protest, I've always lowered my head to stay on the right side of virtue and obedience and faith. But here I am naked, with no one to defend me and no one to speak for me! Promised all the honor of motherhood, and now sterility has reduced me to no more than a maid. Forgive me God for I'm going to blaspheme. They say a woman can go crazy overnight when her husband remarries. It's happening to me. Will there ever be an end to this curse on women?

We come into this world, a flower between our legs. It's a source of fear when we have it, a source of unhappiness when we lose it. It's different for a man. He comes into this world with a gun between his legs. With his first gun, he wins every battle against the flowers . . .

Is this what they call justice? Is it? Is this justice? Is it my fault I was born a flower? Is it my fault I'm not a gun? Am I crazy to be talking to the wall? There is evil in this world, but I know none of it, I've done nothing wrong.

Why have I no right to see a doctor? Haven't I worked enough here? Haven't I served enough? I want to see a doctor, I'm not ashamed! Maybe he will heal me, instead of insulting me! They say a woman's vessel is so narrow it can be blocked by a single hair. Just a hair! And a summer breeze, a gentle wind can free it, a tiny breath! But here I am waiting, searching, and humiliated. They say that when Cadi's daughter was first married, she was so upset when she thought she was sterile that she didn't have children and she became ill with sorrow. God plants children in our minds before he plants them in our wombs. Poor daughter of Cadi! But I envy her, me who covets neither gold, nor money, nor land. She lay in bed until the day they placed that helpless little child in her arms. How that little angel cried with hunger! She woke up and got up to look after it as if she'd done it the day before and the day before that, and before long she became pregnant!

But I have nothing, no child in this womb. (*She slaps her belly violently with the palm of her hand.*) Unknown children, unborn but yet to come, listen to me, little seeds of my womb, children to come, children of the future, children of joy, listen to me! (*She holds her belly with both hands, almost indecently.*) You're still there, but as soon as you come, as soon as the world knows you're coming, I'll be a queen, I'll be given the power and the beauty of a queen! I'll bear the glorious name of mother, I'll be a parent and I'll be sacred! I've waited too long for you, too long I've been waiting, I've waited a thousand years. I'll hold back that awful moment when another mother takes my place. For pity's sake, my little ones, my chicks, my twins, my triplets, my lion cubs, my warriors, don't wait! Wait no more! Don't abandon me, I'll never abandon you, never!

(*She touches her belly in a more . . . specific manner.*) You're there, I can feel you, you're mine, there, there, there . . . From the depths of your being, you can hear me, I know you can! Run to me! Don't stay in the shadows: cast off the shrouds of miscarriage, come to my defense! Come protect me and give me back my honor! Love me now, as I love you! (*Courtyard noises. Voices of women and children. The shutters are closed. Someone is knocking and calling for Taos who, emerging from her nightmare, stands and as if she is sleepwalking, wets a towel to freshen her face.*)

(*She pants as she speaks.*) I'm calling your name, I'm waiting for you! I'm pushing out all my pain so it won't eat me up inside! So it won't harm your precious infant life! I feel you inside me, already so strong! I feel you inside me, already so handsome! Come restore the rule of justice. Let this house be filled with your cries and your laughter and your joy. You there, I see you. All my sons waiting to come, WAIT NO MORE! COME TO ME!!!

(*With this scream, Taos collapses on to her loom and lies motionless.*)

Darkness, end of Act 1

ACT 2
Scene 1

Courtyard noises. Voices of women and children. The shutters are closed. Someone is knocking and calling for Taos who, emerging from her nightmare, stands and as if she is sleepwalking, wets a towel to freshen her face.

THE ANCESTOR (*tenderly*): Wash your heart of all your sorrows of today and yesterday. Wash your heart, and your face will brighten.

TAOS (*rubbing her face vigorously*): Quiet Ancestor! You are wise, but for pity's sake, be quiet! (*The Ancestor returns to her beads. Feverishly Taos arranges her hair and scarves, takes a deep breath, tightens her belt, smoothes her dress and walks over to open the window. Siréna is silhouetted against the light.*)

TAOS (*relieved*): Oh! It's you!

SIRÉNA: Yes, it's me. Back from work. I must show you a book. Am I disturbing you?

TAOS: No, not at all! Would you like some tea?

SIRÉNA: Oh no! I've had more than enough tea. I drink it at home, I drink it at work. I just want a chat.

TAOS: I'll open the door for you.

SIRÉNA: Is it that time right now?

TAOS: What time?

SIRÉNA: The time of the month, of course!

TAOS: Shusshhhh! Do you have to talk so loudly? Let me open the door. (*Taos opens the door. Siréna enters.*)

SIRÉNA (*book in hand*): You look terrible!

TAOS: I'm worried about my mother.

SIRÉNA: You're not pregnant, are you?

TAOS: May God be listening! Bless her beautiful words!

SIRÉNA (*crouching down to embrace the grandmothe*r): Give me your blessing, Ancestor. They say I'm a bad girl when I go out with bare legs, but you know it's not true.

THE ANCESTOR (*stroking Siréna's head*): They do say you're a bad girl, but I know they're wrong. May God keep you and protect you!

SIRÉNA (*getting up*): God already protects us, Ancestor, by watching over you. (*looking around her.*) Where are the girls?

TAOS: Tidying the wood shed. They'll be there for hours.

SIRÉNA: Good. Let's enjoy it then.(T*aos pulls up a chair for Siréna who collapses into it.*) Phew!!! What a day!

TAOS (*going to the loom*): It certainly has been!

SIRÉNA (*raising a leg to massage, almost voluptuously*): Oh that pig! He was at it again.

TAOS: Shhhh! Who are you talking about?

SIRÉNA: My boss at work.

TAOS: The one you call the Postmaster?

SIRÉNA: That's the one. A serious, hardworking family man. Never a day goes by when he doesn't try to put his hand up my skirt.

TAOS: God don't listen! Don't listen to her!

SIRÉNA: Oh! God's heard it all . . . Let me tell you one thing: I have a reputation for being a slut. Well, if one day I actually decide to become one, then I hope at least to enjoy it . . .

TAOS: The sky will fall on our heads!

SIRÉNA: I'm not afraid of the sky. But I am afraid of men and their depravity. And their immense hypocrisy and peculiar taste for social injustice. I can be open with you, I can't be like this with my mother or my sisters. I chose you as a friend because you're a good listener, even though sometimes you'd rather not hear what I say.

TAOS: What about the Ancestor . . .

SIRÉNA (*amused*): Oh, the Ancestor. She knows everything. There's nothing I can teach her about men and their vile infamy and cruelty, even though they do talk about honor and nobility and glory. (*The Ancestor nods in silent agreement.*) Ah! I forgot. At least they acknowledge I have one good quality during these hard times: I earn my living, I bring in honest money . . . But they also criticize me for it . . . Life is never simple.

TAOS: I must get back to work! I have to keep busy! (*She sits back at her loom, working feverishly.*)

SIRÉNA (*laughing*): What are you doing?

TAOS: Keeping myself busy, as you can see. My mother is sick, there are many bad omens, and here you are speaking like a foul-mouthed girl. May God protect us!

SIRÉNA: Couldn't you just sit still for a second? Give your hands a rest?

TAOS: That would do no good! No good at all!

SIRÉNA: What are you playing at? Are you trying to stay pure when the world is rotten to the core? If you don't look at the dirt, you won't have a filthy mind, is that it?

TAOS: Tell me your book stories. They're far more beautiful.

SIRÉNA: Oh, stories of princes and princesses? Well, they don't exist anymore. Poor Taos, apart from your tea, your chicken couscous and your lamb and eggplants, your weaving, the circumcision ritual, and men who go away to work and come back in the summer to marry, what do you know about the world? (*Taos works in silence.*) Taos, what do you know about the world? Tell me.

TAOS: God is great.

SIRÉNA: I know He is, but what else?

TAOS: Mohammed is his prophet.

SIRÉNA: Tell me something I don't know. If you knew just how false this world is, that tea you make every day would taste like bile. And all that weaving that's ruining your eyesight, just as it wore out the eyes of the Ancestor, it would look ugly. But you don't know it. For you, the weaving will always be beautiful and the tea will always taste like heaven on earth. Perhaps it's better that way.

TAOS: Are you trying to make me cry?

SIRÉNA: No. But you are. With that secret pain festering in your heart, you're desperate to cry! (*Still weaving, Taos cries softly but with dignity. Siréna stands up and throws down her book.*) Why the mournful face? Who's died?

TAOS: Me!

SIRÉNA (*going over to her angrily*): I've never hit anybody yet, not even a child, not even that bastard who puts his hands up my skirt, but I could start right now. I'm younger than you and I know I should respect you, but come on now, tell me what's wrong! (*Taos tries to speak, tries hard to say something . . . but fails.*) Have you had an argument with your husband?

TAOS: If . . . if . . . if . . . only . . . it . . . was . . . that simple!

SIRÉNA (*silence*): I think I understand. (*She sits down again and rubs her legs, taking a moment to think.*) Ah! I know what it is . . . it doesn't matter how beautiful or worthy a woman is, if there's no child in the first year of marriage, she's always the one to blame. Unless I'm very much mistaken, he's disowning you.

TAOS (*with a sob*): No.

SIRÉNA: No?

TAOS: No.

SIRÉNA: What then?

TAOS: . . . another . . . wife . . .

SIRÉNA: The swine . . . They're all the same. They've no respect for the mothers of their own children.

TAOS: . . . not . . . him!

SIRÉNA: What do you mean? Who else could disown you or humiliate you with another wife?

TAOS: My mother-in-law.

SIRÉNA (*standing up and stamping with rage*): Ah! A second wife for that weakling? And it's his mother's doing? Poor guy, I mean I wouldn't want him to shine my shoes, but he's not that bad. And what does he have that you haven't? Compared to him you're a lioness! Are you asking for a second husband?

TAOS: Please be quiet! Don't make this pain any worse.

SIRÉNA: Pain? You ask for it! Any opportunity to suffer and you grasp it. The glory of suffering! We women are taught it from an early age. Great pain forges respect! (*Siréna sits back again and tugs her hair in constrained rage.*) What's the use? . . . Even if I tore out all my hair one by one, what good would it do? What do you say,

Ancestor? (*The Ancestor lifts her hand in a gesture of powerlessness.*) Well, you've seen much more than this, that's true. (*Siréna breathes deeply to calm herself. Taos is still weaving.*). As they say, let's speak little, but let's speak well.

TAOS: Exactly.

SIRÉNA: What can I do to help you? I mean, what are you planning to do first?

TAOS: To go crazy.

SIRÉNA: Do you want to hand them the knife to cut your throat? No, look, there must be something better to do. A ruse. Something to play for time . . .

TAOS: Yes.

SIRÉNA: Oh, so you've thought about it.

TAOS: Yes.

SIRÉNA: No sorcery I hope!

TAOS: I must get pregnant!

SIRÉNA: Dreams aren't enough, Taos! We need something real that'll give us time and a good reason to help you hold on for another year while you wait for that miracle. (*Siréna turns toward the grandmother.*) Ancestor, tell me, you've lived more than one life and you know more than all the men in this village put together, tell me . . . Has there ever been any male sterility in the family? (*The Ancestor lifts her emaciated arms and says nothing. She picks up her beads again.*) I see . . . There may have been some cases, but you'd never tell, even on threat of death. You've been calling on death for a long time . . . It's your familiar shadow . . . (*The Ancestor nods her head gently.*) Forgive me.

TAOS: She doesn't like being asked for forgiveness . . . Sometimes she says it's indecent to live so long . . . Thank God, she's not suffering.

SIRÉNA But what about your husband? How did he tell you?

TAOS: He told me nothing.

SIRÉNA: What, was it the old woman who spoke to you?

TAOS: It was her decision. She decides everything.

SIRÉNA: So all's not lost then!

TAOS: I see you don't know her as well as I do.   When she gives an order, it's as if it's already done.

SIRÉNA: And you don't fight back?

TAOS: How?

SIRÉNA: Say no.

TAOS: Who to?

SIRÉNA: Look, let me start again. All you do is say no . . . it's simple! Practice the art of denial in your heart. If you think no, then say no!

TAOS It's easy for you to say, you're young and beautiful. You're free, you go out when you want, no one can disown you. Oh! But I'm poor, I'm an orphan.

SIRÉNA (*angrily leaping to her feet*): That's enough! Enough of your whining. Look, since we're taking stock of the situation, how many hours a day do you work?

TAOS (*blankly*): What do you mean, how many hours?

SIRÉNA: I mean, how many hours do you sit at that loom? (*Taos laughs with bitter incredulity.*) Well. . . you can answer that, can't you?

TAOS I don't know. I never counted.

SIRÉNA: You don't even know if it's eight hours or five hours or even ten hours?

TAOS: No.

SIRÉNA: Well, you don't spend your whole life behind that contraption, do you?

TAOS: Yes, I do.

SIRÉNA: Explain it to me. I don't understand.

TAOS: There's nothing to understand. I learned to weave when I was eight. I'll soon be in my twenty-fifth year and in all that time I haven't stopped a single day. Not even on days of mourning or holidays.

SIRÉNA: And how many hours a day is that?

TAOS: I've no idea. I get up, I do what needs to be done around the house and then I sit down at my loom. In the evening when I get up it's because it's time to go to bed. I thought you knew all this.

SIRÉNA: Don't you even stop to eat?

TAOS: Not to eat, not to drink tea. I can do everything here, from this very spot. My work is weaving, so I weave.

SIRÉNA: You mean you only get up to go to the toilet?

TAOS: Of course, once or twice a day. But that's no time at all.

SIRÉNA: I'm beginning to understand. You're a good weaver and they don't want to lose you. So mother and son won't be sending you away. No. But they do want a good laying hen and so they'll look elsewhere to find one. And if it kills you, well too bad, though they might shed a tear for losing a good worker. Am I right?

TAOS: I suppose so.

SIRÉNA: Stand up.

TAOS: What?

SIRÉNA: I said stand up! Enough of this slavery!

TAOS: I can't.

SIRÉNA (*going over to Taos and pulling her up*): Will you listen to me?
We need to talk. Come sit over here, you talk better when you're
thinking straight. (*Siréna tries to pull Taos up. Eventually Taos gives in;
they both sit down on the ottoman. Siréna smiles.*) Isn't this more
comfortable? Now, relax. (*Taos remains tense, on her guard.*) Alright
. . . since you're so good at following orders, follow this one.
(*Silence.*) Relax. That's an order. (*Strangely, Taos leans back and
appears to relax. Silent tears stream down her face but the conversation
continues.*) Who told you your husband wants to marry again?

TAOS: Does anyone really need to tell me? I saw this misery coming
a long time ago.

SIRÉNA: If you spend your whole life inviting misery, it's bound to
call on you one day.

TAOS: I'm not inviting it, but I am afraid of it. I'm a daughter with
no father, a sister with no brother, a mother with no son. I have no
one to shield me, I go unprotected in public places, I have no
guardian.

SIRÉNA: But your mother-in-law came by this morning.

TAOS: Yes, she was the one that told me. And she said I was lucky
and I should be grateful. Now my husband won't want to confront
me face to face, so I doubt he'll be home for dinner. Courage was
never his strong point. But his mother is strong enough for two . . .
That reminds me . . . (*Taos feels along the ottoman and finds a book,
which she gives Siréna.*) Take this back. I don't want her to find it.

She was already angry this morning . . .

SIRÉNA: Because of me?

TAOS: Because of me, because of you, because of everything that doesn't happen the way . . . she wants it to.

SIRÉNA: Let me tell you one thing. I don't owe your mother-in-law anything. I'll take my book since I don't want to make more problems for you. Besides, I value this book and I don't want her throwing it on the fire.

TAOS: I'm not asking much. All I want is to speak to my husband. I might be able to convince him. He's very kind to me.

SIRÉNA: At night? (*Silence.*) I'm asking you if he's kind at night?

TAOS: Shhhh! The Ancestor's nearly paralyzed and she's blind as a bat, but she's not deaf.

SIRÉNA: The Ancestor's older than our century . . . there's nothing we can teach her. I just want to know if he's nice to you in bed. It's important, isn't it? I want to know if this man is worth your fight to keep him.

TAOS: Nice? I don't know . . . What does that mean? Oh, my God, forgive me these brazen thoughts!

SIRÉNA: Alright. Try looking at it this way . . . Listen carefully and keep calm. At night, when he lies down next to you — imagine . . . there he is lying beside you . . . And then gently, gently, or at least so I hope, in the dark he places his hands on your belly. Right here. Do you follow me? (*Siréna gently puts her hands on Taos' belly. Taos closes her eyes in a moment's reverie.*) There you are lying side by side. His hands on your belly. Now tell me: do you die of joy? . . . or misery? (*Now relaxed, Taos cries, almost from pleasure: it's an admission of joy that can only be expressed in tears.*) Tell me in words. (*Taos is still crying softly.*) I might look young, but deep down I'm like the Ancestor, I'm ancient. I'm weary of a world that's afraid of women, too afraid to let them live. I'm aged by the endless corruption of life. I can forgive you anything, even your happiness. (*Taos still says nothing.*) You won't forgive yourself for being happy, because that kind of happiness doesn't bear fruit. What's worse is that they want to take it all away from you. To speak your language, I forgive you and what's more, I'm happy for you. (*Silence. Siréna, whispering.*) So tell me, is it nice?

TAOS (*dreamily*): If I say no, what would that mean to you? And if I say yes, what could you imagine? You're still a virgin. How could you know?

SIRÉNA: You're right, I am still a virgin. But you can be sure I know more than you and I'm not ashamed to say so. You can talk to me the way you talk to your mother.

TAOS: But I never talk to my mother this way!

SIRÉNA: Well, talk to me! I know what it's like to be condemned, I won't condemn you.

TAOS: But how would you know if it's good or bad?

SIRÉNA: I've learned a lot from books.

TAOS: How can paper tell all the pain . . . all the pain . . . or all the joy of being a woman? Paper isn't flesh or blood.

SIRÉNA: Oh, but it can! And I understand because I know how to look and I know how to listen. Some women say that a man is such misery that to put up with him . . . it's better to be one of many wives. But these women have never known the real joys of the night. Not with a loving husband.

TAOS: My God, why do we have to talk about all this? People don't talk about these things.

SIRÉNA: But other women tell me . . . they often trust me with their secrets . . . They've told me that a caring husband, a loving husband is heaven on earth and they won't share him with another woman. (*Silence.*) So what about you? Do you swoon with joy when he comes near you? Do you long for his presence when he's away? When you're enjoying a ripe fig dripping with sweetness, do you dream of sharing it with him? One half in his mouth and the other half in yours? When you think of his 'divine fruit' while you're weaving away, do you feel like swallowing him there and then, and do your thighs go weak and wet? Do you feel your loins trembling in the middle of a crowd when suddenly you're both thinking the same thing and he's staring at you? Tell me! Tell me, what's a sour-faced mother-in-law compared to that? (*Silence.*) I'll ask you again . . . In the dark, do you swoon with joy when he gently puts his hands on your belly like this? (*Silence.*)

TAOS (*in a cry of pleasure*): YYYYYYEEEEEEESSSSSSSS!!!!!! Yes! Yes! Yyyyyyeeeesssssssss!!!!!

(*Taos collapses in exhaustion on Siréna's shoulder and cries with great sobs of relief. Siréna pats her head gently.*)

SIRÉNA: Well, I think we've taken a great step forward. Now, I'm going to see how I can help you.

TAOS: You can help me?

SIRÉNA (*lifting Taos's face*): Ah! The little schemer! She had it all planned.

TAOS (*wiping her eyes*): No . . . not at all. There's only one thing to do. Only one solution.

SIRÉNA: Well now! Only one? You're not planning to murder your mother-in-law are you? I could do that, but you couldn't.

TAOS: God forgive me for being the cause of such evil words! All because I'm in pain and I need a cure for all this suffering.

SIRÉNA: There, there . . . Let's talk about your runt of a husband. You know, I quite like him now I know he's gentle in the night.

Anyway, what's this cure of yours?

TAOS: You.

SIRÉNA: Ummm . . .

TAOS (*with renewed courage*): I mean it: it's you!

SIRÉNA: Do you mean to say that me, the brazen hussy, is going to convince your mother-in-law that you're her son's one true love?

TAOS: Not at all!

SIRÉNA: Well good, because she hates me. It wouldn't be any help for me to go flouncing about in front of her, speaking in your favor. She'd disown you on the spot!

TAOS: I know that.

SIRÉNA: So, what do you want me to do?

TAOS: Look at me.

SIRÉNA: I am.

TAOS: I'm not crazy.

SIRÉNA: I never said you were.

TAOS: I'm calm and I've thought this through carefully.

SIRÉNA: So it seems.

TAOS: Here it is: I thought that maybe you could, or you might, want to, umm . . . .

SIRÉNA: What?

TAOS: Marry my husband!

(*Siréna bursts into marvelous, splendid, and liberating laughter. It fills the stage and the entire theatre, a laugh on the verge of tears, incapable of entertaining such a notion. She tries to hold it back so as not to hurt her friend, but it clearly shows her rejection of such an incongruous and unexpected request . . . Confused, Taos withers.*)

SIRÉNA (*in fits of giggles*): You must be . . . you must be really desperate, my poor Taos! To come to this! I don't want to hurt you, but I really don't want to marry your husband. Never!

TAOS: Why not? He's very kind. One night for you, one night for me. You'll have children and I'll bring them up . . . You'll live like a princess. I do everything around the house and I never complain.

SIRÉNA: Oh no! No!

TAOS: Like many men around here, I'm sure he dreams of an emancipated girl. I'd rather it be you. You have a good heart; you wouldn't hurt me. And you have light skin and fair hair: my husband will like that!

SIRÉNA: No! No! No! What a ludicrous idea!

TAOS: You'd have anything you want. I'd leave all the jewels to you . . .

SIRÉNA: I'm sorry. This is ridiculous!

TAOS: You could spend all day reading . . .

SIRÉNA: My dear heart, I want to help you . . . not sacrifice myself.

TAOS: Why don't you want to? It would be a fine life for you. You wouldn't have to work anymore and have those hands up your skirt . . . You'd be near your parents.

SIRÉNA: The answer, my dear, is no. There are a thousand reasons why. It just so happens that I like my work. I'm about to be

ack

transferred, I'm leaving for the city — I came to tell you. There are so many beautiful girls in the city, no one will give me a second look, and I'll be left in peace. Besides, I don't want to marry . . . unless my beloved father orders me to . . . and even then . . . I can't stand weaklings who tremble at the sight of their mothers. I'm a girl, and I was never afraid of my father. Let me tell you this: you're young and beautiful, but you don't know it. Tonight, when your husband comes home, tell yourself: "I'm young and beautiful" and you will be. He'll realize that and he won't want to leave you anymore. I have to go now. With all my heart I hold you close, and I give you all my courage and my rebellion . . . I'll see you soon . . .

(Siréna leaves. Taos collapses on the ottoman.)

Darkness

Scene 2

Night. The same décor. A night-light silhouettes objects in the room. The loom looks threatening and ghostlike. The dozing grandmother is silhouetted clearly, flanked on either side by the two little slaves. On the ottoman, Taos is asleep, half sitting and half lying. All is silent. A man's footsteps are heard and the door opens. Driss, the husband, enters. He starts with surprise when he sees his wife in the living room. The Ancestor and the servants Drifa and Draïfa, usually spend the night in the same place where they rest during the day.

DRISS *(groaning)*: Hey . . . What's all this?

TAOS *(waking up)*: Good Heavens, I must have fallen asleep!

DRISS *(standing, angrily)*: Why are you sleeping here?

TAOS *(getting up, confused)*; Forgive me . . . I wanted . . . I wanted to talk to you.

DRISS *(aggressively)*: Well that's an unusual request!

TAOS (*wringing her hands*): It's the situation that's . . . unusual.

DRISS (*amazed*): Since when do you answer me back? Normally you never say more than one word at a time.

TAOS: It only takes one word to obey an order.

DRISS (*incredulous, walking over to examine his wife more closely*): Something's changed you since this morning.

TAOS: Well, that's true.

DRISS: Tradition says I have the right to beat you, but I won't. So unless you've anything more to say . . . I'm an honest man, but it's late and I'm tired.

TAOS: You're a good man, so listen to me. For just once in our life, listen to me.

DRISS: It's been a strange day for listening to a lot of people. A little more strangeness might be a fitting end. Go ahead, woman, I'm listening.

TAOS: Forgive me for remaining seated. I've no more strength left in my body. And forgive me the unforgivable. I've suffered too much today and what I'm about to say might be risky.

DRISS (*pacing the floor*): Risky for who?

TAOS: For me. For you. For us . . . I want to talk about what is usually left unsaid.

DRISS: So why say it?

TAOS: I must say it!

DRISS (*irritated*): Well, say it then!

TAOS: I never had anyone else to love except my mother. All the men in my family abandoned us early on. You know that. I was born virtually abandoned. Then I was married. Now I have neither father nor sons, you are the only man in my life.

DRISS (*shocked*): What the . . . ?

TAOS: It's never said outright, but everyone believes a woman's first true love is her eldest son.

DRISS: Are you crazy? You must be crazy!

TAOS: Yes, I am crazy. I have been crazy since this morning. So let it be my excuse if I tell you that a woman's true love can be her husband! I can say this – before you I had neither father nor brother to love. All my affection was lavished on you the moment I saw you on our wedding night . . .

DRISS: God is listening, woman. Be quiet!

TAOS: I know. It's not decent to speak of love here. But this evening I'd rather speak than wither away and die in silence . . . Legally I have the right to speak to you and I'm asking you . . . (*She shouts.*) I'm asking you to be patient. You and me together is something that exists and mustn't die. Won't you wait a while?

DRISS (*curtly*): Mother says . . .

TAOS: I live with you . . . Tell me what's in your heart.

DRISS (*annoyed*): Everyone says . . .

TAOS: What's in your heart . . .

DRISS: I don't like making decisions . . . I want to go to sleep.

TAOS: Can't you give me . . . a little . . . time?

DRISS: Mother's already decided everything. I don't see why we have to go over it again. It's extremely tedious.

TAOS (*shaking with grief*): But . . . it's about us. This is our business.

DRISS: It's mainly Mother's business. She knows how to deal with this. She's already decided what's to be said and done. She even asked me to be especially kind to you tonight. Now don't make me angry.

TAOS (*desperate*): She, she can decide . . . but what can I do?

DRISS: Do like me. Obey.

TAOS: So you too are abandoning me?

DRISS: Not at all. We're keeping you.

TAOS: Of course . . . for the house . . . for the work . . .

DRISS: Would you rather take up the teacher's satchel and play the fool in schools?

TAOS: I wouldn't. But others would!

DRISS: Here's what I have to say: I could have one wife, two wives, dozens of wives . . . One child, ten children, hundreds. But if I had a choice, I'd abandon all my wives and children any day to stay with my mother. You can change your wife, you can have children well into old age. That's all fine and good, it's a man's place to head the tribe. But a tribe is exchangeable merchandise. You only have one mother . . . one irreplaceable mother. You can't change her, and you're happy to be with her for life. May God keep her for many more years! There . . . My mother has spoken and I'll obey.

TAOS (*heartbroken*) : So . . . in this house, I'm nothing?

DRISS: That's right, you're nothing. I can throw you out right now, in the dead of night and no one would argue with me. Isn't that true? Can't you see? I'm a good-hearted man and I wouldn't throw a dog out in the night. That's my final word . . . I wish you goodnight.

(*Driss leaves. Taos collapses on the ottoman and cries softly. The two servants get up quietly in their half-sleep and curl up next to her, crying with her. The Ancestor is awake now and raises her arms in a gesture of powerlesssness.*)

Darkness

Scene 3

A brief and very animated scene that opens with the arrival of the bride and closes with Taos's lamentations. It is the same set as when the Ancestor is alone, except that when the bride, Mimia, is brought in, another handloom is installed. The ottoman is decorated with a golden cloth and there are new rugs on the floor.

We hear ululations and songs approaching. Enter a richly dressed assembly carrying a heavy palanquin. They parade slowly toward the middle of the room before carefully setting it down. The songs and ululations continue. The group includes Nahnouha, Taos, and the two servants. They open the palanquin and very gently lift out the bride to install her on the ottoman. The bride is enormous, beautiful, fat, and monumental. Nahnouha points to the loom and the two servants hurry to set it up. With a commanding gesture, Nahnouha dismisses Taos who moves to a downstage corner. While the servants are busy with the handloom, Nahnouha oversees the bride with a stern expression. When the servants have finished their work, Nahnouha imperiously points them to a downstage curtain, which until now has remained unnoticed.

Driss appears in the doorway dressed like a prince. With a commanding gesture, Nahnouha indicates his duty by pointing to the bride. Driss approaches his mother without glancing at the bride and bows respectfully. He remains bowed down. The servants run to the downstage curtain and slowly draw it across: it is a vast, immaculate sheet, a symbol of the bride's virginity. It isolates Taos from their conjugal life. She remains alone before the audience. A final ululation is heard.

The stage gradually darkens and only Taos remains, hidden in the shadows, lamenting her grief.

TAOS (*rocking and cradling herself, then striking her face and body*):
Ahhhhhh! Oooohhhhhh! Abandoned, wretched, orphan! I saw it

coming, I always knew I'd be deserted again. I'm a good maid, but I never made a good wife.

Oh!!! Listen all you sleeping people, listen all who are still awake, I don't deserve this punishment. Reduced to the rank of servant, reduced to worthless property. Here I am crying in the wilderness, while my husband, my spouse, the only man in my life, is enjoying his sex in the sex of another woman. They say it's my right to go crazy overnight . . . I'm humiliated, and that's what they wanted: humiliation. It's written in the Holy Scriptures, it says to men: "If you want to debase your wife, bring another woman into your house." Well, here I am debased, here I am dead, here I am useless. I shout out and no one hears, I shout out because no one hears! Tonight I can still play the mad woman. Ahhh! Ahhhh! Ahhh! My God, this brings some relief. I must sleep now, I must get some sleep. Tomorrow morning I have to make crêpes to celebrate the marriage of my husband to my co-wife . . .

Darkness

Scene 4

Stage lights come up on a single white sheet hiding everything. The two servants enter, position themselves on one side of the stage near the sheet, waiting. An ululation gives them the starting signal. They slowly draw the sheet, pulling it across to one side of the set, revealing another sheet — but this one is stained with blood. The deflowering of the bride has taken place. The ululations begin again, reaching a crescendo before dying away. Only then do the two servants draw the blood stained sheet, revealing the same set as the night before, with only the Ancestor present.

The servants leave. Taos bursts in, with a decisive air. She places a chair in the middle of the room and sets up the Qasa, a large wooden bowl into which she briskly pours flour and water and a little salt. She mixes this together to make the crêpe batter, which she stirs noisily (slap . . . slap . . . slap) in the correct manner.

Enter Nahnouha, leaning on a cane. She seems to have aged overnight.

TAOS: Good morning to you.

NAHNOUHA: Good morning to you too. If you want your day to be good, it will be good.

TAOS (*continuing her work*): God is listening.

NAHNOUHA: Let Him listen! I kept watch last night until my son became a real man and I can tell you that it happened at four o'clock in the morning. I'm a proud woman. Some men take as long as a week . . . I'll leave you to your celebrations, I'm going home to rest. It's strange, but sometimes I feel old . . .

TAOS: Go and rest, you deserve it. I'll take care of everything. That's what I'm here for.

NAHNOUHA: I'm happy to see that you're already devoting yourself to your duties as first wife. It's encouraging. If I were less proud, I'd thank you, but I am proud. However . . . (*Taos keeps working in silence.*) However, I do have something for you . . . don't you want to know what it is?

TAOS: No, frankly I don't. My day is dictated by tradition, and I'll keep to it. I want to be a good first wife, since that's my rightful title from now on. When you don't have the means to leave, then you must at least have the humility to stay.

NAHNOUHA: You don't have the means . . . you have no gold . . . and on that subject, I bequeath to you the keys to my garden, in view of your rank as first wife . . . From now on, you have free reign in the garden. Here, take them. With these keys, I'm giving you my entire house and all its secrets.

TAOS (*stopping her work*): The keys to your garden? That patch of ground with those ratty turnips that aren't good enough even for soup? Should I feel honored?

NAHNOUHA: Yes, you should. I'm giving you the keys to all my secrets and all my treasures . . . From this day forth, we're on the same side.

TAOS (*surprised*): The keys to your strength?   The keys to your power?

NAHNOUHA: Exactly. Here! Take them. You won't regret it.

TAOS: Well, alright . . . if that's what you want . . .

(*She takes the keys from her mother-in-law and puts them in "safekeeping" in her bodice.*)

NAHNOUHA I'm leaving now. I'll be back in a few days and you'll tell me everything. Remember, you are mistress of this house now.

(*Nahnouha leaves. Noisily Taos returns to her work. She stirs the batter, but with more vigor, beating her words out in the rhythm of her actions. She weeps and cries out her lament.*)

TAOS: Oh! How right you were, Siréna! My honey has lost its sweetness. From now on, whatever I do, my life will be poisoned. Not only honey, it's the same for sugar and laughter and bread and water, everything's turning sour.   And it'll be more sour by the day . . . (*The two servants approach. Taos angrily.*) What is it? Isn't today like any other day? Do you need me to tell you what to do around the house? (*The two young girls point to the sheets that are still on the line. Taos looking at the sheets.*)   Yes!   Take them down! Everyone's seen them! Everyone knows. (*She returns to her work and the servants delicately take down the sheets and, carrying them like relics, they leave.*

Taos continues to work in silence, but gradually we hear a plaintive lullaby from an uncertain source. The song becomes louder and it becomes apparent that it is Taos who is singing. She sings as she sobs and it is very beautiful. Then she stops singing and stirring the batter. She lifts the hem of her dress to dry her eyes.*). From this day I won't even have time to cry. There will be too much work to do.

(*She picks up the large bowl and leaves.*)

Darkness

Scene 5

Taos and Mimia are weaving. They sit at their looms. Taos is lively and adept, Mimia, on the other hand, is enormously fat, as well as being pregnant, and breathes heavily while fumbling with the wool.

TAOS: Calm down, you're getting too upset! Do you think that's how we make a beautiful carpet?

MIMIA: No.

TAOS: Well then?

MIMIA: But I don't want to make beautiful carpets!

TAOS: Well then, tell me, what do you want to do?

MIMIA: Nothing.

TAOS: Nothing at all?

MIMIA: I want to have the baby.

TAOS: That will come.

MIMIA: Just look at me.

TAOS: I am looking at you.

MIMIA: But you can't see me.

TAOS: You're mixing the purple with the red. Pay attention.

MIMIA: It's true. I don't feel like doing anything. All I want to do is sleep until it's all over.

TAOS: It will soon be over. Be careful.

MIMIA: What?

TAOS: You're tangling all the wool. You're making more work for yourself. Do you want some milk, or perhaps some tea?

MIMIA: I don't want anything. I just want to die.

TAOS: It's lucky we're alone . . . don't ever say that again . . . that kind of language is not welcome here.

MIMIA: But it's true.

TAOS: It's normal for women about to give birth to feel weary and sad. But don't complain about it. You're big and heavy and fat and pregnant, and you're exhausted. I'm sprightly, thin, and healthy, and I never feel tired — but you're far better off than I am.

MIMIA (*stands up suddenly):* I can't take it anymore.

TAOS (*getting up to take her by the arm*): What's troubling you?

MIMIA: Why should I tell you?

TAOS: Because we're family. Remember, we share the same husband.

MIMIA: How could I . . . how could I forget that?

TAOS: What do you mean?

MIMIA: It's all I ever think about! There I am knocked out from sheer exhaustion, laid out like a heavy lump snoring, and all the time my life is feeding another life inside me, and what's he doing? He's with you! He's taking care of you. Half the time his mind is on you, not to mention his body. And now I can't be his woman, maybe he's keeping it all for you.

(*After a moment of stupefied silence, Taos lets go of Mimia's arm, moves away ,and bursts into uncontrollable laughter.*)

TAOS (*in fits of laughter*): My God, my God . . . Are you . . . are you

. . . are you . . . jealous???!!!

MIMIA: Yes . . . yes I am . . . and it's killing me. I'm dying of jealousy.

TAOS (*taking her gently by the arm again*): Come, sit down. There . . . there. If somebody comes in they'd see us chatting away and doing nothing useful. That would bring shame on the house.

MIMIA (*sitting down again*): How can you stay so calm when he's away all day and night? He only comes home to sleep and to eat and to . . .

TAOS: Quiet! Don't let your thoughts run away with you.

MIMIA: He's our husband, but he lives without us.

TAOS: What's unusual about that? All husbands live that way. Men live outside the house and only come home for their bodily needs.

MIMIA: So we're just a bodily need?

TAOS: It's better to see it, since it puts things into perspective.

MIMIA: You never went to school, where do you know all this from?

TAOS (*whispering*): I've spent a lot of time talking with a girl who knows how to read.

MIMIA: How lucky!

TAOS: That's not all! She comes from a good family. She's a friend. She's shown me books with photographs and drawings.

MIMIA: Oh!

TAOS: But no one knows!

MIMIA: Ah! That's good.

TAOS: That's how I know how a man is made.

MIMIA: What do you mean . . . you've seen?

TAOS: Yes. In a book . . . inside and out.

MIMIA: What's it like?

TAOS: HORRIBLE! Just horrible! I wouldn't want you to see it, my dear.

MIMIA: I don't want to see it!

TAOS: Ah! I've made you forget your misery.

MIMIA: No. I'm still jealous.

TAOS: Who of?

MIMIA: Of you!

TAOS: You should be jealous of his mother — she's the real woman in his life.

MIMIA: The old cow, I couldn't care less about her. The moment I hand her a boy, she'll be at my feet. But all those women out there . . .

TAOS: Poor man. He never even looks at them.

MIMIA: How do you know? He doesn't take you with him.

TAOS: I know him.

MIMIA: But what about you?

TAOS: What?

MIMIA: You? What do you do with my husband at night?

TAOS: Oh! My dear, I expected anything but this. I can't imagine you're jealous of a tree that bears no fruit, when you carry all the promises of the earth. You're carrying life within you, the promise of life, the proof of love, the future itself! You should pity me.

MIMIA: Tell me what he does to you, tell me what he says to you!

TAOS: You're persistent, but since no one can hear us . . .

MIMIA: Except the Ancestor . . .

TAOS: The Ancestor is a living tomb, she won't harm us . . .

MIMIA: Well then tell me! Tell me the truth! Tell me now!

TAOS: Would you believe me?

MIMIA: Yes.

TAOS: He talks about . . .

MIMIA: Who?

TAOS: You!

MIMIA: The nights he spends with you he talks about me?

TAOS: Yes.

MIMIA: You want me to believe that?

TAOS: I don't want you to believe anything. I'm answering your question.

MIMIA: And you're not jealous?

TAOS: I can't read, but I have a good memory.

MIMIA: What's that got to do with it?

TAOS: The book that Siréna showed me was very complicated, but I remember some of it. One section was all about a man with several wives.

MIMIA: In writing?

TAOS: Of course. One of the women said that in that situation a wife can't possibly be jealous.

MIMIA: Really!

TAOS: Yes! She claims that you can't be jealous in a "democracy" of the absurd.

MIMIA: I don't understand.

TAOS: The main thing is, you should be reassured. Do you feel better?

MIMIA (*examining her co-wife*): Umm . . .

TAOS: See, everything's fine. Let me just say this: I'm an orphan, with no father, no brother and no honor . . . so I'm glad I haven't been disowned. I have a roof over my head and food on my plate. So you see, in the end I don't really care about your husband.

MIMIA: So you're saying that . . .

TAOS: He's more like a troubled brother with me. He talks about you, your pregnancy, he laughs, tells me his worries, asks my advice, and then falls asleep feeling better. I'm becoming his mother. And that suits me fine. These days I sleep soundly . . . And now you're giving me a little one. What more could I ask for?

MIMIA: Swear on it! Give me your word, so that I can sleep at night.

TAOS (*comforting Mimia*): Well, I sleep peacefully, and from now on, so will you. I swear you will!!! (*They hug each other. The servants' mischievous laughter is heard from the courtyard. Suddenly Mimia has a bad turn and collapses silently onto her loom. Taos responds immediately: with soft reassuring words she carefully lifts her up, and with some difficulty, leads her over to the ottoman. Mimia is having difficulty breathing and Taos, somewhat unnerved, pulls a handkerchief from her bodice to fan and wipe her face.)* You'll bring me our little one, won't you? You'll bring him to me, say you will!

(Mimia moans softly. Taos loosens her dress a little and tries to make her more comfortable by lying her down. The two servants come running in, one behind the other. Taos chases after them. All three exit. From the courtyard we hear Taos' scolding voice.

Mimia has fallen asleep. The grandmother seems to be listening carefully as if to be sure no one else is in the room, except Mimia who is snoring softly. Then she freezes: someone is coming. Enter Driss brusquely, holding a piece of meat in his hand. He seems upset to see his wife sleeping, but puts down the meat without a word.

Enter Taos, who hides when she sees Driss. Thinking he is alone, Driss stands over the sleeping Mimia admiring her. Then, leaning forward, he touches her belly with fear and adoration, as if it were molten gold).

DRISS *(murmuring)*: Thank you for making me a man. *(He stands and exits.)*

(Taos appears, but freezes again when the Ancestor, encouraged by Driss's departure, begins to move. The grandmother coughs, listens carefully, then waits. She coughs and listens again. In the silence of the room, Mimia's regular breathing can be heard clearly. Then, with slow but confident movements, revealing a sure knowledge of the room, the Ancestor drags herself along, feeling her way with objects and furniture, going directly over to Mimia. Reaching the sleeping young woman, she pulls an amulet out from her bodice and makes mysterious gestures intended to protect the pregnant woman and her offspring.

It is a silent, touching scene. The blind woman who, with great dignity, has shuffled over on her backside, engages in an extremely impressive ritual: she sits at Mimia's feet, while she sleeps peacefully. The Ancestor makes circles over the young woman's great belly with the amulet. She lifts her dead eyes to the sky in prayer, puts away the amulet, kisses the tips of her fingers, as at the end of a prayer, and leaves a little kiss on Mimia's lap as a sign of her love.   She goes back to her corner, unhurriedly.

Taos has seen everything, but returns to the courtyard to give the Ancestor the impression that no one has seen her. She is heard calling for the servants again, with little conviction. The Ancestor takes up her beads.

Enter Nahnouha, raising her cane over Mimia).

NAHNOUHA (*angrily*): God forgive me for raising an angry stick to a childbearing woman. My anger is justified, but I won't hit the mother of my little ones. You're sleeping instead of working, using pregnancy as an excuse. Pregnant horses work, pregnant cows work, I won't let you ruin my house just because you come from an important family. I won't allow it! Where is my first daughter, Taos? I left her in charge of this honorable house, and here it is abandoned!!! Ah! This will be my ruin!..(*She removes the shawl that serves as her veil and loosens her clothing as if she were suffocating. She shakes her cane at the Ancestor.*) This is your fault, old woman. You're as guilty as any female in this house. You let this happen. You watched it all fall apart. It's total chaos! And you tell me nothing! You give me no information at all. In fact I wonder just who's side you're on. (*To Mimia*) Get up! That's an order, get up! I know you're weighed down but this is scandalous, sleeping all day! Besides, no woman in my house — and this is still my house — no woman sleeps while the sun is up, except this relic. (*She points at the Ancestor. Mimia tries in vain to stand up. Nahnouha, still shouting.*) I'm utterly ashamed. I hope no one ever sees sleeping like this in my house. I'd have to display my shame in public. Stand up. (*Mimia, still sleeping, stirs.*) I said stand up!

THE ANCESTOR (*pleading*): Help her.

NAHNOUHA: What? Are you giving me orders now?

THE ANCESTOR: God can see you, old woman. Don't forget that one day you'll be just as ancient and feeble as me. And then you might regret all the evil you've done.

NAHNOUHA (*scornfully*): Such insolence! What can I say, words fail me. Old woman, you'd be without food or drink if it wasn't for me. I'll find a way to punish you. But now, I want that woman, fed by my son's own sweat and toil, to get up and get back to work. (*Mimia sleeps on. Enter Taos, who hurries over to Mimia to shake her awake.*) I'll suffer everything before I reach old age: are you leaving your greeting for tomorrow?

TAOS: (*calming down, she embraces her mother-in-law*): Forgive me if you will. I'm not thinking straight. The servants are a nuisance, they won't get down to work, we can't get the fire started, and Mimia has fainted from the heat! I'll wake her up.

NAHNOUHA: At last some sense! Wake her up immediately! I've had enough of all this! (*Nahnouha sits down on the ottoman. Taos leans over to fan Mimia's face with a scarf.*) When I think . . . I'm not even sure she has a boy in that great belly of hers. Did she really have to eat so much and get this fat?

TAOS: She's stopped eating since she's been pregnant. She can't even keep anything down.

NAHNOUHA: So she says. I don't remember being so fat myself.

TAOS: It's her nature. She comes from an obese family. Maybe there are two in there.

NAHNOUHA: Two girls? Disaster!

TAOS: Two boys!

Darkness

Scene 6

Great excitement and panic. Drifa enters with the midwife.

TAOS (*taking Mimia's hand*): Draïfa, boil up some water, quickly.

NAHNOUHA: Goodness me, you're speaking like a matron now

you have another wife to command. I hardly recognize you!

MIMIA: Taos, it hurts. I think I'm going to die. My heart is failing.

TAOS: If we died every time we gave birth, there wouldn't be many people left in the world.

MIMIA: In the name of God and the Ancestor, I give you what's in my belly, Taos, my sister.   Take good care of him.

NAHNOUHA: What's in your belly belongs to me, whether you live or die.

TAOS: I'm holding tight. I'm right here.

MIDWIFE (*touching Mimia*): I think it's coming.

Darkness, then light

Set: Mimia's bedroom. It is large and painted pastel pink. The gentleness of the setting should contrast with the violence of the events that follow. On a rudimentary bed, tipped up towards the audience, Mimia squats in front of the mid-wife, with her head up so we can see her face.
    Taos stands next to Mimia, holding her hand. On the other side, one of the servants stands at Mimia's head. At Mimia's feet, on one side Nahnouha, with her back to the audience, leans on her cane; the other servant stands on the opposite side. The women all have their dresses tucked up, as if about to cross a river.

MIMIA: Hold me . . .

TAOS: I won't let you go.

MIDWIFE: I think it's coming.

MIMIA: No. Noooooo.

MIDWIFE: There, there, my dear. Keep God in your heart . . . and let your child come to me.

NAHNOUHA (*to the midwife*): I hope for your sake it's a boy. If it's a girl, you can leave her where she is . . .

MIDWIFE: Don't blaspheme so loudly, grandmother. At delicate times like this . . . God might take offence.

NAHNOUHA (*raising her cane*): God is on my side. For four years now He's watched my heart bleed, but today He'll give me my reward. A boy. That's what I want! I demand it! Keep that in mind, lady, if you want a handsome sum of money, instead of your usual cup of coffee.

MIDWIFE: It's nature's work . . .

MIMIA: Ahhhhh! No!

MIDWIFE: Come on, deary, help me. Push with all your might! Push with everything you've got. Tonight your sleep will be empty and light.

MIMIA (*suffering*): I see Him. It's the end.

TAOS (*holding her hand*): I'm right here. Can you feel me here? Come on now, give me the little one. Give him to me and bring your suffering to an end.

MIDWIFE: Bring me the towels . . .

(*The servants obey.*)

MIMIA: Oh my God, help me.

MIDWIFE: Yes God, help us! Let this little gift of life come to us. Let this long awaited life come into being. We'll protect him . . .

TAOS (*bringing Mimia's hand to her mouth*): And we'll raise him.

THE SERVANTS: We'll feed him and care for him.

NAHNOUHA: To protect him from the evil eye, he'll be small and puny, ugly and dull.

TAOS (*whispering so the evil spirits don't hear*): He'll be protected from the evil eye and will be big, strong, handsome, and brilliant.

NAHNOUHA: He'll be stupid, and we won't love him.

TAOS (*whispering*): He'll be intelligent and we'll adore him.

MIMIA: My God, I've never failed you . . . never let you down . . . Why all this suffering, why are you tearing me apart like this, ahhhhhhhh!

NAHNOUHA: Shut up and stop bellowing like a cow! You'll bring down all the evil spirits!

TAOS: The evil spirits are busy elsewhere . . .

(*Mimia howls and arches back*).

MIDWIFE: She won't let it happen. Hold her down.

TAOS: No! I'll take her. I'll hold her in my arms. She's my sister. She's my daughter. She's in pain. She needs me.

NAHNOUHA: Be quiet, first wife! No one's asking you to do that much!

TAOS: I promised her!

NAHNOUHA: Silence. Let's get on with it ladies! . . . (*In a single movement, the servants pull the sashes from their aprons and tie Mimia's hands and feet to the bed, lashing them firmly. Nahnouha, unsatisfied*) That won't stop her screaming. (*Pulling scarves from their pockets, the servants gag Mimia. Nahnouha is now satisfied.*) Now we can work in peace.

TAOS (*horrified*): Look at her, like a sacrificial lamb!

NAHNOUHA: Yes. A sacrifice she freely consented to.

MIDWIFE: Ah! I can feel him. The little man's here. Is this earth ready to welcome him?

(On stage left, the servants set up a long mattress on which all the babies who are to be born will be laid. They return to their sentinel positions. What follows is somewhat mechanical: a torrent of blood . . . Mimia screams, followed by a baby's cry.)

MIDWIFE *(lifting up the baby, hands it to Taos, then cuts the umbilical cord with giant scissors, saying):* It's a girl!

TAOS *(laying the baby on its bed):* Chems! I name you Chems, after my mother, since you're a girl. You'll be Chems, the sun to brighten my life!

NAHNOUHA: A girl! God has turned his back on this house.

TAOS: It's a girl! And she has a place in this house. *(A light goes out: the stage darkens slightly. A servant weeps. The choir of servants becomes increasingly mournful, marking the unwanted births, as well as the passing of time. An older Chems is present at her mother's labors. Taos lines up the baby-dolls along the mattress.)* It's a girl! My daughter! A gift from God; she will live.

(The same flashing moment is repeated six times. Each time, a light goes out and the pink room takes on an air of mourning.)

THE CHOIR: Another girl! It's the year of the locusts.
            Another girl! Here come the floods!
            A girl again! It's the summer of drought!
            A girl again! They say it's war!
            Another girl! There are earthquakes!
            Another girl! The crops have failed! The year of all
              hardship!

(The seventh time, things are even worse. The torrent of blood is heavier. Mimia screams louder and longer. The baby's cry is more painful. The

midwife has greater difficulty extracting her from her mother's belly. Finally, she hands the baby to Taos and cuts the umbilical cord).

MIDWIFE: It's a girl.

NAHNOUHA: You've failed. Where is the male child you promised me?

MIDWIFE: Lift your eyes to the sky and talk to your Maker. I act only as intermediary, and I'm very tired.

NAHNOUHA: It's another girl, it's the seventh girl, I can't wail out my cry of joy, I can't wail my cry of victory!

MIDWIFE: You weren't the one giving birth.

NAHNOUHA: The pain of lost honor is greater than the pain of giving birth.

MIDWIFE: The time that has turned your hair white has dulled your memory: you've even forgotten the pain of childbirth.

NAHNOUHA: Find me a boy in that worthless, fertile belly. See if there's some forgotten fruit, a male child to fill me with pride.

MIDWIFE: There's nothing left. This woman's exhausted. I fear for her life.

NAHNOUHA: Her life isn't important. Look again. Cut with your scissors and scrape with your knife. Bring me the final fruit of the harvest, so I can cry with joy and be heard from afar!

TAOS: The mother's resting. She more than deserves it.

MIDWIFE: We must free her. Take off that gag and those ties. Her breathing is weak.

(With infinitely gentle gestures, Taos frees her co-wife, singing a sad lament. The midwife gets up, covering Mimia's seemingly sleeping body with a blanket.)

NAHNOUHA: It's a disgrace! Tell me, abortionist, are you going to leave this house without giving us anything?

MIDWIFE *(touching Mimia's forehead)*: It would be better for all of us, Grandmother, if once and for all you'd be quiet, before things are said that can't be undone . . . death is lurking. Let's not encourage it by inviting it in with desperate words.

NAHNOUHA *(raising her cane)*: Be quiet yourself, you incompetent woman! You'll not even have your cup of coffee!

MIDWIFE: Quite right . . . I never ask for money where there's mourning.

TAOS: Don't say such things, kind woman. You know the pain of life. You frighten me. I must see to the children.

MIDWIFE: Fear is futile. I hear the gates of heaven opening.

TAOS: No! No!

MIDWIFE *(looking at the mother)*: Now you are free of all earthly bonds. Your body is with us but your pure spirit is already flying toward God's heaven, where you are welcome. Forgive me for the suffering I inflicted on you, even when your heart could no longer bear it. I was only doing my work. You purified yourself through childbirth and torture. Sleep now, since you are no longer with us. *(The mid-wife takes off one of her scarves, closes Mimia's eyes and, folding her scarf length ways, makes a chin strap for her. The women all fall to their knees and weep.)*

Slow fade to black, end of Act 2

ACT 3
Scene 1

Time has passed . . .
The stage is empty, except for the presence of the Ancestor.
Enter Siréna, book in hand, looking despondent.

SIRÉNA: Ancestor? (*The Ancestor lifts her head and turns towards the visitor.*) Ancestor? . . . where are you today, closer to life or to death? (*The Ancestor beckons. Siréna approaches, takes the old woman's outstretched hand and sits down facing her.*)

ANCESTOR (*whispering*): Why is your heart crying in silence? Why cry, my child of laughter?

SIRÉNA: My father . . .

ANCESTOR: Your father is a good man, they broke the mould when he was born. He wouldn't harm you.

SIRÉNA: No . . . he's ill.

ANCESTOR: God is all powerful! He brings misfortune, and he can take it away.

SIRÉNA (*holding back the tears*): Seriously ill. Maybe incurable.

ANCESTOR: Everything is cured by death, take this to heart my child. But your father is too young for that.

SIRÉNA (*waving the book about*): Even these learned words can't help me cure my father.

ANCESTOR: How can books cross the line between life and death? If you wish to rid yourself of pain, do it now, strong daughter, while all the women are busy. Let it flood out.

SIRÉNA (*on the brink of tears*): The flood would drown us both!

ANCESTOR: What does that matter? You'll soon feel better.

SIRÉNA: Is crying all that is left?

ANCESTOR: Resign yourself. Sometimes we have no choice.

(*A somewhat unreal scene follows, where Siréna cries like a baby, twisting and turning in the Ancestor's lap, while the Ancestor maintains her eternal calm, consoling and soothing her pain with soft words and gentle gestures. Like a baby, Siréna eventually falls asleep, curled up with her head on the Ancestor's belly, her thighs uncovered and the book resting against her crotch. The Ancestor may also fall asleep. Enter Driss hurriedly*).

DRISS: I want it grilled. Taos? Where are you? I want my meat grilled today. Didn't I tell you already? I'm sick of stew! Taos!

(*Silence. Driss approaches, noticing nothing at first, but gradually makes out the Ancestor in her corner with an unfamiliar shape in her lap. Intrigued, Driss walks over silently, he stops, leans over to take a closer look, and then slowly steps back, stunned and delighted. He returns to center stage, not believing his eyes, and then goes back to look at Siréna again, this time more closely and for longer. She is a stunning woman, revealing voluptuous thighs, but hiding her crotch beneath a book.*

Driss is smitten and dumbfounded. He turns, comes back, seems irresistibly drawn, walking on tip toes to avoid making any noise and putting an end to his state of rapture. He dares not wake Siréna; he just keeps staring at her, on offer and inaccessible at once.

He moves back down to front of stage, and utters a sigh of well-being. The Ancestor, wakes and lifts her head, listening, she knows who is there. In his excited state of bliss, Driss fails to notice, and comes back to Siréna. He tries to take the book, tries to touch it, but doesn't dare, he just can't manage, he stands back and looks around to see if anyone is coming; he tries to touch Siréna's thigh, fails again, and then after a final smitten gaze, he steals away like a thief.

The Ancestor nods her head and gently pulls Siréna's skirt over her thighs, just before the girl awakes.).

SIRÉNA: My God . . . I fell asleep . . . you soothed away the pain.

ANCESTOR: Go now, life beckons.

SIRÉNA: My father will feel better just seeing me this way. Now I can go to him with a light heart, since you have the goodness to carry my burden.

ANCESTOR: Go where your good heart can help my daughter.

(*Siréna stands up and leaves, forgetting the book that has fallen to the floor. The Ancestor picks up the book, holds it before her with both hands as if in prayer, then hides it away.*)

Darkness

Scene 2

The living room. Driss sits on the ottoman. His mother, leaning on her cane, paces back and forth in front. From the courtyard comes the laughter of children.

DRISS: Mother, I'm not ready to think about this. Not yet.

NAHNOUHA: You've been speaking to that Cyclist again!

DRISS: No. I'm tired and worried. Out of the blue, here I am, father of seven girls. It's a burden.

NAHNOUHA: Have some more cake.

DRISS: No.

NAHNOUHA: Oh, I see. You don't love me any more.

DRISS: Mother, don't keep confusing things this way. It's tedious.

NAHNOUHA: That's what I mean. You speak to me as if I'm a servant. You never listen to what I say anymore, and you never obey me.

DRISS: I do! Do I want to marry again? Yes, of course. I want a boy. You're not the only one!

NAHNOUHA: I want a boy now! I want lots of boys, and I want to be around when they're all grown up!

DRISS: Here you go, calculating again.

NAHNOUHA: Exactly! It's now the end of spring. Today I'll let everyone know that I'm looking for your new wife. For a week or two we'll pretend to prepare for the wedding. That'll give me enough time to find a woman from a local family who'll give you the most boys . . . Your wedding will come with the summer.

DRISS: The proper period of mourning is not yet over — the mourning that made me a widower that is. The mourning for being father of seven girls is never ending . . .

NAHNOUHA: Who's in mourning? Are you? Am I? No one is! I'm talking about parties and joy. What are you thinking?

DRISS: I'm thinking about my daughters. They're growing up fast.

NAHNOUHA: That's not your problem. It's mine. I'll take care of those little females when the time comes. They're worthless livestock.

DRISS: I don't like it when you refer to them as a commodity.

NAHNOUHA: They are a commodity. So you agree with me about early summer?

DRISS: Well . . .

NAHNOUHA: So that's settled then. A nice young girl, not too fat, obviously not thin, with plenty of brothers and uncles. She must be from a long line of men, so we can be sure the male line will continue. All the luck's on our side. Perhaps I'll even dig up a few bracelets.

DRISS: Mother, no one's ever seen these famous bracelets of yours, do they really exist?!

NAHNOUHA: You doubt my word, apple of my eye?

DRISS: You gave your keys to Taos.

NAHNOUHA: She doesn't know where the jewels are, and unless you tell her, she'll never know.

DRISS: So why did you give them to her?

NAHNOUHA: For an illusion of power. An abandoned woman needs some recompense. She loves your home and your children, and that mustn't change. She works like an animal, and she's hopelessly in love with you, all thanks to a simple illusion: a bunch of keys that open nothing . . . Shhh! Here she comes. (*Enter Taos.*) I'm leaving now. I've said enough for one day.

(*Driss gets up to embrace his mother. Taos also greets her. Nahnouha leaves. Taos busies herself. Driss watches her silently for a moment.*)

DRISS: Woman, do you never stop?

TAOS: How could I? I can't stop, even at night!

DRISS: My mother's right. You're irreplaceable.

TAOS (*surprised*): She said that?

DRISS: Absolutely.

TAOS: Goodness me, that's nice to hear!

DRISS: She also said you'd appreciate a young girl in this house to make us some boys.

TAOS (*frozen*): A girl?

DRISS: I mean, a wife.

TAOS: Am I not a wife?

DRISS (*assertively*): A wife for children.

TAOS: I am a wife for children: I have seven, as you know.

DRISS: I mean . . . a young wife.

TAOS (*approaching him*): Ah! Now I understand. Your mother wants a young wife because I'm an old wife that's not worth sleeping with and has no hope of getting pregnant. So what did you say?

DRISS: Did I need to say anything?

TAOS: Didn't you tell her you're a father and I'm a mother and we don't need anyone else to make us happy?

DRISS: I don't see it that way.

TAOS: So how do you see it?

DRISS: Well, this house is becoming too lifeless. It wants youth.

TAOS: What about your daughters?

DRISS: My mother said girls are like their mothers, they don't count.

TAOS: I see, you want a replacement for Mimia. So she died for nothing then. She wanted me to be the only mother of her children.

DRISS (*angrily*): I'm not looking for a mother. The children already have one: you. Have I ever tried to take them away? God gave you those girls and because of them you'll always be mistress of this house. You didn't know it, but their maternal grandfather has been asking for them—I could have given them to him, and I can always change my mind. He's been heartbroken since his daughter died.

TAOS: And your heart needs comforting too?

DRISS: Yes, by a woman.

TAOS: And what am I then?

DRISS: Property.

TAOS: I stepped aside because of my friendship for Mimia. Now she's in a better place, I want my place back. I was the first and I'll always be first. First and last.

DRISS: It's lucky my mother's gone. If she heard you talking this way, you'd be out on the street, forced to spend the night like a dog. But I'm willing to forget what you've just said. I won't disown you, it would be a nuisance to be left alone with the children. Now go and pray to the prophet for patience and consolation. I'll marry at the beginning of the summer.

TAOS (*Raising her voice and lifting her arms*): Ohhh! What a poor abandoned orphan I am! I should have grieved for Mimia longer than I did, but from this day on, I'll mourn her death, because it's her you're betraying, her memory and her kindness. She left us responsible for seven lives!

DRISS: Woman, you're deluded! I'm not responsible for anything! I'm not a mother. But I do have what it takes to be a man.

(*Enter Chems, Mimia's eldest daughter, now ten or twelve years old. She runs over to Taos and hugs her.*)

CHEMS: Are you crying Mama? (*Taos wipes her face in silence. Chems looks at her father.*) Did you make Mama cry?

DRISS: Which Mama?

CHEMS: My Mama, Taos!

DRISS: Mama, you mean that sterile woman?

CHEMS: My nourishing earth. She's my nurse mother and she brought me up. She didn't bear me, but she saved me. I owe her my life. She's my mother and I'm her daughter.

DRISS: Ahhhh! You're all I need. My mother and my wife are enough to be dealing with, without you bothering me as well! Go learn to weave, that'll be more useful than all this talk.

CHEMS: Papa, I said Mama's crying, don't you see?

DRISS: I haven't raised my hand to you yet, but I can start now.

CHEMS (*stepping forward*): Go on then Father, start now!

DRISS: If your mother's crying, that's my concern, not yours.

CHEMS: So why is she crying?

TAOS (*crying*): But I'm not, I'm not crying.

DRISS: Your mother's crying and it's none of your business. It's between your grandmother and me.

CHEMS (*crossing her arms*): So I don't count. My mother's crying and it doesn't matter?

DRISS (*with a commanding gesture, points to the door*): Get out! Get out before I lose my temper! Get out before I hit you, you brainless girl!

CHEMS: I'm leaving, but remember one thing, Papa: I'm on Mama's side and every day that you grow older, so do I. Soon I'll be stronger than you, even if I am just a girl.

DRISS: I can't believe my ears.

CHEMS: I know I'm the boy you always wanted and never had. I'm just as smart as any boy and one day I'll have my say in this house.

DRISS: Get out!

CHEMS (*Embracing her mother*): I'm going, but don't forget I'm growing older every day.

(*She leaves. Taos dries her tears.*)

TAOS :You're the man of this house, but now you must listen to me. I've never spoken to you this way before and I know what's at stake. Repudiation. And that's as good as death since there's no one out there to feed and protect me.

DRISS: Are you complaining? You've brought up a tigress to protect you and you've done a good job of turning her against me.

TAOS: I did not! She surprised me as much as you . . . So you want a woman in this house. Not me, but a woman to your own tastes. Well, I'll do everything I can to stop you marrying again.

DRISS: What? Witchcraft?

TAOS: No. Just good sense. I'll try to convince you, but if I can't, if I really can't . . .

DRISS: Then what?

TAOS: I want to choose my co-wife myself.

DRISS (*after a silence*): Ah . . . Well, that could be an interesting suggestion . . . in fact it almost makes sense . . . After all, mother's becoming old, perhaps her judgement's not what it used to be . . . With some diplomacy on my part perhaps you'll have your say . . . There's no question, you're a good wife . . . Do you have someone in mind already?

TAOS: No.

CRIES FROM THE COURTYARD: Taos! Taos!

TAOS: Shhh! It's our neighbor.

DRISS (*leaving*): Well, none of this is worth missing my afternoon at the café.

(*He walks past Siréna, and comes back to stare at her, dumbstruck.*)

TAOS (*Arranging her hair*): Be gone, man! Leave us women alone!

SIRÉNA: Hello neighbor.

(*Driss leaves.*)

TAOS: Welcome back! We don't see much of you in this house anymore, we miss you.

SIRÉNA (*embracing Taos*): I've got so much to tell you!

TAOS: Sit down, let's chat. I need to get something off my chest. You may look young and brazen, but you're already so wise and mature . . .

(*They whisper, laughing together as they sit down.*)

TAOS (*becoming serious again*): You know, he wants to do it again!

SIRÉNA: Do what? You mean your husband? What does he want now?

TAOS: The same thing! Another marriage!

SIRÉNA: He has a one-track mind.

TAOS: Before he wanted children, now he wants boys.

SIRÉNA: And when he's got boys, he'll want something else.

TAOS: A younger woman, younger every time . . .

SIRÉNA: From a foreign country, a beautiful blond . . .

TAOS: Or even a little girl . . .

SIRÉNA: His daughter's age . . .

TAOS: Or even younger . . .

SIRÉNA: Or even two little girls . . . has he ever tried it on with the servants?

TAOS: Never . . . He's not like that.

SIRÉNA: I don't want to disillusion you, I'm too fond of you for that. After all, illusions make life sweet. But I think all men are like that, though maybe your husband's an exception, and in that case I'm happy for you.

TAOS: You still don't have one?

SIRÉNA: What?

TAOS: A husband. Don't you want one?

SIRÉNA: No! I have a father and he's all I want. His love is immense and irreplaceable. When I'm sad, he wants me close by and I stay with him. A husband? I could have ten if I wanted. They're all the same. Besides, you can't have a good job and a good husband, or a good father and a good spouse. I'll keep my job because I like it. I don't need a spouse. Over time, a job gets better, but a husband only gets worse! A father matures, but a spouse just shrivels up!

TAOS: It's a pity! You could keep a good husband.

SIRÉNA (*getting up*): Let me show you something. Look . . . It's strange . . . when I'm with you I forget my father is dying. (*Showing off her breasts and buttocks, Siréna dances about, making sophisticated, elegant gestures.*) See how you should communicate with your husband? Act as if it's nothing, but while you're doing the housework, remind him of the joys of the night, the dark joys.

TAOS (*shocked*): The dark joys?

SIRÉNA: Yes! Do I have to explain everything to you?

TAOS: I mean . . .

SIRÉNA: Don't tell me that . . .

TAOS: You know, I look after the children, that's enough for me.

SIRÉNA: But not enough for a man! Do you think a man's happy to be the one that's always giving? It's a game of give and take you know.

TAOS: We share a concern for our girls.

SIRÉNA: That's not enough. You're lucky I'm honest! Otherwise, I'd show you just how easy it is to drive a man to distraction. They have a shaft between their legs, but the slightest sensuous breeze, the slightest whiff of a woman, and they go crazy. They think they're strong but just one little pair of boobies makes their eyes pop right out of their heads.

TAOS: I don't want to think about it.

SIRÉNA: If you bury your head in the sand, the world will still be there. Shall I continue?

TAOS: Yes.

SIRÉNA: Your husband's looking for some sex. Offer him what he wants.

TAOS: Shhhhhhhhhh!

SIRÉNA: It does happen in marriage you know!

TAOS: Would you do it?

SIRÉNA: What, with your husband?

TAOS: He's a man, isn't he?

SIRÉNA: He has as about as much effect on me as a broom—and in bed I think I'd prefer the broom.

TAOS: My God, my God . . . You say such awful things. The house will fall upon us.

SIRÉNA: Listen. I'm going to be staying at home. You know, my father's been sick for a long time . . . I want to see his face, from morning till night. I'll come by to see you, and I'll teach you a little elegance, a few tricks . . .

TAOS: But I'm a respectable woman. What are you going to teach me?

SIRÉNA: Do you want to keep your husband or not?

TAOS: I want to keep the father of my children.

SIRÉNA: You can put it that way if you want . . . Is the old woman still bothering you?

TAOS: Less than before.

SIRÉNA: Does she listen to you now?

TAOS: Oh no. But she's not so quick to criticize me. Though she still wants to remarry her son.

SIRÉNA: He's your husband more than her son.

TAOS: I don't know.

SIRÉNA: Well, do you mean he's more her husband than her son?

TAOS: Ayayay! Be quiet. Sometimes you go too far. What will our punishment be?

SIRÉNA (*prancing around*): Come on, you'll be alright. If you're determined, I can help you. I'm not afraid of anything anymore . . .

TAOS: Go . . . go now . . . May God preserve us. (*Siréna leaves. Taos raises her arms to the sky, then puts her hands together in prayer before kissing them.*) Mimia . . . Oh Mimia . . . Where you are there is no more suffering . . . Look down on me from a better place and tell me what to do. This man of ours wants yet another woman. She'll give him boys, and he'll prefer his boys to our girls. Come to me and tell me. Should I play at being the young girl to seduce him, or should I accept our common fate? Speak to me!

Darkness

Scene 3
The Women's Conspiracy

The living room, steeped in shadow. Two old women are sitting down, while Chems and the servants move around talking. Everyone is angry.

TAOS'S MOTHER: What does he want another wife for, he already has one, and why more children, he has seven already? He's crazy!

MIMIA'S MOTHER: Did my daughter die for nothing? She chose a mother for her children before she went to heaven. A last wish is sacred.

CHEMS: There'll never be more than one mother in this house, I swear to God.

MIMIA'S MOTHER: My naïve child, you show great courage, but you can do nothing alone.

CHEMS: Well, let's work together then.

TAOS'S MOTHER: Daughter of my daughter, I agree, but what can we do? We're not in the habit of making decisions about men. If your father wants to marry again, we can't stop him, but let's at least minimize the damage.

CHEMS: Never!

THE SERVANTS (*together*): No! We don't want another mistress! Not another mistress in this house!

MIMIA'S MOTHER: Oh! You soothe my heart, little ones. Sweet words that heal these bitter wounds. Taos, what do you have to say?

TAOS: My daughter speaks for me. She's fearless.

THE SERVANTS: We won't serve another mistress!

CHEMS: And my little sisters don't want another mother.

TAOS'S MOTHER: They don't count. Nothing counts in this house except a man's wants and desires. What do you say, Taos?

TAOS: I can't say more than that: nothing does count here except a man's desires.

ANCESTOR (*raising her arms to the sky*): No! I do!

ALL (*amazed*) : Ancesssssstor!

ANCESTOR: Help me up! (*She grasps a book to her chest.*)

(*The servants hurry over, lift her up and take her to the mothers, dragging and carrying her. The mothers stand up to make space on the ottoman..*)

THE MOTHERS: Ancestor, you do us a great honor by breaking your silence to share your great wisdom. Sit with us.

TAOS: Have you broken your silence in my defense, Ancestor? Then, I am saved!

ANCESTOR (*aside*): I don't have long to go now. I see you all as I've never seen you before. At long last, the gates of heaven are open and drown me in light. Now . . .

CHEMS: Ancestor, your beauty is eternal. I've never seen you this way before. Will you help us now before your eternal sleep?

ANCESTOR: Hold me tight, pure-hearted little slaves. You've never uttered a word of disrespect. Now, are you all listening?

ALL: Yes!

THE SERVANTS: We're saved!

ANCESTOR: I could curse this third wife, and she would die after the marriage. But that's no solution. The man of the house would only marry again. Mourning for lost love is short lived in men's hearts.

ALL: And so then?

ANCESTOR: We must pretend to play the game. Whoever this future wife may be, she must be our accomplice. She must be a woman with no vested interest here. A generous woman, not afraid of losing her reputation.

CHEMS: Ancestor, you're twelve or fifteen times my age, I feel unworthy asking you, tell me who?

ANCESTOR: Never search far and wide for what's already in your hand.

CHEMS: Ancestor, please, give us a name at least!

TAOS: Is it who I'm thinking of?

ANCESTOR: I've already said too much. The Angels are calling. Leave the mothers to think, my child. I'm sure they understand. You're still too young to be concerned with your father's marriage.

CHEMS: I'm not too young, I haven't been too young for a long time, Ancestor. I've been suffering for years.

ANCESTOR: You must suffer a while longer to fully understand. Give thanks to God that your father's thinking about his own marriage, not yours. You should take care now. Make full use of your spring days before a man steals them away forever.

THE MOTHERS (*prostrating to kiss the Ancestor's feet*): You've helped us greatly. We'll keep the secret.

TAOS: The women's secret!

ANCESTOR: Now I can leave peacefully. My place on the hill has been ready for a long time. (*The mothers rise and return to the ottoman.*) Come, little slaves, help me leave this blessed house . . . Wives and daughters, I leave you all in peace. The servants usually do the cleaning, so I'll go with them.

(*The Ancestor leaves with the servants. Taos and the mothers start whispering and making plans. Then they get up.*)

THE MOTHERS (*to Chems*): Daughter we're leaving now, we have things to do.

CHEMS: What about me?

THE MOTHERS: You are guardian of the house, you and your mother. Now we embrace you. We ask you say nothing about what was said here.

TAOS: She won't tell a soul.

CHEMS: Go peacefully, my grandmothers.

THE MOTHERS: May peace be with you, granddaughter. May peace be with you, our brave, brave woman. (*The mothers leave.*)

CHEMS (*parodying the Ancestor as she leaves*): The servants usually do the cleaning, so I'll go with them.

TAOS: You'll be a fine woman, filled with a spirit of resistance and never afraid to speak your mind.

(*They leave.*)

Darkness

Scene 4
The Wedding

Enter Driss, in an agitated state.

DRISS (*looking over his shoulder, moving cautiously*): Easy now, careful. There . . . (*The stage is gradually lit, and we see that Nahnouha has taken the place of the Ancestor. Enter the mothers and the two servants, carrying a palanquin, which they set down carefully. The servants withdraw. The mothers stand side by side. Driss bows before the two mothers.*) I thank you, mothers of today, for replacing my mother of yesterday. Thank you for coming around to my way of thinking and for skillfully keeping my wife and daughter away, so I can consummate this sublime marriage. I admit I didn't expect such indulgence and understanding, but you are mothers and I am your son. I thank you both for remembering this.

THE MOTHERS: Stand up, son! Now show some understanding yourself toward your wife and daughter: they'll be here soon. May peace be with you.

DRISS (*raising his head with a delighted expression*): Peace go with you.

(*The mothers leave.*)

DRISS (*talking to Nahnouha*): I know, I know . . .

NAHNOUHA (*raising her arms in a gesture of powerlessness*): Oh! What a disgrace!

DRISS: I know you disapprove, but you're powerless now. I'm going to prove I was right. This unexpected marriage will make me a thousand times the father of a thousand sons!

(Taos and Chems burst into the room.)

TAOS *(stupefied)*: Ahhhh! What's this? Am I dreaming? No, this is no dream! Can this be real? No, my eyes deceive me. It's impossible!

CHEMS: Mother, calm down. Let's try to understand. Perhaps it's not as bad as you think.

TAOS *(walking toward her husband in a threatening manner)*: Don't ever say that . . .

CHEMS: Mother, we should wait and see . . . It might not be as bad as you imagine.

TAOS: Ooooh! What a poor abandoned orphan I am!

CHEMS: No! What a poor abandoned orphan I am!

DRISS *(gesturing to the servants to go to the palanquin and bring out the bride)*: Come on, let's get on with it. I don't have time to argue, today. This is a celebration. No, don't move! First, I'll go and make sure the bridal suite is ready! *(He moves upstage and disappears through the door leading to the bedrooms. As if enjoying a good joke, Chems, Taos and the servants immediately begin to jump for joy and embrace each other, in silence. They peer into the palanquin, giggling. Then they stop, just as abruptly as they began, and go back to their places, adopting serious expressions. Driss returns, satisfied and tri-umphant.)* Servants, get to work! *(The servants carry the bride from the palanquin, and settle her on the ottoman. Then they stand behind her, and in a single movement, unveil her face.)*

TAOS AND CHEMS *(feigning surprise)*: Siréna!!!

NAHNOUHA *(raising her arms to the sky in defeat)*: A woman of the streets in this house! A common trollop who's brushed up against every man in the town and village!

DRISS (*annoyed*): Mother, you shouldn't be speaking this way. You're an Ancestor now. You've crossed into the time of powerlessness and meditation. You should speak with the wisdom of the oracles.

NAHNOUHA: A whore. A hussy. A woman who's been displaying her body in the streets for years. You poor blind fool. You think you're marrying an untouched woman? There's nothing left for you to take.

DRISS: But she's beautiful.

TAOS: Ayayayaay! It's a day for celebration! Let's wail for victory. Come daughters, all together.

(*Taos, Chems and the servants ululate with true feeling. Driss applauds, half delighted, half astonished.*)

Darkness

Scene 5

A white sheet is hanging, hiding the set. When drawn back by the two servants, it should reveal the bloodied sheet behind, but this time the second sheet is immaculately white. Upstage, coming from the bedrooms, Siréna and Taos arrive, giggling and chattering.

TAOS (*to the servants*) : Go fetch the midwife.

(*The servants leave. The two women sit down laughing. Nahnouha raises her arms to the sky.*)

SIRÉNA: I hold nothing more against you, old woman. Nothing more. You've said a lot of bad things about me in your life. But now you've become a phantom, I'll do you no harm. But you should know this: your son will never have me! The moment he sees me, he's paralyzed. He can't do a thing!

NAHNOUHA: That I should bear witness to this before I die: my son destroyed!

SIRÉNA: Even better! Ridiculed!

NAHNOUHA: It's your fault, you've no more blood to give. You gave it away a long time ago!

SIRÉNA: Don't get carried away. I'm still a virgin, and he'll never have me! I'm too fantastic a dream for him!

TAOS: I hope you'll manage to hold out long enough to keep him at bay!

SIRÉNA: Someone's coming!

TAO: It's the midwife. That was quick.

(The two women stand. Enter the midwife, followed by the servants.)

THE MIDWIFE: Good day to you all. You're calling me so early in the morning, is there a birth already?

SIRÉNA: Far from it, it's to prove my virginity.

THE MIDWIFE: Ah! My God. Are there still men around incapable of doing their duty?

SIRÉNA: And who never will. *(She bursts out laughing.)*

TAOS: A man can't do what he can't do.

THE MIDWIFE: Really! And why not?

SIRÉNA: Abuse! Something that's over-used soon wears out!

THE MID-WIFE: Oh you young ones, none of this is new to me. Come on then, let's see if this hymen is still intact.

SIRÉNA: I'm ready, wise woman, I'm willing, but what will you do to me?

(Siréna sits down like a nervous young girl, facing the public on the ottoman. She raises her legs in the air. The midwife sits between her thighs for the examination. Then she gets up and nods her head.)

MIDWIFE: Perfect! This girl is still a virgin. No man has touched her. I declare this in the name of God, the one true witness of all our actions.

TAOS (*giving her a few coins*): Go and spread the news in the village. The poor man is no longer capable of doing anything . . . to anyone.

THE MIDWIFE: Well! It just goes to show, the punishment always fits the crime. It's too big a secret to keep. Many thanks to this generous house. This sheet should be openly displayed every day for all to see. On the evening of the seventh day, if this marriage is still unconsummated, then this young girl, whose integrity I guarantee, may return to her parent's home. This is our custom, and we observe the commandments. I leave you all in peace.

TAOS AND SIRÉNA: May peace go with you.

TAOS (*to the servants*): Seven days, is that clear?

(Siréna laughs. Nahnouha sobs softly.)

Darkness

Scene 6

This scene represents Siréna's seven days of patience, during which she teaches Taos how to be more alluring in order to seduce her husband. Each time the servants draw the sheet, revealing the immaculate sheet behind, Siréna begins her lesson of the day. The lessons are as follows:

The First Day

SIRÉNA: Sit down. Taos, are you listening? There. Sit here. Now lift your dress over your knees. What do you mean, no? Now, don't look at your knees! Keep your mind on what you're doing, your weaving or your baking. No! I didn't tell you to cover your knees. Alright, let's start again!

The Second Day

Today we'll work on your shoulders. That dress you're wearing is too stiff, too restrictive, too sensible . . . Here, I'll lend you one of mine. In our country, husbands rarely see shoulders. You know, when women go to the beach, they wear swimming costumes that show off their shoulders. Shoulders are beautiful. They're nice and round. Touch them! I said touch them! You see . . . Aren't they soft? Don't blush, silly! Go on, feel them. The right one, then the left one. There, nice and relaxed. Now, feel this silk and satin. Tell the dressmaker to make you a "boat neck" dress, and let it drop to one side while you're working. One shoulder at a time. It'll catch his attention, make him dream, give him warm thoughts. It's alright, you won't go to hell for it!

The Third Day

Some days wear a low cut dress, the way young nursing mothers do. Wait, let me feel your breasts. Well, there you are, you do have some! Why are you so keen to hide them? Really, Taos! Take that stifling dress off! That's better. The neckline of your slip is far more inviting. Are you wearing a bra? What's that? A traditional corset! Do me a favor, stop wearing that thing. It's crushing your lovely breasts. It's a crime to mistreat them that way. Don't be afraid, I'm not going to eat them, you know. They're just like a young girl's because you've never had children. See, sterility does have some advantages! Now, listen to me. When he comes back this evening, first of all, don't hide under the covers. Luckily it's summer, so I'll give you one of my sheer nighties. Stop muttering. Even if you do go to hell, I guarantee you'll go to Paradise first. Good, now you're beginning to relax. You have such a beautiful bosom. Show it off, open it up a bit. That's better. Men love to suck them. You've never nursed a baby, you'll see how nice it is. How do I know? It's written in books. Besides, I'm a sensitive girl. He'll gaze at your breasts and he'll fondle them with his hands. Men just love toying with them and nuzzling them. He'll lick them and be happy as a child. Let him do what he wants. Promise me!

The Fourth Day

Today we'll talk about your rear end. I don't know why, but men are turned on by a nice backside. Stop laughing, silly, it's true. Feel it. Ah, you want to feel mine? Go ahead. Yes, mine's bigger. Now feel yours. It's far more cute — nice and tight and pert. The problem is you can't see it with those dresses you wear. So we need to find a solution for that. It's not that important. We have other weapons.

The Fifth Day

Of course, your face is very important, that's why it's hidden beneath a veil. You've got a beautiful brown face with fine features, big eyes, and a young girl's mouth. Don't you wear kohl anymore? You should start wearing it again, it makes you more mysterious. You already have a dark look, a flash of kohl would give you that edge of mystique. You think all this will make you a witch? Alright then, I'll join you. We'll go to hell together and have a great time! Now, when you're alone with him and you're eating together, look at him, move your lips, and slide out your tongue, slip it out gently. No, not like that. Very slightly. Just an insinuation . . .

The Sixth Day

Of course, all this leads us to your general appearance. Put your dress back on and tell me what you look like. Do you look like the mother of a family? Not in the least. You look more like a servant born to this house. You're too at ease with domestic concerns and have the same bearing as your little maids. This is your home, you're the mistress of the house. Show it! Look confident and well-cared for, from dawn till dusk. And remind him constantly of the joys of the night, show him how comfortable and at ease you are in your body. When night falls and work is over, make yourself desirable, wear only sheer, see-though cloth. Reveal some of your nakedness, but always hide a little so in his mad dreams of pleasure, a man's convinced he can go even further . . . Shall I start again? No? You're learning quickly . . . poor husband ridiculed by the whole village! He daren't show his face in his own home during the day anymore.

The Seventh Day
Last but not least, what goes in the soup! Spices, especially hot peppers. You're a good cook, so make sure it's hot, especially at night. And always plan to go to bed early, because men often have the urge during meal times. If you overfeed them, well, these gentlemen will be snoring before bedtime! And there'll be nothing left for you except the dishes.

NAHNOUHA: Ah! The youth of today are destroying our traditions!

SIRÉNA: Shhh! Leave us be. We're trying to give your son his honor back. Finally he'll become a man. He has to; he can't hide behind you anymore!

NAHNOUHA: My son deserves seven wives!

SIRÉNA: He doesn't need that to be happy. Taos is worth ten wives! Especially now she knows how to make a man happy!

TAOS: May God always keep you. You brought me back to life! My gratitude will be eternal. Come back any time to heal your wounds or rest in my house: from now on we're blood sisters.

SIRÉNA: Taos, my sister, our time together has been so enjoyable. People in the village have been wondering why I accepted a marriage that brought me nothing. Well, you could say I'm distracting myself, trying to forget my father's imminent death. But who would understand that?

THE SERVANTS (*Together*): A marriage that brings you nothing. No gold, no silver, no honor or respect.

SIRÉNA: Exactly! I accepted this union to put the world back in place. It's not only the privilege of the wise. Crazy women and fools like me also have their uses . . . Even if one day I do become an orphan . . . oh, sad sorrow!

TAOS: I'll be able to thank you one day. I'm going to be rich . . .

SIRÉNA: Keep your riches for your children and your children's children. You have a duty to them . . . It's time for me to go. I'm happy to leave you now that you're mistress of your own house. Lift your shoulders and let your bosom glow with pride.

TAOS: I'll help you gather your things.

SIRÉNA: No. On second thought, I'll leave everything here. There's nothing I could take with me that would be of any use for crying. All I need for that are my eyes. You need the dresses more than I do. I leave you your husband. For me, he's more like a brother. I took his name but I didn't take his seed. He has the power to disown me, and if he does, I'll give him back his name. So I'm leaving as I came: untouched . . . just a little sadder because the party's over.

(*Affectionately, Taos accompanies Siréna to the door, hugging and embracing her. They look happy. Siréna leaves. Enter Chems.*)

TAOS: Here you are, my daughter. You look so tired.

CHEMS: Oh! It's this exam that's coming up.

TAOS: Will your father let you to take it?

CHEMS: He can't allow me or stop me from doing anything any more.

NAHNOUHA (*raising her arms*): Ah! Perversion and shame-lessness have corrupted this generation as well!

CHEMS: Where's Siréna?

TAOS: She's gone back to her father's house, as custom allows. She's still a virgin, and as a virgin she reclaims all her rights . . .

CHEMS: Good for her and good for us!

TAOS: Your father wants to remarry.

CHEMS: Mother, so long as I have a breath of life left in me, have no fear of that.

TAOS: You're my own flesh and blood child, but you don't know your father like I do.

CHEMS: No, I know him better! I don't indulge him the way his wives do. I won't pamper him and I won't submit to him. We have to stand our ground.

TAOS: His pride has been hurt. He'll want to mend that as soon as possible.

CHEMS: He can do that by being a good father, and a good husband to you!

TAOS: Careful, he's here!

(*Enter Driss. He sits down without greeting them.*)

DRISS: Tea! (*The servants busy themselves.*) Call my wife!

(*Taos and Chems stand on either side of the ottoman, like judges.*)

CHEMS: Do you mean our neighbor . . . Siréna?

DRISS (*seething with anger*): I've decided that today I'm going to give all the wives of this house a good beating, and all the girls too. Shall I start with you?

CHEMS: I only wanted to inform you that our neighbor has returned to her father's house, on the evening of the seventh day, as common law dictates.

DRISS: Ah, so that's how it is! Well then, I'm going right back out! I'm going to look for another wife, as common law dictates. Good thing I have a clever daughter to remind me of my rights.

CHEMS: No!

DRISS (*getting up*): Did you say no? To me, your father? Are you saying no to me? You were born from a drop of my good humor, and you're saying no? Have you forgotten that your father has every right over you?

CHEMS: No.

DRISS: Well I'm glad about that!

CHEMS: No. You don't have every right. You don't have the right to be violent and you don't have the right to be arbitrary. But you do have rights to kindness and you've never taken advantage of them. You're the father of seven girls. Where are they? What are they doing? What do they think about? How do they see you? Do they love you or hate you? How old will they be when they make that first mistake, the one that will ruin your honor once and for all?

DRISS (*threatening*): What's this I'm hearing? Such vile words from your precious mouth!

CHEMS: They're true words. If they're vile, that's because they speak of our vile lives. The life you impose on us.

DRISS: I'll deal with you later. But now, I'm going out again. And when I come back to this house, it'll be with my fourth wife. And this time she'll be the right one.

CHEMS: Never!

DRISS: If you were my grown son, perhaps I'd listen, but . . .

CHEMS: No, I'm only a girl! A girl whose dowry will be expensive and who'll never bring anything into the house. Wait, there's more! Fortunately she'll change her name so that any future dishonor will be her husband's, not her father's! I'm the boy you always dreamt of and never had. You must be really suffering to reject your own flesh and blood this way. Even though I'm not a boy, I have all the qualities of a modern girl. I do! I'm strong, I have willpower and determination, I'm not afraid to make decisions, I like schoolwork and everything I learn outside, and I'm skillful at home. Didn't you know? Of course not. You've never bothered to look at me, never listened, you never even noticed me growing up. I'm the son you'll never have, because that's the will of God. You'll accept His will for so many petty things that we could change or improve ourselves, so why can't you accept . . . a daughter with good qualities, and an extraordinary wife? And that's not to mention your other daughters — my sisters — who have always obeyed you in silence.

DRISS: I have no wife. And I won't take lessons from anyone, especially not from female offspring! I said I'm leaving and that's exactly what I'm doing!

CHEMS: No!

DRISS: My poor mother no longer has the right to speak, but she was absolutely right! You leave an opening and revolution comes charging in! I was too stupid to understand it then, but I won't forget it now. Good-bye.

CHEMS: I said no! (*Driss, who was about to leave, turns around. Chems running towards the door.*) Wait there . . . you'll see! . . . (*She goes out. We hear noises from the courtyard, a door slams. Chems returns brandishing an axe. Chems to her father.*) Just you watch what I'll do to another marriage. (*She goes over to the second loom, and with a final burst of energy, attacks it with the axe, shouting.*) See what I'm doing! There'll never be more than one mother in this house. No other marriages, not today, not tomorrow. Am I an unworthy daughter? Well, let my unworthiness at least serve the interests of this house.

Grandmother said that daughters are like their mothers:they don't count! Starting from today, under this roof, mothers will be like their daughters: they will count! . . . You're a father and a husband, and we're going to teach you to be a good father and a good husband. And God, who is our God too, will guide us in our actions. There, Father, that's knocked you off your pedestal! From now on, you'll just be an ordinary man! . . . (*Exhausted, she throws the axe down by the destroyed loom. Taos's loom remains intact. Chems walks threateningly toward her cringing father who sits down cautiously on the ottoman, holding his head in his hands. Chems, taking her mother by her shoulders, smiles at her and declares*) From this day I name you mistress of your house! (*As she embraces her mother, the servants prostrate themselves at Chems's feet. Then the three young girls go over to broken loom and start picking up and playing with the pieces. Chems to Taos.*) Unless you want to go and find a second husband, another father, for me?

(*The three girls laugh. The parents are frozen: Taos, the serious mother; Driss, the defeated father.*)

Black. Curtain.

END

Tayeb Saddiki

THE FOLIES
BERBERS

by Tayeb Saddiki

Translated by Marvin Carlson

THE FOLIES BERBERS

(We Were Created to Understand Each Other)

by Tayeb Saddiki
1993

CHARACTERS

SCHEHERAZADE	NARRATOR
A GIRL	MOLIÈRE
THE STORYTELLER	BOILEAU
DADA	ONE-ARMED MAN
BEN AÏCHA	ONE-LEGGED MAN
BEN SOUSSANE	M. JOURDAIN
DE BRETEUIL	MME JOURDAIN
THE BARON DE SAINT-OLON	YOUNG SAILOR
TAGHARI	SAILOR
PETIS DE LA CROIX	RAJA
MADEMOISELLE DE CONTI	MARJANE
MADEMOISELLE HERVE	YAQOUT
MADEMOISELLE DU PARC	SERGEANT
MADEMOISELLE DE BRIE	TURKS
MADEMOISELLE HERVE	AUSTRIANS
MADEMOISELLE DU PARC	COURTIERS
MADEMOISELLE LE CAMUS	

SCENE 1

Prologue

SCHEHERAZADE: Two poles of power and glory, brought to their position as if by an irresistible force, here and there, on one side and the other of the Western Mediterranean.

GIRL: In France, a king, Louis the Fourteenth by name, spreading his sun-like rays over all Europe in a central, sovereign act.

SCHEHERAZADE: In Morocco, an Emperor drawing up in energetic, definitive strokes, those of a nascent modernity, the outlines of a national territory,

GIRL: Two wills who wove together the century in a Promethean effort, sowing their furrows with the rich nourishment of pride and dreams.

SCHEHERAZADE: How could these two flamboyant figures, whose fates were so disturbingly similar, who so surprisingly resembled each other, know so little of each other or so completely misunderstand each other?

GIRL: It was written in the great book of history that a dialogue must occur between them, that some exchange must take place!

SCHEHERAZADE: Amid the tumult, the listening, the storms, the questions, the enthusiasm, the suspicion, there was only a single encounter between Sultan Moulay Ismail and his double across the sea. What might have been the effect on such prominent symbols and on the clearest tracks on the sands of the future whose traces could already be seen?

GIRL: We will recount by anecdote, chronicle, legend, memories, the peripeties of the coming together of these two rulers, two great rulers whose interlocking observance prefigured, in a manner of which they were unaware, a later intertwining with its own drams, passions, and rich revelations.

SCHEHERAZADE: Two leading contemporaries—neither of them knowing anything about the restraints of that simplifying Oriental/Occidental dichotomy, a symbolic reduction for textbooks. Moulay Ismail Emperor of Morocco and Susa and the Emperor of France and Navarre Louis XIV.

> *France is a stronghold, safe, secure*
> *Her banners bold the world can face*
> *Her steps to glory firm and sure*
> *Of all the lands she is the ace*
> *Her fame, her words all pain can cure*
> *Her guests she greets with warm embrace*
> *Her people bow in homage pure*
> > *To Louis, ruler of that place.**

The special, extraordinary, plenipotentiary Envoy of his Imperial Majesty, the Sultan, utilized his extensive and unshared power to turn his mission in a new direction, since he wanted to place the imprint of his overflowing imagination in the service of bringing together these two powers.

DADA: This evening, the exercise that we propose to offer to your sagacious appreciation is a capricious and casual, yet impassioned promenade through this seventeenth-century episode, when something was within an inch of being tied together between Paris and Meknes. Let us speak of this past without haste and without priggish pedantry. Let us speak frankly, and if we do not recount history, at least let us recount a chronicle of history.

Darkness

SCENE 2

Homage

DADA: This evening, in a preliminary and symbolic homage, Morocco, through our voices, honors the memory of that great Frenchman, Lois Hubert Lyautey!

SCHEHERAZADE: And if there are among you some forgetful or ignorant souls who don't know who Lyautry was, we do not hesitate to scorn them.   Better yet, we will reduce them to shame by informing them that in Morocco, in every village and throughout the countrywide everyone, from the youngest to the most aged, knows that Lyautry held the position of the first Resident General of France in Morocco.   That was in 1912.   You know that this did not rejuvenate us.   And if he was only Resident General, if he resided with us only in the capacity of General, that was only because it was only much later that he was elevated to the dignity of Marshall of France.

GIRL: Yes, everyone in our country knows who Lyautey was.   His patronym soon became common, indeed, almost dynastic.   Those Residents who followed him at Rabat were known as Lyautey II, Lyautey III, etc.   According to this reckoning, Juin (note, another Marshall) and General Guillaume bore the numbers seven and eight in this series.

> *The new ambassador's well known*
> *His life is full of wondrous deeds*
> *His desert armies strong have grown*
> *His peaceful talk our hearing feeds*
> *Manners and wisdom he has shown*
> *Religious folk admire his creeds*
> *To friendship with us he was prone*
> *Fulfilling all our hopes and needs*
> *A man full of testosterone*
> *Like hirsute Lyautey he succeeds.**

ONE-ARMED MAN: Honor to the one who permitted some of us to participate in the European wars. Mektoub! I am a one-armed man, Mektoub! A monomaniac!

ONE-LEGGED MAN: Honor to the one for whom I lost my leg!

BLIND MAN: Honor to the one who brought us syphilization!
> *I'm not your brother, why should I*
> *To the Moroccan army hie?**

ONE-ARMED MAN: Desport the history of the 7/15 gun,

THE SARGEANT (*sotto voce*): The 7/15 gun is divisioned into seven principled parties which are to wit:
    First party: scarpshooter
    Secondary party: disgusting ammunition clips
    Turd party: unstable mechanisms
    Forth party: distorted engine
    Fifth : Sheathed bayonet
    Should I replete?

BLIND MAN (*sotto voce*): Fuckitall!

> *If Madame comes to see our mission*
> *Then offer her a hearty meal*
> *If Monsieur comes give him permission*
> *In written form with sign and seal.**

DADA: This evening we are gathered, we Moroccans, to render homage first to the most intelligent ex-colonized people and then to the most dangerous colonizer.

> *Let us hold glory in our view*
> *The victory is on our side*
> *Whatever enemies may do*
> *Our flag will always wave in pride.**

SCHEHERAZADE: Homage, homage to Lyautey, who, long before he received the star-spangled baton, brought about with his magic baguette great changes in Morocco.

GIRL: Homage to the prestigious soldier, to the proud man of Lorraine who, speaking like Jesus, the savior himself, modestly confessed one day that "Everything that has developed here has become one with me."

DADA: And good God! How we have developed every day, and we continued, we Sunni Muslims, to be one with this passionate Christian. A miraculous symbiosis, a divine entente, based on a respect for the dignity of each as the jargon of the official communiqués expresses it.

THE WOMAN STORYTELLER: Thus, many thanks, Monsieur Marshall, for having refused to tame the Moroccan soul. Thanks for all you have done to allow Morocco to maintain its Arab-Muslim culture and its identity.

DADA: Thanks for having dechristened the town of Sidi Kacem du Gharb (an important saint among us), a great marabou, as you express it so well in French! Sidi Kacem became Petit-Jean. Yes, simply Petit-Jean. So straightforward, nothing chichi about it: Petit-Jean. And along the same lines, Benslimane became Boucheron and Al Youssoufia, Louis-Gentil.

THE WOMAN STORYTELLER: How charming they all are! And we must not forget Kenitra, which had the supreme honor of becoming Port Lyautey! The founding father himself!

(They sing.)
Even the Zulus cannot be
More dense then we
Even the Zulu eyes can see
Obscurity.

SCHEHERAZADE: Whatever may occur, whatever the operations of chance, despite all past, present, and future circumstances, our homage to Resident Lyautry would be hollow if it did not emphasize forcefully and at the outset the clear and evident truth that you, the Occident, and we, the Orient, were created to understand each other. One might even go so far as to say that we were created only for this. Everything, absolutely everything, draws us together. Nothing separates us and our view of the world is almost identical. The proof of this is that we are gathered together this evening and that we tolerate each other with the most exquisite good manners.
(They sing.)
Even the Zulus cannot be
More dense then we

*Even the Zulu eyes can see
Obscurity.*

DADA: Good! Good! You write from left to right and we from right to left. What of it? We all know that left-handed and right-handed people are never in opposition or conflict for that reasons. So what is the problem?

THE GIRL: Entering the church, you may say. We take off our shoes at the entrance to the mosque. But this does not at all prevent us from walking with head high at the same pace. We were created to understand each other!

THE WOMAN STORYTELLER: You are irreverently referred to as "frog-eaters." Please don't take offense. We ourselves eat grasshopper when we have the misfortune to see them swarming over the countryside. And although moved by a legitimate spirit of revenge, we hold their abdomens swollen with frozen gold in as high esteem as you do the fine thighs of your inoffensive amphibians, We were created to understand each other!

DADA: Your women, when marrying, bring a dowry. With us it is the opposite. It may be that you somewhat undervalue women! We consider ourselves too proud to accept a gift. But after all this amounts to the same thing and proves once more that we were created to understand each other!

SCHEHERAZADE: Certainly real misunderstandings arise from time to time, but these never last long. We are, on both sides, too civilized to get hung up on subaltern contingencies. Consider, for example, there is a king of fig produced by a cactus that you call a Barbary fig. Very well! We, in exchange, speak of it simply and literary as the Christian fig! You see, we were created to understand each other!

DADA: What does all this prove? It proves first of all that, both of us have little regard for this fruit with its unpleasant spines. At the same time, it shows our mutual desire to transfer its paternity onto the other side, a necessary evil. And good heavens, there is no evil in this.

THE GIRL: Even our two languages unite us. Oh, it is true that only an infinitesimal part of the French people speak or understand Arabic, while millions of Moroccans speak and write French. The French want us to be ourselves, that is ourselves as they wish we were, good descendents of the Gauls!

SCHEHERAZADE: Look, this great quarrel which is raging among you about franglais simply gives us Arabs a good laugh. What's the point?

THE WOMAN STORYTELLER: Basically, we aren't afraid to admit it; we are underhanded. Or rather, it is not us, but the Arab language which, without making waves or engaging in polemics, has for several centuries shamelessly mixed in with the beautiful language you speak and which we love because we find so much of ourselves in it.

DADA: Sitting on sofas or divans, we taste a well-sugared cup of coffee, or a lemonade in a carafe, accompanied with an apricot tart or a few bananas.

SCHEHERAZADE: You poor souls think you are speaking French, but these divans, these sofas, these mattresses with carmine material are all Arab. The coffee and the coffeepot are Arab, as is the sugar and the carafe, your alcohol and your lemonade, your orange or apricot sorbet, your bananas. Not to mention the vegetables, your artichokes, your spinach.

THE GIRL: Yes, that's the way it has been for a long time. If its any consolation to you, you should know that in almost the entire civilized world these things still bear their Arabic names.

SCHEHERAZADE: The French are famous for their refinement and their beauty, but where would they be without our mousselines, or cotonnades, our supple and downy mohair? Not to speak of our satins, our taffetas, our damask. Nor of the whole range of nuances from saffron to lilac passing through orange and cramoisi. The atmosphere is perfumed by our camphor, musk, and amber. Yes, for centuries Arab words have taken root in the French language. Sometimes a bit of humor gets mixed in so that we see a political man running madly in pursuit of a maroquin (minister's portfolio), that false God that he seeks and with whom he is given a public accolade.

THE GIRL: And please do not forget that these Arab words which dot your language refer to articles in common usage whose existence then necessarily we have revealed to you. Otherwise you would have had no need for these expressions.

DADA: Give us thanks therefore for these furnishings and materials, these items of food and drink, the perfumes and colors whose original is Oriental and which make your everyday life healthier and richer in comfort and elegance.

SCHEHERAZADE: Words, even the word "love," can reveal contradictions. Love, for you, involves by preference the heart. This is also true for us. But in the Orient, the liver is also worthy of being the receptacle of this exquisite and yet painful feeling. Thousands of the livers of Arab poets have been consumed by passion, while their hearts continued to beat!

THE WOMAN STORYTELLER: And note this: when the success of your amorous designs warms your heart—as you put it—that same success for us "cools the breast." In your cold climate you dream of sunlight while, in our deserts, we are nostalgic for the snow.

THE GIRL: And all these French-Arabic words, these Arabic-French words, with their meanings, their nuances, their sounds and their silence, all are made up of flesh, blood, and sweat. Constantly corrupted, removed from their first meaning, mangled, twisted, turned, they are still the base and vehicle of our understanding. And it is in part thanks to them that we rediscover the common sources of our being and our becoming. And since both language and music are open to unknowable changes, one can truly see that we are created to understand each other!

SCHEHERAZADE: Monsieur Marshall Lyautey, according to the saladins of usage, the best way to do justice to your memory and to prove that we are created to understand each other is, it seems, to quote the epitaph which you drew up for yourself:

"Here rests Louis-Hubert Lyautey, who was the first Resident General of France in Morocco (1912–1925). Died in the Catholic faith, of which he received in good faith the last sacraments, profoundly respectful of the ancestral traditions of the Muslim religion, maintained and practiced by the inhabitants of North Africa. God keep his soul in eternal peace." Amen

> *The new ambassador's well known*
> *His life is full of wondrous deeds*
> *His desert armies strong have grown*
> *His peaceful talk our hearing feeds*
> *Manners and wisdom he has shown*
> *Religious folk admire his creeds*
> *To friendship with us he was prone*
> *Fulfilling all our hopes and needs*
> *A man full of testosterone*
> *Like hirsute Lyautey he succeeds.**

Darkness

SCENE 3

Brest

THE NARRATOR: And now, let the performance begin, with images depicting the relations, not always easy, between these two sovereigns of such immense stature. It is a prestigious page of a common history, under the gaze of the genial Jean-Baptiste Poquelin, better known under the name of Molière.

BEN AÏCHA: Gentlemen, praise God for having brought us safely into port.

BEN SOUSSAN: We should salute the people of this place, the

beneficial Djinns.

TAGHARI: As opposed to the evil Djinns.

BEN AÏCHA: Come, gentlemen, we are in France. There are no Djinns here!

BEN SOUSSAN: Still, I would like a conditional salute so that I won't regret it later.

DE BRETEUIL: This way, Monsieur Ambassador. Welcome to Brest.

BEN AÏCHA: After a long and painful voyage, here we are at last at Brest. It has been two months since we left our lovely town of Salé.

DE BRETEUIL: The Baron de Saint-Olon and the Consul Petis de la Croix will not be long.

BEN AÏCHA: This chandelier is dripping; there is a spreading pool of wax beneath it.

DE BRETEUIL: Ah! Here they are! Sir, allow me to withdraw.

SAINT-OLON: Do so! (*to BEN-AÏCHA*) Sir!

BEN AÏCHA: Sir!

SAINT-OLON: Monsieur Ambassador of Morocco, I wish you a pleasant stay among us. I receive you by order of my Master, the most high, most excellent, most powerful, most magnificent, most invincible, and most victorious Louis the Great; Emperor of France and Navarre, first born of the Church, defender of the faith, refuge and protector of kings, arbitrator and grand conqueror of Europe.

BEN AÏCHA: I thank you, Monsieur Ambassador, in the name of the Emperor of Morocco, the most humble servant of God. Pardon me, Monsieur Baron de Saint-Olon, but your long speech seems to suggest that Moulay Ismaïl, my master, is seeking something, and your Prince is a superior figure who is condescending to listen to his requests.

SAINT-OLON: I have come, Monsieur Benach, to verify your power before entering into any negotiations with you.

BEN AÏCHA: A copy of the letter from Chérif concerning me has been sent to your Consul Jean-Baptiste Estelle. This letter provides my accreditation. You will of course understand that I can only show it to the King, the great King of France.

SAINT-OLON: Must I insist?

BEN AÏCHA: Baron, do you understand Arabic?

SAINT-OLON: Monsieur Petis de la Croix will be delighted to translate the contents . . .

PETIS DE LA CROIX: Ana outarjimou Al Arabia bil Faransaouia.

BEN AÏCHA: Ten clumsy fellows have trouble tying up a single chicken.

SAINT-OLON: I will report this. Monsieur!

BEN AÏCHA: Monsieur!

PETIS DE LA CROIX: Monsieur!

BEN AÏCHA: Monsieur!

(*PETIS DE LA CROIX and SAINT-OLON leave*)

TAGHARI : One must cut the wood while it is green.

BEN SOUSSAN: Once it dries out, the hatchet can do nothing.

BEN AÏCHA: I must respect the dogs out of consideration for their master.

BEN SOUSSAN: The loudest voices have the least to say.

BEN AÏCHA: Gentlemen, be calm! It is the ignorant man who cannot alter his views. The head that never turns is a hill. *(to SAINT-OLON)* I have my orders and my head is at stake. I can only show this letter to His Majesty in person.

SAINT-OLON: I will so inform his Majesty. Monsieur!

BEN AÏCHA: Monsieur!

PETIS DE LA CROIX: Monsieur!

BEN AÏCHA: I must remind you, Monsieur Saint-Olon, that when you came to Morocco, we took you to our master Moulay Ismaïl without asking anything of you and without giving you any difficulties. I might add that the first Moroccan ambassador, Haj Mohamed Temim, was freely given an audience with Majesty Louis XIV. A parallel honor can hardly be refused me, especially in light of my considerable position. I repeat, my head is at stake. I have no option but to go to the court or to return home.

SAINT-OLON: I will so report. Monsieur!

BEN AÏCHA: Monsieur!

(SAINT-OLON leaves)

BEN AÏCHA: Gentlemen, I have the impression that our path will not be easy.

TAGHARI: This Saint-Olon is tough.

SOUSSAN: Tough and unsympathetic.

BEN AÏCHA: If this goes on they will end up closing their borders. Visas will be doled out like eye drops.

TAGHARI: Our master will not accept that.

BEN AÏCHA: Long live Moulay Ismaïl!

My master Ismaïl

> *Ismaïl, our potentate*
> *God's light on you has descended*
> *You have made our country great*
> *May your life be long extended*
> *Evil you eliminate*
> *For your people's peace contended*
> *Foes you kept outside the gate*
> *Ports and cities you defended*
> *Master, live in high estate*
> *And your reign be never ended*
> *May your children share your fate*
> *And be stars in heaven suspended.**

Darkness

SCENE 4

Paris

NARRATOR (*reading*): Praise be to God! From the servant of God the Prince of Believers who fights on the side of God the Master of the Universe.

Seal of the Sultan, bearing in the center in letters of gold "Ismaïl, son of Chérif, of the line of Hassan, whom God has assisted and made victorious."

To the Emperor of the French, the very Christian Louis XIV, the greatest of all the Christian Kings and Emperors who have been and who shall be.

This letter is given to our dear and well-loved vassal, the greatest of our captains, Admiral Abdellah Ben Aïcha, to whom we delegate our power over all matters and all regulations concerning the sea, which are familiar to him, to be enforced by him according to accepted maritime practice and in the manner authorized by the revelations of divine law, accepted by good sense and arrived at by reason, zeal, good advice, and determination, on all occasions when he must conclude or confirm a treaty or negotiate a peace with any Christian nation. We have given him complete power and have given him leave to negotiate with you, promising to confirm, approve, and ratify what he does, and to put into action completely any agreement.

BON SOUSSANE (*singing and dancing*):
"Oh God of Heaven and Earth!!
Root out the demon, the blockage, from my entrails!
Oh God of sea and winds!
Remove the black mist from my heart!"

BEN AÏCHA (*entering*): What are you saying, Bensoussan? Do you think we are in some Zaouia? Get a hold of yourself, my friend. We are in France now. The country of the Nazarines. (*to Monsieur de Breteuil*) For five days now I have not been able to leave this Hotel. Monsieur Baron de Breteuil, Ambassadorial Liaison, you arranged for us to arrive by night and without ceremony. You welcomed us and gave us greetings in the name of the King and then you disappeared for five days.

DE BERTEUIL: Alas! Monsieur Ambassador, French protocol does not allow our guests to leave these quarters except for the presentation of letters of commission.

BEN AÏCHA: I have also noticed that you have had removed from here the elegant furnishings which were provided for other ambassadors, in particular those from England which my predecessor described in the greatest detail in his well-known book *Biladu Al-Ajaybe*.

DE BERTEUIL: Monsieur Ambassador, how dare you . . .

BEN AÏCHA: Yes, you have carried off the furnishings and provided in their place these mediocre and uncomfortable chairs. This is not Louis Quatorze, even less Louis Quinze, it is Louis Crass!

DE BRETEUIL: Let's let that go, if you please, and discuss your audience. I am charged to say this to you. His Majesty the King of

France, in his extreme kindness, will receive you the sixteenth of November in the Year of Grace 1699 in the Throne Room with, standing behind his chair, the Duke d'Anjou, the Duke de Berry and Monsieur . . .

BEN AÏCHA: You mean the King's brother?

DE BRETEUIL: And you will make your presentation.

BEN AÏCHA: In Arabic, please, as protocol requires.

DE BRETEUIL: Monsieur Petit de la Croix will translate it into good French.

PETIT DE LA CROIX: Ana outarjimou mina Al Arabiya ila Al Faransaouia.

DE BRETEUIL : His Majesty will rise and remove his hat if he approves of your presentation. He will accept your letters of commission and give them to the Marquis de Torcy. Then, smiling, the King will tell you that he is most pleased to see you.

BEN AÏCHA: I have no doubt.

DE BRETEUIL: I have been charged, after this audience, to lead you, Monsieur Ambassador, by way of the grand gallery to the council chamber where there will be several other rooms prepared for your lunch and that of your retinue.

BEN AÏCHA: I will sit at the table only to respond to the honor His Majesty does me. But I cannot eat or drink anything, since we are in the month of abstinence, Ramadan.

DE BRETEUIL: Good heavens, Monsieur Ambassador, you are in France. No muezzin is watching you here.

BEN AÏCHA: You are a man of wit. What a pity that no one is laughing.

DE BRETEUIL: Good evening, Admiral.

BEN AÏCHA: Good evening, De Breteuil.

DE BRETEUIL: Monsieur.

BEN AÏCHA: Monsieur. Please tell me . . .

DE BRETEUIL: Yes?

BEN AÏCHA: Don't you find this room badly lighted?

DE BRETEUIL: Ah! (*He lights the candles.*) Monsieur, I will return to conduct you personally in the Royal Ambassadors carriage to Versailles, where you will be dazzled by the Very Great Sun King, His Majesty the Fourteenth.

> *France is a stronghold, safe, secure*
> *Her banners bold the world can face*
> *Her steps to glory firm and sure*
> *Of all the lands she is the ace*
> *Her fame, her words all pain can cure*
> *Her guests she greets with warm embrace*
> *Her people bow in homage pure*
> > *To Louis, ruler of that place.**

Darkness

SCENE 5

Versailles

NARRATOR: Ben Aïcha's presentation demonstrated that he had more wit and style than one had any right to expect from a Barbary pirate. He was a man, the chronicles report, of much wit and intelligence, polished, humane, and wise. Louis XIV enjoyed his presentation, arose, removed his hat, received Ben Aïcha's letters of introduction, and gave them to the Marquise de Torcy, Secretary of State for foreign affairs, then, smiling, told the Moroccan

Ambassador that he was very pleased to see him,

DADA: During the ceremony, the Ambassador was closely observed, but contrary to all expectations, he gave little occasion to smile, since this individual committed no indiscretions and was quite adept at finding his way through the garden of elegant manners and flowery rhetoric.

NARRATOR: The rooms were magnificent and well lighted, the assembly numerous and select.   Many women were present. Madame de Saint-Olon offered a reception this evening in honor of the Ambassador Ben Aïcha.

BEN AÏCHA: It is an adhesive with a base of Arabic gum. We Orientals use kohl to prevent the falling of hair from the eyebrows.

LITTLE RAJA: Monsieur Ambassador, how do you like Saint-Cloud?

BEN AÏCHA: Admirable! It is the best I have seen!

LITTLE RAJA: How can that be, when you have seen Versailles?

BEN AÏCHA: I love what pleases me, not what astonishes me.

PETIS DE LA CROIX: Will you have a little tobacco, Monsieur Ambassador?

BEN AÏCHA: Gladly! Tobacco cures boredom, irritation, and other disagreeable things.

PETIS DE LA CROIX: As Molière says: "It is the passion of all honest men. He who lives without tobacco is not worthy to live."

MME CAMUS: Are you not too warm, Monsieur Ambassador, with that great crowd of people surrounding you?

BEN AÏCHA: Madame, in paradise, things are as they are here, and the number of angels that I witness here at this moment represents heaven perfectly.

PETIS DE LA CROIX: *Ajib. Ajib.* Compliments!

M. CAMUS: Monsieur Ambassador, do you feel a natural attraction for the fair sex?

BEN AÏCHA: Monsieur! If the fire of love that I feel for the fair sex were directed toward mountains of rock, it would melt them like water.

MLLE DE CONTI: I observe in you, Monsieur, more manners and gallantry than one normally sees in the people of your nation.

BEN AÏCHA: A man cannot enter a perfumer's shop and remain there long without carrying away some scent. The same is true of those of my nation, who cannot remain long among the ladies of France without taking on some of their manners.

(*They laugh and applaud.*)

MLLE DE CONTI: What memory, Monsieur Ambassador, will you keep of your visit with us?

BEN AÏCHA: There are three things I have seen in France that cannot be surpassed, nor even equaled. They are the King, Jean-Baptiste Poquelin, and Monsieur's ball.

MLLE DE CONTI: Does it surprise you to see the women and girls of France mixing with the men with their faces uncovered?

BEN AÏCHA: The women being virtuous, the men perfect, they create a mixture of musk and amber that can only produce a good odor, while for we Moroccans, musk and amber have an aphrodesiac effect.

THE MARQUISE: Is it true what they say, that the people of your country eat with their fingers?

BEN AÏCHA: Madame, for us as for you, the charms of the table are infinite and the art of appreciating good food is highly prized throughout the world. The one who appreciates them is considered superior. Moreover all the senses, yes, all, should be brought into play — the pleasure of sight at the arrangement of the dishes and the refinement of the presentation; the pleasure of hearing, from time to time, the fading away of the last crackling of the grill; the pleasure of smell, deliciously involved; the pleasure of taste. The king in the palace is dedicated to pleasure. Why not add touch, true possession and pure sensuality?. But before taking nourishment, of course, one must wash one's hands carefully.

MLLE DE CONTI: How gallant and full of wit this man is!

PETIS DE LA CROIX: He is perfect!

BEN AÏCHA: Oh, no . . . I am neither good nor virtuous, and as the Brothers of Purity say: "The perfect man is a good, virtuous, intelligent, and insightful being. He must be Persian in origin, Arab in religion, Hanafit in ritual, Iraqi in education, Hebrew in experience, Christian in bearing, Chemite in asceticism, Greek in knowledge, Hindou in expression, Sufi in creed, royal in morality, divine in judgment.

THE MARQUISE: Is it true, Monsieur Ambassador, that you are the Admiral of the Barbary pirates?

MME LE CAMUS: Ah, a Barbary pirate, famous for his spirited deeds, full of style.

BEN AÏCHA: I am only a simple Ambassador, the faithful servant of my master the King of Morocco, and my mission has as its central concern peace and friendship between France and my country, a friendship which will make the Moors French and the French Moors! (*They laugh.*) Ah, you will be astonished to find yourself Berberians!

> All of my hopes are set on thee
> Have mercy, bless my coming, dear

From far I come, a deputy
Hoping to win your favor here
Daughter of manly royalty
None equals you in grace, 'tis clear
Wisdom, charm, propriety
Joy reigns whenever you appear
My duty calls; I must to sea
*My queen, my goddess, keep me near.**

Will you do me the honor, Madame, to tell me the name of this charming person?

MME LE CAMUS: Why, that is the dowager princess of Conti, Marie-Anne de Bourbon, the legitimate daughter of the King and of Mademoiselle de la Valière.

BEN AÏCHA: One need only see her to know whose daughter she is. A charming person. I am enchanted by the beauty and the gracious manners of this princess.

MME LE CAMUS: You should know that the lovely Conti, daughter of the gods, daughter of Love, has lost her young husband, carried off, alas, by smallpox. Boileau himself sang of the litheness of her body and the delicacy of her bearing. As for La Fontaine, he considered that:

> "The very grass bore her up
> Not a flower received
> The mark of her step."

BEN AÏCHA: She shows off at the court what master of the gods she has received each day.

MME LE CAMUS: She has refused in addition to French suitors the son of the King of Cologne, the Duke of Parma, the Prince of Denmark, the Doge of Genoa, Prince Clement of Bavaria, and many others . . .

BEN AÏCHA: Perhaps for this beauty with her lovely dimpled

cheeks, perhaps her freedom is worth more to her than all their crowns.

> *What a life the French pursue*
> *Sweet scents and color fill the air*
> *Their vistas beautiful to view*
> *Their palaces beyond compare*
> *Heavenly Paris, always new*
> *The Louvre with its stunning Square*
> *Great art in every avenue*
> *Young people dancing free of care*
> *Drama they study and review*
> *Their Shakespeare is the great Molière*
> *Who shows what evil men can do*
> *Their sins and cunning he lays bare*
> *Dastardly doctors, and priests too*
> *Misers unwilling gold to share*
> *These are his foes and but a few*
> *Of those whose guilt he strives to air.**

Darkness

SCENE 6

The Rehearsal

MOLIÈRE: Yes, Monsieur, I tell you straight out, the art of courtesans serves only to encourage the weaknesses of the great!

BOILEAU: Let your rivals growl!

MOLIÈRE: Yes, Monsieur, I prick those who are ridiculous; I attack vices. I hold up mirrors. Some look into them, some hide from them, and some want to smash them.

BOILEAU: If you knew a little better how to please, you would not displease them so much.

A MARQUIS: We approve of all these follies which have been

criticized so well and with so much good sense, but believe me, we will have to destroy what we have worshipped.

A MARQUISE: Take courage, Molière. Here is real comedy!

BOILEAU: The soul that knows itself and which flies the light if it makes fun of God fears Molière and his *Tartuffe*.

BEN AÏCHA (*entering*): Ah! Monsieur Jean-Baptiste Poquelin, what a pleasure to see you. The Kingdom of France is indeed fortunate to possess a man like you. How are you doing with all the enemies that are attacking you?

MOLIÈRE: In this world, Monsieur Ambassador, one must live by cunning . . .

BEN AÏCHA: I have attended with delight what you call comedy, and I particularly loved this phrase: "I hate those cowardly souls who are so concerned with the consequences of things that they do not dare undertake anything."

MOLIÈRE: The task of comedy is to correct men while amusing them.

BEN AÏCHA: This reminds me of the speeches of our storytellers in the public squares. These storytellers are real poets. They are the depositories of the wisdom of the ages which they pass on sincerely and without hypocrisy.

MOLIÈRE: Alas! Monsieur, in our world hypocrisy is a fashionable vice, and all fashionable vices pass as virtues.

BEN AÏCHA: Monsieur! (*He bows.*)

MOLIÈRE: Monsieur!

BEN AÏCHA (*to his companions*): This Molière is a bit like our entertainers in the Jemma el Fna square in Marrakesh.

MOLIÈRE (*to his company*): Come now, Ladies and Gentlemen, are you making sport of me with your indifference? Aren't you all willing to come here?

MLLE HERVE: They're coming.

MOLIÈRE: I think these people will drive me mad.

BRECOURT: What do you want us to do! We don't yet know our parts.

MOLIÈRE: Ah! What strange animals to lead these actors are!

MLLE DU PARC: What are you thinking?

MLLE DE BRIE: Since we are all in costume and will not be here for another two hours, let us spend the time rehearsing our business and deciding how best to perform things.

MME JOURDAIN: Ah! Good Heavens! Mercy! What is all this! What an appearance? Are you going to wear that coat, and is this the time to go masked? Speak up, what is all this? Who dressed you up so badly?

M. JOURDAIN: What impertinence! To speak in this way to a Mamamouchi!

> *Monsieur Jordan, Mama mouchi?*
> *Monsieur Jordan, keep your loot-chi*
> *Monsieur Jordan, Mama mouchi?*
> *Monsieur Jordan's mucho mouchi.**

MME JOURDAIN: What's that?

M. JOURDAIN: Yes, I must be respected now. I have just been made a Mamamouchi.

MME JOURDAIN: What are you talking about with your Mamamouchi?

M. JOURDAIN: Mamamouchi, I tell you. I am Mamamouchi.

MME JOURDAIN: What sort of creature is that?

M. JOURDAIN: Mamamouchi. In our language, a paladin.

MME JOURDAIN: A Baladin? You're going to sing ballads?

M. JOURDAIN: What an idiot! I said "paladin." It is an honor which was just conferred upon me, with all due ceremony.

MME JOURDAIN: What sort of ceremony?

M. JOURDAIN: Mahameta per Iordina!

MME JOURDAIN: What does that mean?

M. JOURDAIN: "Iordina" means Jourdain.

MME JOURDAIN: Well, what of it, Jourdain?

M. JOURDAIN: Voler far un paladina de Iordina!

MME. JOURDAIN: What?

M. JOURDAIN: Dar turbanta con galera.

MME. JOURDAIN: What does that mean?

M. JOURDAIN: Per defender Palestina!

MME. JOURDAIN: What are you trying to say?

M. JOURDAIN: Dara dara bastonara

MME. JOURDAIN: What is all this gibberish?

M. JOURDAIN: Non tener honta; questa sar l'ultima affronta!

BEN SOUSSANE: Mamamouchi?

BEN AÏCHA: This Molière is tremendous!

TAGHANI: In any case, I don't understand a word of it.

BEN AÏCHA: What you have seen here the French call "theatre."

BEN SOUSSAN: Theatre?

TAGHARI: Is it legal or illegal?

BEN AÏCHA: That I can't answer. All I know is that this Molière is something like our Jouha.

MME JOURDAIN: What is all this?

M. JOURDAIN: Hou La bb ba la chou ba la ba ba la da . . .

MME. JOURDAIN: Alas! Dear God! My husband has gone mad!

M. JOURDAIN: Silence! Insolent woman, show proper respect to Monsieur the Mamamouchi.

MME. JOURDAIN: Has he lost his wits, then? Hurry, keep him for going out. Ah, ah, this is really the last straw. I see nothing but trouble on all sides.

MOLIÈRE: I'm outraged!

MLLE BÉJART: If this frightens you, you should be more careful and not take on what you have in eight days.

MOLIÈRE: How could I defend myself when the King demanded it?

MLLE BÉJART: How? A respectful excuse based on the impossibility of the task, on the small amount of time given you. Anybody else in your position would have protected his reputation better and would have been reluctant to commit himself as you have done. Yes, what will you do, I ask you, if this business turns out badly? What advantage do you think that all of your enemies will gain from it?

MLLE DE BRIE: Truly, we have to excuse ourselves to the King, with all due respect, or else ask for more time.

MOLIÈRE: Good lord, Mademoiselle! Kings like nothing so much as prompt obedience, and they are not at all pleased to encounter obstacles. Things are not good except at the time they expect them, and to dare to postpone this divertissement is to remove all its charm for them. They want entertainments that they need pay no attention to, and they find those most agreeable that are the least well prepared. We must never think of ourselves in what they want from us, we are only there to please them, and when they order something from us, we must profit from the desire they feel. It is better to do badly what they ask of us than not to do it quickly enough, and if one suffers the shame of not having done well, one has always the glory of having promptly fulfilled their orders. But let's think about rehearsing, if you please. (*They go out*)

BEN AÏCHA: What a nice compliment!

BEN SOUSSAN: What did he say, Monsieur Ambassador?

BEN AÏCHA: It would take too long to explain . . . We will have plenty of time to discuss it during our trip back.

TAGHARI: It will be a long trip. Our dear Morocco is far away!

Darkness

SCENE 7

The Hotel des Ambassadeurs

THE NARRATOR: While the King's actors are rehearsing the new comedy, another comedy, of a much more serious aspect, is being played on another chessboard where the black spaces are nights and the white ones days. The King moves the player and the player moves the piece. An agile knight, a devious bishop, a Homeric castle, a desperate queen, and a confrontational pawn. All these pieces are present to put the central piece, the King, in check. The players are Monsieur le Baron de Saint-Olon and the Ambassador Ben Aïcha. Check or mate? Mate or check?

BEN AÏCHA: Do you remember, Monsieur Saint-Olon, the last interview that my master, the Emperor of Morocco, granted you?

SAINT-OLON: Ah! I am not about to forget it; it took place under false pretenses.

BEN AÏCHA: The Shereef, however, told you that he would set free his French captives if his own subjects were returned to him, as the Spanish had just done.

SAINT-OLON: Yes, but the Shereef added that it was only on this condition that he would sign the Peace Treaty that the King of France requested.

BEN AÏCHA: What was wrong with that?

SAINT-OLON: The King of France never requests peace treaties. Sometimes he grants them.

BEN AÏCHA: To his enemies. The eagle does not pursue flies . . .

BEN SOUSSEN: . . but a gentle tongue is needed for spicy food.

TAGHARI: Be careful. A rope stretched too tight may finally break.

SAINT-OLON: Meaning what?

BEN AÏCHA: I am saying that we are not the King's enemies.

SAINT-OLON: It was his majesty, the King of Morocco, who asked for peace in the letter carried to Paris by the Consul Jean-Baptiste Estelle.

BEN AÏCHA: We were quite mistaken to trust that greedy tradesman. That Jean-Baptiste Estelle had neither intelligence, nor breeding, nor eloquence.

SAINT-OLON: Monsieur Estelle is our Consul at Salé. He was appointed by His Very Magnanimous Majesty Louis XIV the Great.

BEN AÏCHA: Please, Monsieur Baron. Spare me these outbursts, these lies, these dissimulations.

SAINT-OLON: You dare to insult . . .

BEN AÏCHA (aside): It's another rat trick.

SAINT-OLON: What's that?

BEN AÏCHA: I said the funeral was impressive, but the corpse was a simple rat.

SAINT-OLON: But again, what is your meaning?

BEN AÏCHA: It's an old Chinese saying that we have also. Our Spanish neighbors, who, however, have no love for us, the Spanish who are still occupying our Ceuta and our Mellilia, these Spanish, I say, have proven less intransigent than you. Could the King of Spain be better than the King of France?

SAINT-OLON: No prince in Europe would dare to say such a thing. I demand that you retract those words immediately and use less offensive ones.

BEN AÏCHA: To whom do you think you are speaking? Moulay Ismaïl is not the Dey of Algiers, of Tunis, or of Tripoli.

SAINT-OLON: Do you want me to be totally frank with you, Monsieur Ambassador? It would be scarcely possible for me to do anything in your country. It is a country where laws, good faith, and honesty are upside down. And where you are made to wait for weeks before one deigns to receive you.

BEN AÏCHA: Have you forgotten, Monsieur Baron, your mission to Genoa where for two long years you remained confined to your residence, where your own people were scarcely able to poke their noses out of the French consulate without being severely beaten. Has the Gentleman in Ordinary forgotten that?

SAINT-OLON: I have always thought that it was inconceivable to expect to come to a reasonable agreement with you.

BEN AÏCHA: Our legendary hospitality . . .

SAINT-OLON: I beg you, spare me these affectations. It's too much an honor . . .

BEN AÏCHA: Too much of something is also a lack of something. A little green tea, Monsieur Baron?

SAINT-OLON: Gladly! (*Two attendants serve mint tea*) I would have preferred black tea.

BEN AÏCHA: Black tea encourages backbiting and scandal. Just look at the English, men and women alike; when those parasites of teahouses drink tea, it stirs their passions. That's why they are called Sanglo-Saxons.

SAINT-OLON: This tea is a bit too sweet for my taste.

BEN AÏCHA: Did you know, Monsieur, that the Great Gilgamesh defiantly cut off his eyelashes to avoid sleeping? Those eyelashes, falling to earth, engendered that heavenly plant that has been named tea. In the amber liquor which fills my glass, I discover the exquisite taste of Abla's kiss, the piquancy of Amina, and the fragrance of Laal Zeïneb.

SAINT-OLON: Let's get back to our sheep!

BEN AÏCHA: Let's get back to our camels! We were speaking of arrangements between states . . .

SAINT-OLON: Precisely.

BEN AÏCHA: We have come to reasonable arrangements with others, such as the Portuguese, who are far from being fond of us. Two priests came to Meknes to negotiate for the freeing of their countrymen. My master, the Shereef, gave the responsibility of dealing with them to the Jewish financial advisor Abraham Maimorane. Their agreement led to us giving up to Lisbon one hundred and thirty Portuguese slaves in return for the freeing of sixty Moorish captives by Portugal

SAINT-OLON: It was a truly base treaty which fed the vanity of your Shereef, but Portugal is not France and King Pedro is not the Sun King.

BEN AÏCHA: I hold you responsible for the eventual failure of these negotiations. You are determined not to reason with a Moor as you would with a Frenchman. You do not give enough consideration to the ideas and feelings of someone else.

SAINT-OLON: To speak frankly, I must tell you that we have renounced the general exchange of captives to go back to the principle of a head for a head filled out with a reciprocal exchange in the amount of one hundred and fifty piastres.

BEN AÏCHA: I am going to tell you, Baron, what you expect from us, or rather what you demand from my master: a peace treaty which protects French merchant ships from the operations of those you call the Barbary pirates without giving us anything in return. You intend to dupe us by giving us captive Turkish invalids, so thin and skeletal that people cry out whenever they are seen: "The Ottomans! The Ottomans!" At the same time, you keep our Moroccans chained up in your horrible galleys. You speak of an exchange in the amount of one hundred and fifty piastres. My Master wishes to receive Moors in exchange for Frenchmen, not money. Or else send us the Arabic books that are in the Royal Library, as well as those in the Sorbonne and the Collège des Quatre Nations. In return, we will set free all the Frenchmen held captive in Meknes.

SAINT-OLON: Pooh! The Arabs have written so little!

BEN AÏCHA: In the twelfth century, Monsieur de Saint-Olon, when Europe was plunged in the depths of ignorance and obscurantism, there were six hundred and twelve bookshops around the Koutoubia in Meknes, close to today's Club Mediterranean.

SAINT-OLON: Don't let us get lost in discussing affairs of the marketplace. Let's speak about what concerns us here, the exchange of prisoners.

BEN AÏCHA: I tell you again that Moula Ismaïl will never accept his subjects serving as galley slaves, rotting away among gangs of convicts. Failing that, send us arms and munitions and we will speak no more of it.

SAINT-OLON: The Papal Bull *Ina Cina Domini* forbids all Catholic nations to sell anything to . . . to . . .

BEN AÏCHA: To infidels. Don't be afraid to say it. We certainly call you unbelievers!

SAINT-OLON: The Bull forbids us to sell arms to our adversaries for use against us.

BEN AÏCHA: A Bull is so light. It needs only a pin, a single pin.

SAINT-OLON: You have seen for yourself the state of our forces, the greatness of our power both on sea and on land. It is in your own best interest and that of your country to accept peace on the conditions sent by the orders of our King. It not, there will be war!

BEN AÏCHA: War or peace with you matters little to us since our warehouses are, by God's grace, full of treasures and riches, unlimited, uncounted arms and weapons of war. We are not afraid of making enemies. And as the Arabs say: Many problems we have solved by not considering them.

SAINT-OLON: Monsieur! (*He leaves.*)

BEN AÏCHA: Monsieur! Ah! These cursed negotiations! I should have applied the saying: "The beard that you accept for one dirham, add another dirham and pluck it out." Gentlemen, I fear for the success of our mission. If there are no new developments, we are headed straight for failure. We must get word as quickly as possible to our master, Moulay Ismaïl, by whatever means possible: telex, fax, but especially by Arab telephone.

Darkness

SCENE 8

Madam Le Camus

THE NARRATOR: Poor Ben Aïcha was submitted to every sort of pressure. A young widow, Charlotte Le Camus, famous alike for her beauty and her wit was selected especially to brighten from time to time the gloomy hours of our Ambassador. This evening she is accompanying him to the Opera, where *Thèseé* is playing.

BEN AÏCHA (*with a slight cough*): Very well . . . We have worked long enough. It is growing late. Good evening, Monsieur.

BEN SOUSSANE: The report that I am preparing is not yet complete.

BEN AÏCHA: We will complete it tomorrow, God willing.

BEN SOUSSANE: It is an urgent report that I . . .

BEN AÏCHA: Tomorrow, Monsieur Ben Soussane.

BEN SOUSSANE: But Monsieur Ambassador . . .

TAGHARI: Monsieur Ambassador has told you tomorrow. Do you understand?

BEN AÏCHA: Good evening, Monsieur!

BEN SOUSSANE and TAGHARI: Good evening, Monsieur Ambassador. (*They go out.*)

BEN AÏCHA: What's this? Madame, are you growing sad after the obliging kindnesses that you had the goodness to give me? Alas, I see you sighing! Is it in regret? Tell me?

MME LE CAMUS: Dear Monsieur, I cannot regret all that I have done for you. I felt myself carried along by a gentle urging and I quite lacked the power to wish that things had happened otherwise.

BEN AÏCHA: What could you fear, tell me, from the pleasures you have given me?

MME LE CAMUS: Alas! A hundred things at once. The reproaches of my circle, the gossip, the censorship of society, who knows what else? But more than all else the change in your heart and that criminal coldness with which those of your race, so they say, often repay the too ardent confessions of an innocent love.

BEN AÏCHA: Ah! Do not do me the wrong of judging me by the actions of others. You may suspect me of anything, Madame, rather than of lacking in anything I owe you. I love you too much for that.

MME LE CAMUS: Ah! My good friend. Everyone says the same. All men in every country are alike in their words; it is only in their actions that they reveal their differences.

BEN AÏCHA: Since only our actions reveal us for what we are, at least wait to judge my heart by them, and do not seek crimes in the unjust fears of a mistaken presentiment. Allow me, Madame, the time to convince you by a thousand and one proofs of the honesty of my passion.

BEN SOUSANNE (*sings*):
    "Oh my gazelle, if you must choose
    Do not exchange me for a low-born Bedouin. "

MME LE CAMUS: What is he singing?

BEN AÏCHA: He sings of lost love, of nostalgia, of despair, of annihilation.

MME LE CAMUS: And you! Have you nothing to say to me, your little Parisian gazelle?

BEN AÏCHA: "Arise and see; the silver petals of the almond
            spread out on all sides!
        The zephyrs scatter then through the valley, the dew places
            pearls on them!
        When the core is made fertile, the message of happiness
            arrives!
        And the orchard is a marvel of color. Arise my dear one
            again,
        Oh let us go together into the garden, to enjoy an instant of
            this world below."

MME LE CAMUS: Alas! How easily we let ourselves be persuaded by those we honor. Yes, my excellent friend, I feel your heart incapable of loving me but equally incapable of harming me. Leave me. I am not for you.

BEN AÏCHA: What is Madame saying? Am I to understand that another occupies your heart? Oh, Madame, if you must choose, do not exchange me for some base fellow, some fool who feels love only for the smell of cold meat.

MME LE CAMUS: Let us profit still from these happy moments. Life is short.

BEN AÏCHA: Life, Madame, is a tarboosh. Some put it on and others take it off.

MME LE CAMUS: Do you really love me?

BEN AÏCHA: If the full moon loves you, what do you care for the inclinations of the stars ?

MME LE CAMUS: Would you be generous enough to risk your life for me?

BEN AÏCHA: That would be inadequate in my eyes to represent my immense love.

MME LE CAMUS: I have no wish at all to doubt you . . . If you love me, forget everything, friends, parents, country, and all. If you love me, share with me this gentle nectar. (*She offers him a glass of alcohol.*)

BEN AÏCHA: If in order to love you, Madame, I must separate myself from heaven . . . as one says of this nectar where I come from: "Evil messenger. I sent you to my stomach and you climbed up to my head . . ."

MME LE CAMUS: "The shades of night flee in defeat around the sleeping . . ."

BEN AÏCHA: Sleeping!

MME LE CAMUS: "And the light that follows them appears and expands . . ."

BEN AÏCHA: Expands!

MME LE CAMUS: "The burning torch weeps over our separation."

BEN AÏCHA: Separation!

MME LE CAMUS: "The bird sings, the flowers smile."

BEN AÏCHA: Smile! (*He offers her some cakes.*)

MME LE CAMUS: Ah ! My goodness, my favorite treats: Loukoumes !

(*She sings*)
Rahat Loukoume, charming sweet
In our eyes is such a treat
That it changes, in our books
Corsairs into candycooks!

Darkness

SCENE 9

Molière

MOLIÈRE: The duty of comedy being to correct men while diverting them, I have always believed that in the trade I follow I had nothing more important to do than to attack the vices of my time in ridiculing portraits. Hypocrisy is beyond a doubt one of the most common, most troubling, and most dangerous of these.

BEN AÏCHA: Yes, but under certain circumstances . . .

MOLIÈRE: I dare to hope, Monsieur, that in your society, though it is called barbarous . . .

BEN AÏCHA: It is called Berber . . .

MOLIÈRE: I dare to hope that the people in your country are less given to hypocrisy.

BEN AÏCHA: Under certain circumstances: sometimes certain people are obliged to indulge in a few minor falsehoods. It is from the total lies that a man is capable of that his level of accomplishment is determined.

MOLIÈRE: Hypocrisy, hypocrisy . . . only truth is good to speak.

BEN AÏCHA: Truth offers certain inconveniences, while falsehood has sometimes slight advantages.

MOLIÈRE: Our prelates, Monsieur, have pronounced their

judgment. My comedy *Tartuffe*, although they have never seen it, is in their opinion diabolic, and my brain is diabolic as well.

BEN AÏCHA: You too have your Ayatollahs, your fanatics.
MOLIÈRE: I am a demon wrapped in flesh and dressed as a man, a libertine, a heathen deserving an exemplary punishment.

BEN AÏCHA: Monsieur, you need only to place your interests in the hands of the King and respectfully wait for whatever it pleases him to do about them.   Enlightened monarchs have no need to be informed what is expected from them.

MOLIÈRE: You are right, Monsieur. Happily we live under a prince who is the enemy of hypocrisy, whose eyes cast daylight into men's hearts, and who is never misled by the art of imposters. You see, Monsieur, my affairs are going badly, but I hope that for you . . .

BEN AÏCHA: In respect to my mission, I know how to show my Lord and Master what sort of stewards you have, who want war and not peace. Ah! If only your prince was aware of the disloyalty of some of the rascals in his entourage.

MOLIÈRE: What, Monsieur, have you also been the victim of this strange entourage? Of this Jurassic Park?

BEN AÏCHA: Alas, my dear Monsieur, my mission is falling apart. Many difficulties remain. You see before you a very disappointed man. I have received an infinity of examples of the incompetence of Consul Estelle!

MOLIÈRE: I know his reputation, a complete rascal!

BEN AÏCHA: The Consul is a virtuoso of plots and scheming. He has a great capacity for causing trouble. Allow me to open my heart to you. Monsieur Torcy and Monsieur Torpus and the intolerable Jean-Baptiste Estelle presented me with a document, a treaty based on that of 1692, and asked me to sign it without any sort of discussion. We have already refused to sign this treaty, two years ago at Meknes. And I have just heard that I have been recalled from

France. Despite a few considerations and some small initiatives, the Ambassador of Morocco is being recalled. The dream is apparently shattered before it has even begun.

MOLIÈRE: And yet, Monsieur, everyone praises your qualities and your and your delightful flashes of wit. The court has appreciated all the compliments you have offered it.

BEN AÏCHA: But I merely spoke aloud what I have from time to time heard in private. Hospitality requires it.

MOLIÈRE: Hypocrisy requires it, too !

BEN AÏCHA: No, simple tact. I can say this to you because you have created some comedies. That perhaps may be of service to you. I confess to you that some of the customs here have astonished me. For example engaging in affairs, having affairs.

MOLIÈRE: Ah! I see which way the wind is blowing.

BEN AÏCHA: Those in high positions in your country require special sedan chairs for affairs . . .

MOLIÈRE: Prepared for them by their head valet.

BEN AÏCHA: And this is considered a mark of rank!

MOLIÈRE: Yes, that's quite true.

BEN AÏCHA: And how can such luxury in dwellings and furnishing, such refinement of manners, allow the public use of portable toilets? And gambling, my dear Molière, this madness of gambling, with the women worse than the men . . .

MOLIÈRE: And the old worse than the young . . .

BEN AÏCHA: Farewell, my good friend, farewell.

MOLIÈRE: Before leaving us, Admiral, tell me, is it true that the sulpher that the Marseilles ships sell to you is used in your cannons?

BEN AÏCHA: French merchants know that sulpher is indispensable to us for bleaching our woolens and our burnous, especially when one has been sweating in the burnous. Farewell, Molière . . . All our little troubles will be swept aside by history. All that will remain perhaps are your lovely comedies: *Tartuffe, l'Avare, le Malade Imaginaire* . . . Molière, you have done much for the glory of France. Farewell, Jha!

MOLIÈRE: And Mademoiselle de Conti?

BEN AÏCHA: She is charming, she is divine, and she sparkles with brilliant colors that are not seen anywhere else. Pure and white as ermine, she eclipses all flowers, even the lily of her origin.

MOLIÈRE: She is certainly a perfect being, in dance as well as in music. As for her figure, it is certainly divine.

BEN AÏCHA: I will take her portrait to my master. I will speak of her qualities, of her courtesy, of her lively wit, of her regal air and of her perfect intelligence.

MOLIÈRE: Madame de Conti and the Prince of Morocco! What an amusing idea, what a strange idea, what a great subject for a comedy! The Follies Berberes!

> *All of my hopes are set on thee*
> *Have mercy, bless my coming, dear*
> *From far I come, a deputy*
> *Hoping to win your favor here*
> *Daughter of manly royalty*
> *None equals you in grace, 'tis clear*
> *Wisdom, charm, propriety*
> *Joy reigns whenever you appear*
> *My duty calls; I must to sea*
> *My queen, my goddess, keep me near.**

Darkness

SCENE 10

Mademoiselle de Conti

MLLE DE CONTI: What do you know, Admiral?

BEN AÏCHA: I know that very soon you will be surrounded in your salon with financiers, poets, and diplomats in view.

MLLE DE CONTI: And what else?

BEN AÏCHA: You will enchant your entourage with much fine repartee and by a thousand lovely little things that emerge from your pretty mouth.

MLLE DE CONTI: And what else?

BEN AÏCHA: At the age of fourteen, they married you to Louis Arnaud, Prince de Conti, a marriage which they say . . .

MLLE DE CONTI: Is an unhappy one. Everybody knows it!

BEN AÏCHA: You have found consolation and favor at the harpsichord and the dance, which steadily increases your admirers and your gallants.

MLLE DE CONTI: You exaggerate, Admiral.

BEN AÏCHA: Oh ! Madame ! Words cannot express the dazzle of your beauty. You will see, poets of the future will call the Princess de Conti a masterpiece whose divine shape surpasses imagination.

MLLE DE CONTI: Let that go, I pray you, and tell me how women live in your country?

BEN AÏCHA: In our society, Madame, there is a tacit understanding which makes the woman mistress of the home and the man master of the street.

MLLE DE CONTI: Poor creatures! Condemned to be shut up within four walls . . .

BEN AÏCHA: That is why, Madame, we have created interior gardens within our homes bursting with orange, jasmine, and pomegranate trees and where a thousand and one birds sing near fountains of the beauty of the roses of paradise.

MLLE DE CONTI: Is it true, Admiral, that you have several wives?

BEN AÏCHA: If we have several wives, as you say, it is to discover in each of them qualities that are united in Mademoiselle de Conti.

MLLE DE CONTI: Charming! But tell me, is it true that among you there is a saying: "Beat your wife every morning. If you do not know the reason, she does."

BEN AÏCHA: That saying, Madame, was invented much later by those bastard *pied noirs*, but that is another story.

> *Dearest love, I honor thee*
> *Have sympathy, kiss me my dear*
> *I come from across the sea*
> *Hoping to find affection here*
> *Daughter sweet of royalty*
> *Your charms, your elegance are clear*
> *Wisdom, charm, propriety*
> *Joy reigns whenever you appear*
> *Words fail thy divinity*
> *My queen, my goddess, keep me near.**

This song, dedicated to the glory of Mademoiselle de Conti, as I can bear witness, is a song that our troubadours, all aquiver, sing in far-flung towns and villages, from Meknes to Marrakesh, from Tangiers to Agadir. The people of my country still hum it today. We heard it hummed most recently in the famous market of Taoujtat by the singer Moula Addi Bizizi!

Darkness

SCENE 11

The Marriage Proposal

THE NARRATOR: Upon his return to Morocco, the Ambassador Ben Aïcha gave a laudatory report to King Moulay Ismaïl. All this remained engraved in his heart and caused him serious thought. Then, the Emperor of Morocco, Amir Al Mouminine, Prince of the Believers and descendent of the Prophet of Islam, asked for the hand of the daughter of the Most Christian King, elder son of the Church, and desired to contract a matrimonial alliance with him!

PETIS DE LA CROIX (*outside*): Anna la outarjimou . . . la outarjimou. Are you a child ? Louis XIV would never consent to give his daughter in marriage to the Emperor of Morocco and thereby provide for his enemies in England the occasion for them to spread the word that he has allied himself with an infidel. Mademoiselle de Conti, a Muslim!

BEN AÏCHA: I appeal to the spirit of tolerance in Islam, which allows Muslims to marry a Christian or a Jew without forcing her to become Muslim.

PETIS DE LA CROIX: How is that possible? Kaïfa hada ?

BEN AÏCHA: The Princess will keep her religion, interests, and manner of living. Must I remind you, Monsieur, that we Muslims believe that the Messiah Jesus is the son of Mary, who was still a virgin, totally pure, and that is why the spirit of God breathed in his breast.

PETIS DE LA CROIX: La Youmkin!

BEN AÏCHA: Father Diego, who lives in our country with a dozen brothers of his order, is a Franciscan whom our King has authorized to establish himself at Meknes with the mission of caring for captives and giving them medicine. There are convents at Fez, Tetouan, and Meknes which enjoy a real privileged status.

PETIS DE LA CROIX: This is all very well, but Mademoiselle de Conti, a Muslim!

BEN AÏCHA: Prayers, processions, and religious hymns are pursued with fervor. There are three Christian cemeteries in Meknes.

PETIS DE LA CROIX: Three cemeteries! It seems that Christians die a great deal in Meknes.

BEN AÏCHA: We are ready to build a cathedral for Mademoiselle de Conti.

PETIS DE LA CROIX: To insist on this matter is to emphasize how ridiculous and foolish this marriage proposal is . . .   Anna la outarjimou!

BEN AÏCHA: The Emperor of Morocco, Amir Al Mouminine, Prince of Believers and descendent of the Prophet of Islam, wishes you to know that he wants very much to make an alliance with such a Great King and that all the ports, cities, and lands of the Empire of Morocco will always be open to him and to his subjects.

PETIS DE LA CROIX: This is simply the pipe deam of an oriental potentate, eager to enrich his harem. Hadid hamakat-hamakat!!!

BEN AÏCHA: Deluded by grandeur, it is what I would call megalomania.

MOLIÈRE: The court, dying of boredom, where everything becomes known eventually, learned the news. They guffawed, they sneered, they made songs, rhymes, and verses . . .

DADA: *Your great beauty, great Princess*
       Bears the traits that wound and bless
       Even the most savage places.
       Africa admits your graces
       And your eyes, across the seas
       Conquer more than Hercules.

MME LE CAMUS: Why refuse the glorious homage of a King who awaits you and who knows you so well? Since Hymen summons you to Morocco, go. Perhaps in that land you will find a faithful lover.

Darkness

SCENE 12

The Farewell

THE NARRATOR: Moulay Ismaïl's request was not taken seriously. There was perhaps a great opportunity offered there, but the pride of the great King and his agents completely missed it.

BEN AÏCHA: Madame, I come with a sorrowful heart to bid you farewell. I am leaving you and leaving France, where I have never ceased to be the object of such great honor.

MME LE CAMUS: The day when I met you was one of my happiest. I will never forget your courtesy and your wit.

BEN AÏCHA: I leave you this letter, Madame, in which I express the happiness of my fate. I am embarrassed by the fire in my heart but I can allow nothing of that to be seen.

MME LE CAMUS: Your absence will be painful to me, but in the depths of my soul you will always be present.

BEN AÏCHA: Oh, light of my eyes . . .

MME LE CAMUS: Continue to call me what you did before: my rose.

BEN AÏCHA: My rose! All the mysteries and the beauty of life are found in the rose.

MME LE CAMUS: Again . . .

BEN AÏCHA: Oh, my rose! The rose lives a day and the palm tree ninety-nine years.

MME LE CAMUS: More, more . . .
BEN AÏCHA: Oh, my rose! Who can make me forget the tenderness of your soul, the generosity of your heart, and the perfection of your friendship?

MME LE CAMUS: Oh, my handsome favorite pirate, take this letter case and this golden snuffbox in memory of the happy moments that we have spent together.

BEN AÏCHA: Allow me, Madame, to place at your feet this ancient manuscript, *The Guide to Good Things*, that has been kept jealously in my family since time immemorial.

MME LE CAMUS: A king served by a subject like you can rest easy about any affairs he puts in your hands.

BEN AÏCHA: Alas, my rose! I did not achieve the success I expected due to your officials who wanted war and not peace with us. I fear my master will reprimand me.

MME LE CAMUS: Certain reprimands are worth more than any praise.

BEN AÏCHA: If, God forbid, war comes to our gates, the bombardments can only touch dwarf palms. But I will report what I have seen in your country: the palaces I admired, the beautiful architecture, and the skill of its designers. It is well known: as the proverb says, "a thing is not well done except by the hand of a Christian." I would do anything to bring some architects to whom we would give great rewards and salaries for them to build a bridge as a symbol of our future friendship, a bridge which would connect the Paris of Louis XIV with the Meknes of Moulay Ismaïl.

MME LE CAMUS: There are certain things that cannot be refused among kings.

BEN AÏCHA: And kings make of these things a glory between themselves. My lord and master is accustomed to say: "Good and evil do not know how to march in step." Return good for evil and you will see your enemy change into a faithful friend. Perhaps we have shown a bit of vehemence. Farewell, Madame. I have succumbed to your pleasing charms. O, my rose! Oh, wise creature with burning kisses.

MME LE CAMUS: Farewell, my gentle friend.

BEN AÏCHA: I must confess to you, my rose, that when my master selected me to come as Ambassador to France, I wept with joy. But now, I know that I will weep even more in leaving it, for leaving you, Madame, I leave behind a part of my heart. So that you do not forget me, noble lady, allow me to send you each month a small amount of the sweet loukoum.

MME LE CAMUS: Ah! Rahat loukoum.

BEN AÏCHA: Noble lady, accept, in homage of your sublime beauty which has so ravished my soul, this loukoum which the French view as such a delicacy!

MME LE CAMUS (*sings*):
> *Rahat Loukoume, charming sweet*
> *In our eyes is such a treat*
> *That it changes, in our books*
> *Corsairs into candycooks!*

:

BEN AÏCHA (*sings*):
> *Sweet its scent as lovers' dreams*
> *Sweet its taste as love's own thought*
> *Savor it as if it seems*
> *Love's own sweetness it has brought.*

Darkness

SCENE 13

The Royal Gift

SAINT-OLON: Monsieur Ambassador, I have come to make my farewells.

BEN AÏCHA: Farewell, Baron. Please be so kind as to serve as my spokesman, take, as we say in Arabic, my tourjman to the most excellent, all-powerful, most magnificent, invisible, and victorious Louis the Great for the gifts that he was so kind as to have sent to my master Mouley Ismaïl. In return, allow me to offer to the great and generous state of France, these.

SAINT-OLON: Good Lord! Ostriches!

BEN AÏCHA: I am first intended to offer you camels, but alas, I was not able to find any.

SAINT-OLON: Ostriches!

BEN AÏCHA: I must admit that in Barbary we are at presently suffering from a serious shortage of dromadaries. The desert dockyards are no longer producing vessels.

SAINT-OLON: An admirable gift, but how do they live?

BEN AÏCHA: They will eat anything, digest anything, even nails, especially nails of garlic, which give them a sweet breath.

SAINT-OLON: A gallinaceous wonder!

BEN AÏCHA: Please note, Baron, that this does not mean that in our future relationships we will practice Austrichan diplomacy!

Darkness

FINAL SCENE

MME LE CAMUS: Louis XIV and Moulay Ismaïl, whom we have had the pleasure of presenting to you, in your company have remained glorious in the memory of their people.

SAINT-OLON: From age to age their names will echo profoundingly in the imagination of the descendents of their subjects, overwhelmed by the magnificence and dazzle of their reign and by the fierce conviction of these kings that they were the shadow of God himself projected on earth.

MME LE CAMUS: History, they say, is the science of things that are not repeated, since what have we done before you this evening if not shown you that history can never be withdrawn from repetition?

THE GIRL: Time, setting, and characters can, must change. But the inspiration of men and their noble and authentic ambition, do these not continue to be the seeking of alliances, the daughters of peace and harmony?

SAINT-OLON: History may perhaps be the science of things that do not repeat, but the theatre is also a science, grave and humorous, profound and frivolous. This theatre loves to repeat things, especially when it is believed that they were said once for all time.

MME LE CAMUS: It is true, my friends of this evening, that theatre loves to repeat things to say and say again that they are living, not fixed, faded, immutable. The most immediate, the most contemporary become, as if by magic, of unquestionable age, just like the memories of the past become deliciously contemporary. Magic! Magic!

SAINT-OLON: The magic of theatre, one of the reigning words of which, both at its beginning and end, is no other than the word "repetition."

DADA: To you, oh magic of the theatre, thanks be given, excellent lover who knows how to mix history and fiction with assured skill.

MME LE CAMUS: We are all servants of the sublime, even if this evening we have given you only a caricature of it. But at the theatre, is not complicity a right that can be assumed?

DADA: And just as in France, everything ends with bonbons, let us sing and celebrate together the Rahat Loukoume.

ALL (sing) : *Rahat Loukoume, charming sweet*
      In our eyes is such a treat
      That it changes, in our books
      Corsairs into candycooks!

      Over our festival today
      Not a trace of blame will loom
      Please give us without delay
      Glorious Rahat Loukoume
      Taste its flowery essence, pray,
      Rahat will remove all gloom
      To this candy don't say nay
      It's the very latest boom
      Help yourself, go on, you may
      *Rahat Loukoume!**

Curtain

*Translator's Note: The songs and poems marked with an * are in Arabic in the original; the others are in French. The translator wishes to thank Khalid Amine and Dalia Basiouny for their advice on the Arabic passages.

TRANSLATORS

Marvin Carlson

Marvin Carlson is the Sidney E. Cohn Professor of Theatre and Comparative Literature at the Graduate Center of the City University of New York. He has previously translated plays from French, German, Italian, and Arabic and is the author of many books and articles on theatre and performance history and theory. He edited in this series *The Arab Oedipus: Four Plays* in 2005.

David Looseley

David Looseley is Professor of Contemporary French Culture at the University of Leeds, UK, and Director of the International Popular Cultures Research Group, based at Leeds. He has published widely on French theatre, popular culture, and cultural policy. His translation of Armand Salacrou's play *Nights of Wrath* (*Les Nuits de la culture*, 1946) was put on by Horizon Theatre Rep in New York in 2005, after a staged reading of the play at the Martin E. Segal Theatre Center at the Graduate Center of the City University of New York in 2004.

Carolyn and Tom Shread

Carolyn Shread teaches French at Mount Holyoke College, after completing her doctorate in French and Francophone Studies at the University of Massachusetts Amherst. She is currently also translating Haitian Marie

360

Chauvet's novel *Les Rapaces* for an M.A. in Translation Studies. Tom Shread earned an M.F.A. in Dramaturgy at the University of Massachusetts Amherst and now works as a dramaturg and sound designer. This translation of *Les Co-épouses* was first performed in the University of Massachusetts Curtain Theater in November 2000. Originally from the U.K., Carolyn and Tom Shread now live in Northampton, Massachusetts, with their two daughters, Sylvia and Pearl.

A number of friends and colleagues helped make this publication possible. We would especially like to thank Karim Alloula, Khalid Amine, Rafael De Mussa, Shonni Enelow, Fabienne Gallaire, Sophie Proust, and of course, the authors who generously granted permission for us to present the English translations of their work.

The Martin E. Segal Theatre Center (MESTC), The Graduate Center, CUNY, New York, is a non-profit center for theatre, dance, and film affiliated with CUNY's Ph.D. Program in Theatre. Originally founded in 1979 as the Center for Advanced Studies in Theatre Arts (CASTA), it was renamed in March of 1999 in recognition of one of New York City's outstanding leaders of the arts. The Center's primary focus is to bridge the gap between the academic and professional performing arts communities by providing an open environment for the development of educational, community-driven, and professional projects in the performing arts. As a result, MESTC is home to theatre scholars, students, playwrights, actors, dancers, directors, dramaturgs, and performing arts managers, as well as both the local and international theatre communities. The Center presents staged readings to further the development of new and classic plays, lecture series, televised seminars featuring professional and academic luminaries, and arts in education programs, and maintains its long-standing visiting-scholars-from-abroad program. In addition, the Center publishes a series of highly regarded academic journals, as well as books, including plays in translation, all written and edited by renowned scholars *http://web.gc.cuny.edu/mestc*

MESTC books include *Four Melodramas by Pixérécourt* (edited by Daniel Gerould and Marvin Carlson—both Distinguished Professors of Theatre at the CUNY Graduate Center), *Zeami and the Noh Theatre in the World* (edited by Japanese Theatre authorities, Professors Benito Ortolani and Samuel Leiter), *Contemporary Theatre in Egypt* (which includes the translation of three plays by Alfred Farag, Gamal Maqsoud, and Lenin El-Ramley), *Four Works for the Theatre by Hugo Claus* (the foremost contemporary writer in the Dutch language, edited by David Willinger), *The Heirs of Moliére* (four representative French comedies from the death of Moliére to the French Revolution that are edited and translated by Marvin Carlson), *Seven Plays by Stanisław Ignacy Witkiewicz* (edited and translated by Daniel Gerould), *The Arab Oedipus: Four Plays* (edited by Marvin Carlson), *Theatre Research Resources in New York City* (edited by Jessica Brater, Senior Editor Marvin Carlson) the most comprehensive catalogue of New York City research facilities for theatre scholars, and *Comedy: A Bibliography of Critical Studies in English on the Theory and Practice of Comedy in Drama, Theatre and Performance* (edited by Meghan Duffy, Senior Editor Daniel Gerould). New publications: *BAiT-Buenos Aires in Translation: Four Plays* (edited and translated by Jean Graham-Jones) and *roMANIA AFTER 2000. Five New Romanian Plays* (edited by Saviana Stanescu and Daniel Gerould—translations edited by Saviana Stanescu and Ruth Margraff.)